CW00505362

Holman *QuickSource*™

GUIDE TO

THE DEAD SEA SCROLLS

Holman *QUICKSOURCE*™

GUIDE TO

THE DEAD
SEA SCROLLS

Craig Evans

HOLMAN
REFERENCE

NASHVILLE, TENNESSEE

Holman QuickSource Guide to the Dead Sea Scrolls
© 2010 by Craig Evans
All rights reserved

ISBN: 978-0-8054-4852-8

A Holman Reference Book
published by
B&H Publishing Group
127 Ninth Avenue, North
Nashville, Tennessee 37234
http://www.bhpublishinggroup.com

Dewey Decimal Classification: 296.155
Subject Heading: DEAD SEA SCROLLS \ QUMRAN COMMUNITY \
SACRED BOOKS

Cover Design by Greg Pope
Interior Design by Doug Powell

Acquisitions Editor: Dr. Terry Wilder
Editor: Dr. Jeremy R. Howard

Unless otherwise indicated, all Scripture passages are taken from the
Holman Christian Standard Bible®,
© copyright 1999, 2000, 2002, 2003 by Holman Bible Publishers.
All rights reserved.

Scripture quotations marked NASB are from the New American Standard
Bible. © The Lockman Foundation, 1960, 1962, 1963, 1968, 1971, 1972 ,
1973, 1975, 1977. Used by permission.

Scripture quotations marked NRSV are from the New Revised Standard
Version of the Bible, copyright © 1989 by the Division of Christian Education
of the National Council of Churches of Christ in the United States of America.
Used by permission. All rights reserved.

Scripture quotations marked RSV are from the Revised Standard Version of
the Bible, copyrighted 1946, 1952, © 1971, 1973.

Scripture quotations marked KJV are from the King James Version.

Printed in the USA

3 4 5 6 7 8 9 • 19 18 17 16 15

Dedicated to

. . .

My cousin, Ron Eoff

Table of Contents

Preface......................................18

Part I:
Discovery and Importance:
Basic Facts About the Scrolls

1 Lost...................................24
2 Found..................................30
3 Why the Scrolls Matter.......................44
4 The Dead Sea Region........................49

Photo: Hoyasmeg.

Part II:
The Science of the Scrolls

5 The Science of Dating the Scrolls...................56
6 Restoring and Preserving the Scrolls..............68

Photo: Berthold Werner.

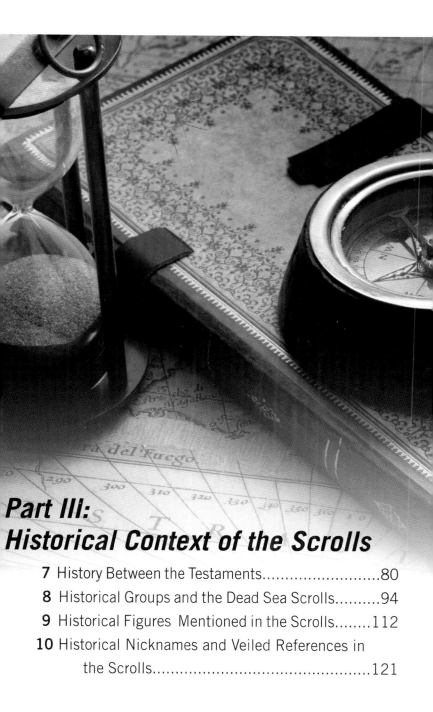

Part III:
Historical Context of the Scrolls

7 History Between the Testaments............................80

8 Historical Groups and the Dead Sea Scrolls..........94

9 Historical Figures Mentioned in the Scrolls........112

10 Historical Nicknames and Veiled References in
the Scrolls...121

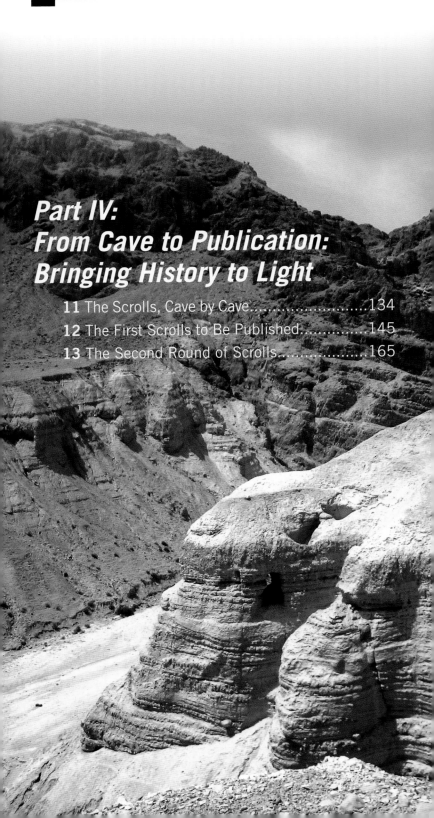

Part IV:
From Cave to Publication:
Bringing History to Light

11 The Scrolls, Cave by Cave..........................134
12 The First Scrolls to Be Published...............145
13 The Second Round of Scrolls....................165

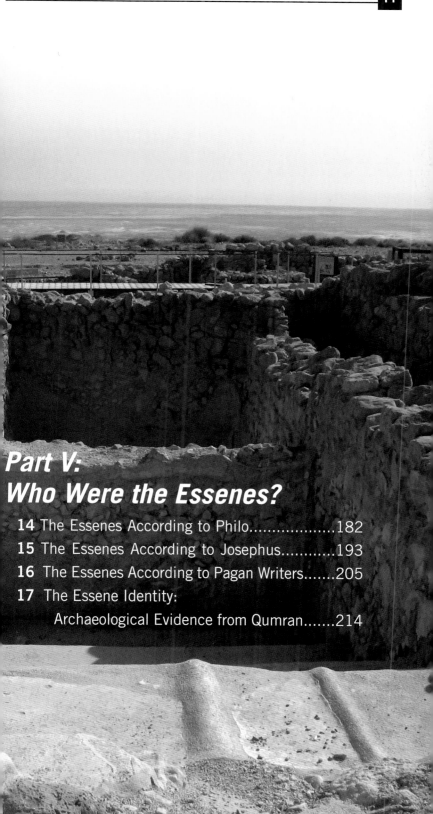

Part V:
Who Were the Essenes?

14 The Essenes According to Philo...................182
15 The Essenes According to Josephus............193
16 The Essenes According to Pagan Writers.......205
17 The Essene Identity:
    Archaeological Evidence from Qumran.......214

Part VI:
Faith and Practice According to the Scrolls

18 How the Essenes Interpreted Scripture....................230

19 How the Essenes Worshipped God.........................236

20 How the Essenes Related to the
   Priests of Jerusalem..247

21 The Essenes and the End Times............................254

Photo: Berthold Werner.

Part VII:
The Scrolls and the Old Testament

22 How Well Is the Bible Preserved in the Scrolls?.....266

23 The Scrolls and the Canon of Scripture................277

24 The Scrolls and Popular Bible Figures..................285

Part VIII:
The Scrolls and Jesus

25 The Scrolls and John the Baptist.....................304

26 The Scrolls and the Coming Messiah..............308

27 The Scrolls and the Teaching of Messiah........327

Part IX:
The Scrolls and the
New Testament

28 The Scrolls and Paul.............................346

29 The Scrolls and Hebrews, James, and Jude........357

30 The Scrolls and Revelation......................365

31 Are Some of the Scrolls from the
New Testament?..................................369

Part X: Conclusion

32 Summary Q&A on the Dead Sea Scrolls.............376

Appendix 1 Major Scrolls Publications....................382
Appendix 2 Major Scrolls Players...........................388

Preface

The Dead Sea Scrolls (DSS) first caught my attention as a seminary student about 35 years ago when I took a class on how Scripture was interpreted in the time of Jesus and the early Church. This introduced me to the allegorical-prophetic style of biblical interpretation (usually called *pesher*) practiced in many of the scrolls. I found it fascinating.

As a doctoral student at Claremont, I had the good fortune of working with several proven DSS scholars, including William Brownlee, James Sanders, and John Trever. Anyone who is familiar with the scrolls and their discovery will recognize these names. Brownlee and Trever were actually in Jerusalem the year the first scrolls came to light (1947–48). Trever made beautiful photographs of several Cave 1 scrolls; they remain among the very best. Brownlee produced some of the first scholarly studies on the scrolls. Sanders became one of the original editors of the scrolls, producing an excellent volume on the Cave 11 Psalms Scroll for the Discoveries in the Judaean Desert series. He went on to serve as founding president of the Ancient Biblical Manuscript Center in Claremont, whose important work continues to this day.

A "Qumran spring" dawned in the early 1990s thanks to the long-awaited publication of the many fragmentary scrolls from Cave 4. At this time the Dead Sea Scrolls Institute was founded at Trinity Western University in British Columbia, where I served on the faculty. The directors of the institute were Martin Abegg and Peter Flint. These were heady days for scrolls enthusiasts. We held conferences, published books, traveled to Israel and elsewhere in the Middle East, and collaborated with scholars around the world.

I have contributed to and edited my fair share of books on the DSS, given countless lectures at popular conferences and learned symposia, and for many years have had the privilege of serving on the editorial board of *Dead Sea Discoveries*, a scholarly journal devoted to the scrolls and their impact on biblical scholarship and the world of early Judaism and Christianity. And yet the scrolls are as fresh and interesting to me as they ever were.

The Purpose of This Book

The purpose of this book is to help you understand what the DSS really are and how they shed light on Jesus and the Jewish people of 2,000 years ago. For example, the scrolls will help you understand better how the Jewish people yearned for the dawning of a new day, a day when God's people would live in righteousness and justice, a day when the Messiah would reign as king and evil would be banished from earth. You will also read about the interesting events surrounding the discovery of the scrolls, the controversies surrounding the publication and implications of the scrolls, and the major scrolls scholars. Other important topics include:

- The region of the Dead Sea
- The contents of the scrolls
- The date of the scrolls
- The science of restoring and preserving the scrolls
- The scrolls and the Bible
- Who wrote the scrolls
- The scrolls and the end time
- The scrolls and the messianic hope
- The scrolls and Jesus
- The scrolls and Old Testament (OT) interpretation
- The scrolls and New Testament (NT) interpretation

In keeping with the purpose of the Holman QuickSource series, the *Guide to the Dead Sea Scrolls* is organized and written in a user-friendly style, accompanied by many photographs, text boxes, and other aids. Read on and enjoy!

My English quotations of the DSS are from *The Dead Sea Scrolls: A New Translation* (HarperCollins, 1996), a fine work put together by Michael O. Wise, Martin G. Abegg, and Edward M. Cook.

Finally, I express my thanks to Terry L. Wilder for extending to me the invitation to write this book and to Jeremy Royal Howard for his expert assistance and advice as it was being written. I also salute my cousin Ron Eoff, to whom the book is dedicated. Ron served the public in law enforcement in southern California for more than 30 years.

Craig A. Evans

Acadia Divinity College

Photo: Hoyasmeg

Part I

Discovery and Importance: Basic Facts About the Scrolls

Photo: xta11.

Chapter 1
Lost

"The able-bodied fled, the feeble perished, and everything left was consigned to the flames."

–Josephus, *War* 4.489, in reference to the Roman capture of Gerasa in AD 68

Date: AD 73

Place: Qumran, on the northwest shore of the Sea of Salt (or Dead Sea)

It was early morning. There was a haze over the blue waters of the Sea of Salt to the southeast. Inside the compound Eleazar, the chief scribe, looked wistfully upon the rows of neatly organized scrolls. Hunched over their writing boards, his younger colleagues Yehudah and Yehohanan labored away making fresh copies of Scripture. Dipping into the inkwells and scratching away on the smooth leather skins. Another Isaiah scroll and another copy of Genesis. But these faithful scribes would not complete their task. They did not know this yet, but Eleazar did.

He had learned from the overseer what everyone had

feared: the Romans were approaching. It was to be expected. The last rebel stronghold was atop Masada, Herod's mountain fortress and palace. To reach it the Romans would have to march south, right past the compound at Qumran. Nothing in their path would be safe. Eleazar loved the community, and now he feared for it. The Romans had showed no pity when they took Gerasa and nearby Jericho five years ago. Why would they now? The Romans had fought a long and bitter war and now were filled with thoughts of final revenge.

Roman camp near Masada. Photo: Ester Inbar.

Eleazar believed with all his heart that someday God would raise up his Messiah, who with the community's faithful high priest would defeat the Romans and subdue the ungodly of Israel. Israel would once again be exalted among the nations. There had been talk of this among the rebels, of course. The riots in Jerusalem over debt had given the rebels and zealots the opportunity that they had longed for. They gained control of Jerusalem, and soon all of Israel was seething in revolt. They restruck coins so that they now declared "year one of the liberation of Israel." Eleazar had seen some of these coins. But after "year two" and the Roman advance south, no more of these coins found their way to the community.

Eleazar had had no confidence in the integrity and righteousness of the rebels. From the beginning they were divided, at each other's throats, and their armed followers were scarcely more than disorganized mobs. No, the salvation of God would not come through these men. And indeed it had not. In short order the Romans had subdued Galilee, Samaria, and parts of Judea. The enemy had established camps in nearby Jericho to the east and Haditheh to the west. Jerusalem had been hemmed in, awaiting the inevitable siege. Rome's great general Vespasian was ready to march against the Holy City.

The death of Rome's wicked emperor had delayed the final advance. One emperor after another seized power. Even the faithful at Qumran, so mindful of the shortcomings and worldliness of the rebels, could not help but wonder at times if the rebellion was truly of God after all. Would the wicked empire crumble? Alas, no. When Vespasian became the new emperor, the war was quickly and decisively resumed. Within a few months Jerusalem had been surrounded, and in the summer of "year five" of the self-proclaimed Jewish liberation, Jerusalem had been captured, her temple destroyed, and her people enslaved or put to the sword. The few stragglers who evacuated to the Qumran compound reported these things.

The Triumph of Titus by Lawrence Alma-Tadema. Titus was also called Vespasian.

As Eleazar stepped outside, he was met by the overseer. "Eleazar, we have little time. Elisha has just returned and tells me the Roman dogs are almost within sight. Gather up our books and hide them, some here and others farther away."

Eleazar did as he was instructed. He had Yehudah and Yeho-hanan gather as many scrolls as they could carry and take them over to the storage room that had been carved out of the sand-stone many years ago. He had others take up holy Scripture and some of the community's precious books of interpretation and rules and take them to caves far away from the compound, caves that could not be easily seen from the road.

Photo: Hoyasmeg.

The young men readily complied but looked worried and perplexed. "Don't grieve, my friends," Eleazar assured them. "We shall return when the danger passes. We shall collect our books and continue our study. Wrap the books in linen and place them in the jars. This will make your work all the heavier, but it is important to protect our library." They did as instructed.

The overseer and some of the community evacuated; oth-ers remained behind, including Eleazar and Yehudah, willing to show the Romans a measure of hospitality, hoping to keep the theft and vandalism to a minimum. In the afternoon a mount-ed Roman patrol approached. When they saw a few unarmed men milling around in the compound, they signaled to the main body behind them.

The skirmish was brief. The brothers stood before the Romans, some calling on God to send fire from heaven to consume them and others simply standing in silence. The ones who called for

God's wrath were felled by arrows. The Romans also hacked to death anyone who attempted to flee or offer any hint of resistance. Eleazar and the dozen others who stood still and unflinching were spared. It seems even Roman soldiers found cold-blooded murder distasteful.

The travel-weary Romans took possession of the compound, making free with the food and drawing water from the pools and reservoirs. Eleazar was disgusted at this defilement but said nothing. The soldiers were speaking Greek, that much he knew, but exactly what he was not sure. In peacetime the Romans had shown the Jews some respect, not flaunting their most offensive, pagan standards and images but taking some care with respect to their behavior. Not this time. Not after years of bloody, costly war. Feeling for the leather strap wound around his arm, Eleazar softly recited the Shema, "Hear, O Israel, the Lord our God is one. . . ."

The Romans relieved themselves wherever they wished. Stripped naked, they flung themselves into the water, laughing and making obscene gestures. They freely ransacked and pilfered the community's goods. Unclean lips tasted pure food. One book that Eleazar's men had overlooked was picked up, held upside down, stared at with mock interest, and then with

Photo: Teqoah

a laugh was torn and thrown into the fire. Yehudah jumped up and tried to save the book, but a soldier rushed forward and pierced the young Jew's body with a sword. Nearby one of the other soldiers discovered one of the storage caves. Eleazar groaned when he saw him dragging books out from the cave, tearing them to pieces and casting them to the wind. He uttered a prayer that the other caves and the books within them would remain hidden.

Once they were refreshed, the Romans forced a few survivors of the community to carry whatever plunder had been gathered for the army's use. And so Eleazar and his colleagues began their march, a march that they knew would end either in slavery or death. Looking back, he saw the flames and smoke. The despoiled and defiled compound would soon be rubble. A soldier roughly shoved Eleazar and warned him of the consequences if he continued to look back at the sacked compound. Eleazar barely heard the threat; he was lost in questions about the future. Would he ever return here? Would the community ever reassemble? He doubted it. And what of Israel? Another exile for God's people? As they marched, he noticed that some of the others who earlier had fled were being rounded up. Eleazar was not surprised. It was easy to hide in the wilderness but not so easy to survive in it. "But God willing the books will survive," he said to himself. "The books will survive."

Chapter 2
Found

Date: AD 1947

Place: The marl terrace along the northwest shore of the Dead Sea

Seized with curiosity, Muhammed edh-Dhib Hasan, known to friends as "the Wolf," lowered himself into the cave. He wondered if he was the first man ever to enter this obscure hole in the ground. He hoped not. The ancients sometimes hid treasures in such places. Might this be his lucky day? As his eyes adjusted to the dim light, he noticed several clay jars sitting along the wall. Expectation surged through him as he began opening them. Here, locked away for untold years, he found dust, dirt, and a few ragged bundles that contained rolls of ancient leather. Oh well. No riches here. Perhaps he would have better luck some other time.

Early Discoveries

Though most people probably have no idea when the first of the Dead Sea Scrolls (DSS) was discovered, a common reply is shortly after World War II. In reality the DSS were discovered at least four times: twice long ago and twice again in modern times.

The DSS were discovered at least four times: twice long ago and twice again in modern times.

We cannot be certain, but the first discovery evidently took place in the early third century. Church historian Eusebius (AD 263–339) reports the following story concerning research conducted by the great Christian Bible scholar Origen (185–254):

> So accurate was the examination that Origen brought to bear upon the divine books, that he made a thorough study of the Hebrew tongue, and got into his own possession the original writings in the actual Hebrew characters, which were extant among the Jews.
> . . . He discovered certain other (manuscripts) in turn, which, after lying hidden for a long time, he traced and brought to light, I know not from what recesses. (*Ecclesiastical History* 6.16.1–2)

Origen.

Eusebius.

Eusebius goes on to mention Origen's production of a six-columned, multiversion edition of the Bible known as the *Hexapla*, in which the Hebrew text of the OT was compared with various Greek translations.[1] Eusebius states that "in the case of one of these [manuscripts] he indicated again that it was found at Jericho in a jar in the time of Antoninus the son of Severus."[2]

Jar found at Qumran. Photo: HolyLandPhotos.com.

Aurelius Antoninus was the elder son of Septimius Severus, and he reigned as Roman emperor from 198 to 217. Thus it was sometime in this 19-year period that Origen came to possess at least one manuscript which had long lain hidden. The fact that one or more manuscripts was discovered "in a jar" is quite interesting in light of the fact that some of the DSS were discovered in jars, as for instance in Cave 1 at Qumran. The practice of storing important documents in jars is mentioned in Scripture: "'This is what the LORD of Hosts, the God of Israel, says: Take these scrolls—this purchase agreement with the sealed copy and this open copy—and put them in an earthen storage jar so they will last a long time'" (Jer 32:14).

Further adding to the intrigue, Eusebius said Origen found a manuscript in a jar at Jericho. Jericho is on the outskirts of the very region in which the DSS were found. Two possibilities suggest that Qumran may have been the ultimate origin of this manuscript. First, it is possible that Eusebius was geographically imprecise when he named Jericho as the place of the manuscript's discovery.

Writers often name the largest known town in a region where an event or discovery has taken place. Thus "at Jericho" may be equivalent to "somewhere near Jericho." Second, it may be that the jar and scroll were indeed found in Jericho itself, but they could very easily have been found closer to Qumran in the first place and then taken to nearby Jericho, where they eventually came into Origen's possession. Given these plausible scenarios, it is certainly possible that Origen possessed a manuscript that belonged to the original group of DSS.

The second discovery of DSS may have taken place in the late eighth or early ninth century. In a letter to Sergius, the Bishop of Elam, Timotheus I, the Nestorian patriarch of Seleucia, mentioned manuscripts found in a cave near Jericho. Again this may be a geographical vagary. Jericho was certainly more widely known than the defunct Qumran community, and so Timotheus may have chosen to mention Jericho in order to give Sergius a general idea of where the discovery had taken place. The cave in question could have been at Qumran, but the only nearby city of note was Jericho.

Finally, some medieval Arab writers and others referred to a "cave sect" in the vicinity of Jericho that possessed Scriptures. The Qumran community fits this description very well, and if it was known that this sect possessed Scriptures, then it only makes sense to conclude that some of the writings had been recovered from the caves at Qumran.

From the above considerations we see that the DSS were possibly known, in part, many centuries before Muhammed edh-Dhib Hasan lowered himself into a cave in search of treasure in 1947.

The DSS were possibly known, in part, many centuries before Muhammed edh-Dhib Hasan lowered himself into a cave in search of treasure in 1947.

Modern Discoveries

In modern times the first scroll was discovered in the late nineteenth century not in the region of the Dead Sea but in a synagogue in Cairo, Egypt. The document in question was found among thousands of mostly medieval texts, stored away in a long-forgotten synagogue storage room called a genizah, a

Part of the Ben Ezra Synagogue. Photo: Zerida.

place where worn-out sacred books were retired. By custom, the Jews refused to burn or destroy documents that contained the name of God, and so they were typically stored away and either forgotten or eventually buried in a reverent burial ceremony. More on this genizah in chapter 12.

The scroll discovered in the Cairo genizah became known as the Damascus Document. We will examine it more closely later. It provided scholars with much data, but it proved to be only the barest beginning of a new era in the study of ancient Jewish writings.

In contrast to the first modern discovery of the DSS, which involved only the Damascus Document, the second modern discovery involved hundreds of documents and dozens of caves in almost as many locations. Furthermore, the discoveries have continued on and off for about a half century.

We think the discovery of the first cave in the region of the Dead Sea came in the spring of 1947, though it was another six months or so before scholars laid eyes on the scrolls extracted from this cave.[3] I say "we think" because some local Bedouin (desert-dwelling nomads) claim that a few of the scrolls were actually discovered a year or more before the spring of 1947. The story of the discovery and eventual sale of the first scrolls recovered from Qumran could hardly be more convoluted and

:onfusing. Here are the basic events in chronological order:

November 1946 to February 1947
Sometime during this period three Bedouin (Muhammed edh-Dhib Hasan, Jum'a Muhammed, and Khalil Musa) discovered the first cave near Qumran while tending their flocks. Eventually called Cave 1, this cave is about one mile north of the Qumran community ruins adjacent to Wadi Qumran. A wadi is a gulch or small canyon. The ruins of the Qumran community itself lie about 20 miles north of En Gedi, an oasis west of the Dead Sea.

March 1947
Jum'a and Khalil offered to sell three scrolls to Ibrahim 'Ijha, an antiquities dealer in Bethlehem. The dealer declined, fearing the scrolls were stolen property. Shortly thereafter Jum'a showed the scrolls to George Isha'ya, another Bethlehem antiquities dealer, and Sheikh 'Ali Subh, chief of the Ta'amireh tribe. 'Ali Subh suggested that Jum'a show the scrolls to Khalil Iskander (a.k.a. Kando Shahin). Kando was a Syrian Orthodox merchant, shoemaker, and later became an antiquities dealer. The scrolls Jum'a possessed were:

- 1QIsaiah^a (the Great Isaiah Scroll)
- 1QpHab (the pesher, or commentary, on the biblical book of Habakkuk)
- 1QS (Serek Yahad, or the Rule of the Community, at one time called the Manual of Discipline)

April 1947
George Isha'ya mentioned the scrolls to the Syrian Orthodox metropolitan Mar Athanasius Samuel at Saint Mark's Monastery in Jerusalem's Old City. Kando and Isha'ya later showed one of the scrolls to Mar Samuel. Recognizing that the scroll was written in Hebrew and was probably ancient, Mar Samuel expressed interest in purchasing it and any other scrolls Kando and Isha'ya possessed.

May or June 1947
Jum'a returned to Cave 1 and recovered four more scrolls.

July 1947
Kando, acting on behalf of the Bedouin, sold 1QIsaiah^a, 1QpHab, and 1QS to Mar Samuel for about $100. Later that month Mar Samuel showed the scrolls to J. P. M. van der Ploeg, professor of Old Testament at the University of Nijmegen, the Netherlands. The professor mistakenly believed that the scrolls dated to the medieval era. He was the first scholar to lay eyes on the DSS, but he failed to recognize their great value.

Late August 1947
William Brownlee and John Trever, postdoctoral students and fellows of the American Schools of Oriental Research, arrived in Palestine.

September 1947
Anton Kiraz traveled with Mar Samuel and assisted him in showing the scrolls to interested parties. In October the two men became partners, with Kiraz providing financial support.

Late November 1947
An anonymous Armenian antiquities dealer contacted Eleazar Sukenik of Hebrew University. Sukenik was shown a piece of leather with Hebrew script. Sukenik, who had excavated burial sites on Kiraz's property, recognized the antiquity of the script. Sukenik was the first scholar to perceive their importance.

November 29, 1947
Sukenik purchased two scrolls: 1QHa (the large Hodayot, or Hymns, Scroll) and 1QM (Milhamah, the War Scroll).

December 22, 1947
Sukenik purchased several fragments of 1QIsa^b, the second Isaiah Scroll from Cave 1.

February 6, 1948
Sukenik attempted unsuccessfully to purchase more scrolls.

February–April 1948
Butros Sowmy, assistant to Mar Samuel, took three scrolls (1QIsaᵃ, 1QpHab, and 1QS) to the American Schools of Oriental Research, where on February 21–22 John Trever and William Brownlee photographed them after they recognized the antiquity and value of the scrolls. On March 6–11 the Isaiah and Habakkuk Scrolls were rephotographed for publication. In April Trever and Brownlee departed Palestine for the United States.

April 11, 1948
News of the discovery of the scrolls made headlines around the world.

May 1948
The British mandate over Palestine ended, and Israel became an officially recognized nation. Israel was immediately attacked by her Arab neighbors. Butros Sowmy was killed in the ensuing war.

August 1948
George Isha'ya returned to Cave 1 and recovered additional scroll fragments.

November 1948
George Isha'ya and Kando returned to the cave and recovered more fragments.

February 1949
John Trever met with Mar Samuel in the United States and assisted in unraveling 1QapGen (the Genesis Apocryphon Scroll).

March 1949
Cave 1 was professionally excavated by Lankester Harding (of the Palestine Archaeological Museum) and Roland de

Vaux (of the École Biblique et Archéologique Française). Pottery and many more scroll fragments were recovered.

Spring 1950
Kando sold the remainder of his Cave 1 scrolls. These included 1QSa (the Rule of the Congregation) and 1QSb (the Rule of the Blessings). To this day his family still possesses pottery from the caves, including a fully intact scroll jar.

November–December 1951
Harding established via archaeological evidence that the ruins at Qumran were related to the pottery and scroll discoveries of Cave 1. This implies that the scrolls were the property of members of the Qumran community.

February 1952
Cave 2 was discovered a short distance south of Cave 1.

March 1952
Cave 3 was discovered about one and three-quarter miles north of Qumran. On March 14 the Copper Scroll (3Q15) was discovered.

September 1952
Cave 4 was excavated and discovered to contain hundreds of scrolls, comprising (it is now estimated) some 40,000 fragments. Cave 5, quite close to Cave 4, was then discovered to contain scroll fragments. Caves 4 and 5 are man-made and evidently were part of the Qumran compound. At the same time Cave 6 was discovered by Bedouin. It was located a short distance west, on the cliff overlooking Wadi Qumran.

June 1954
Mar Samuel ran an advertisement in *The Wall Street Journal*, offering to sell the remainder of the scrolls in his possession. Yigael Yadin, son of the late Eleazar Sukenik, purchased these scrolls for $250,000. Recall that on February 6, 1948, Sukenik had tried but failed to purchase more

scrolls. Thus his son fulfilled his father's wishes.

February–April 1955
Caves 7, 8, 9, and 10 were discovered. All of these are quite close to the Qumran ruins, sharing the same marl terrace on which the ruins are situated.

February 1956
Cave 11 was discovered about one and a half miles north of Qumran. Most of the scrolls found there ended up in the hands of Kando, who sold them to the Palestine Archaeological Museum. Two of the most important scrolls sold at this time were 11QNew Jerusalem and 11QtgJob (an Aramaic paraphrase of Job). However, Kando retained possession of 11QTemple (the Temple Scroll).

June 1967
Israel defeated several Arab nations and gained control of all of Jerusalem and the West Bank. Shortly after the cease-fire, Yadin hired some men to seize the Temple Scroll from Kando at gunpoint.[4] Kando retained an attorney and later received financial compensation for his losses.

Scroll Discoveries Outside Qumran

In all, some 100,000 fragments have been recovered at Qumran, constituting at least 900 documents. However, while Bedouin and archaeologists were excavating caves in the vicinity of Qumran, discoveries were also being made at other sites in the Dead Sea region. I list below these other sites and offer brief summaries of the finds:

In all, some 100,000 fragments have been recovered at Qumran, constituting at least 900 documents.

October 1951
Bedouin found fragments of inscribed leather in caves of the Wadi Murabba'at, about 11 miles south of Qumran.

Harding and de Vaux joined in the excavations. In March 1955 a scroll of the Minor Prophets was found.

July 1952
Bedouin found Byzantine and early Arabic texts in and around the ruins of a monastery at Khirbet Mird, about five miles west of Qumran. "Khirbet" means ruins. In early 1953 and again in early 1955, the site was excavated.

July or August 1952
Bedouin found a few fragmentary manuscripts at Nahal Hever, some 25 miles south of Qumran. In April 1958 another cave was discovered at Nahal Hever, yielding fragments of the Psalter and more than one dozen nonbiblical letters in the Hebrew, Aramaic, and Greek languages. Yadin conducted a series of excavations in 1960 and 1961, uncovering the Babatha letters and the Bar Kokhba letters. Yohanan Aharoni also discovered a Greek Minor Prophets scroll.

March 1955
A papyrus fragment was found at Masada, some 30 miles south of Qumran. In 1963–64 Yadin excavated Masada, uncovering a number of documents, including a work called the Songs of the Sabbath Sacrifice, several copies of which had been found previously in Qumran Cave 4.

1960
Aharoni excavated several caves in Nahal Se'elim (a.k.a. Seiyal) and found a few fragments of text in Cave 34.

1960 and 1961
Pessah Bar-Adon explored and excavated various caves at Nahal Mishmar, uncovering a few papyrus fragments.

February 1962
Bedouin discovered about 40 Samaritan documents inscribed on papyrus in Wadi ed-Daliyeh, about nine miles north of Jericho.

April – June 1986
Hanan Eshel excavated caves in Wadi el-Mafjar, finding some Aramaic and Greek documents.

November 1993
The Israel Antiquities Authority conducted "Operation Scroll," in which a number of caves and various locations were examined. Eshel discovered Aramaic and Greek non-literary documents at Ketef Jericho, near modern Jericho.

August 2004
Eshel purchased Bar Kokhba-era (c. AD 132) Leviticus scroll fragments from three Bedouin. Where the scroll fragments are from and under what circumstances the Bedouin acquired them is uncertain (though it is claimed that Eshel's colleague Roi Porat has located the cave source). The fragments comprise portions of Leviticus 23–24. Eshel also obtained and published fragments of earlier finds that had remained in private hands.

More to Come?

From this overview one should realize that fresh DSS discoveries remain possible. The region around the Dead Sea, lined with many wadis and dry riverbeds, is peppered with natural caves and man-made hiding places that are ideal for storing scrolls. The arid climate protects the leather and papyrus documents from rot, and the sparseness of human population has left most of these treasures undisturbed for millennia.

Modern Storage of the Scrolls

The DSS (from Qumran and elsewhere) are housed in different locations around the world. Here are some of the key locations:

National Archaeological Museum, Amman, Jordan
About 20 documents are housed here, including the Copper Scroll (3Q15).

The Shrine of the Book

This repository is part of the Israel Museum compound in Jerusalem. It houses the major scrolls acquired by Eleazar Sukenik and his son Yigael Yadin. These include the Isaiah Scrolls (1QIsa^a and 1QIsa^b), the War Scroll (1QM), the Hymns Scroll (1QH), the commentary on Habakkuk (1QpHab), the Genesis Apocryphon (1QapGen), the Rule of the Community (1QS), and the Temple Scroll (11Q19).

Bibliothèque Nationale

Some of the scrolls acquired by the École Biblique are stored in Paris.

Rockefeller Museum, Jerusalem

The bulk of the scrolls, including the many thousands of fragments, are housed in the Rockefeller Museum of east Jerusalem (formerly the Palestine Archaeological Museum).

Private and Miscellaneous

A few scrolls are in the hands of private collectors, such as Georges Roux in France and an anonymous collector who may possess one or two Cave 11 scrolls. The Schøyen Collection in Oslo should also be mentioned. Some scroll fragments are in university collections (e.g., Chicago, Heidelberg, and Louvain). Finally, many photographs and digital images of the scrolls are housed in other countries.

Muhammed's Treasure

It is now more than 60 years since Muhammed edh-Dhib Hasan sneaked into a cave in hopes of finding treasure. Whereas he thought he had only found worthless old jars and documents, in reality he found treasure far more precious than gold or gems. In the next chapter we examine why the scrolls are so important.

Notes

1. The *Hexapla* presented the OT text in six parallel columns. The first column was Hebrew, the second was Hebrew transliterated (or sounded out) with Greek letters, and the next four columns were various Greek translations of the Hebrew. Origen's work was of great use to early Christian scholars of Scripture. Unfortunately, only fragments of the *Hexapla* survive today.

2. Eusebius, *Ecclasiastical History* 6.16.3.

3. For up-to-date and very helpful overviews of the discovery of the scrolls, see W. W. Fields, "Discovery and Purchase," in L. H. Schiffman and J. C. VanderKam (eds.), *Encyclopedia of the Dead Sea Scrolls* (2 vols., Oxford: Oxford University Press, 2000), 1:208–12; idem, *The Dead Sea Scrolls: A Short History* (Leiden: Brill, 2006); and J. C. VanderKam and P. W. Flint, *The Meaning of the Dead Sea Scrolls: Their Significance for Understanding the Bible, Judaism, Jesus, and Christianity* (San Francisco: HarperCollins, 2002), 3–19. One should also consult J. C. Trever, *The Dead Sea Scrolls: A Personal Account* (Piscataway, NJ: Gorgias Press, 2003), as well as G. Kiraz (ed.), *Anton Kiraz's Archive on the Dead Sea Scrolls* (Piscataway, NJ: Gorgias Press, 2005). Anton Kiraz worked with Mar Samuel, Eleazar Sukenik, and John Trever, leaving behind 20 years of correspondence and notes (mostly 1948–67) that help fill in the many blanks in the fascinating and complex story of the discovery and eventual publication of the DSS.

4. Sometime later a sanitized version of this remarkable incident was reported on the front page of the *Jerusalem Post* (October 22, 1967).

Chapter 3
Why the Scrolls Matter

The Dead Sea Scrolls (DSS) have fascinated people around the world since April 11, 1948, when headlines everywhere announced their discovery. Part of the fascination has to do with the physical makeup of the scrolls themselves. Rather than books made up of bound pages that you turn as you read, the ancients put their manuscripts on scrolls that were unrolled as they were read. Thus the scrolls are long sheets of inscribed leather rolled up and bound shut by strips of linen.

The larger cause for fascination has to do with the origin of the scrolls. To the delight of anyone interested in biblical studies, the DSS date all the way back to the era before and during the lives of Jesus and his disciples. Such a discovery seemed impossible. Could scrolls

The DSS date all the way back to the era before and during the lives of Jesus and his disciples.

this ancient really have survived down to modern times? Yes, they did. Dating methods such as Carbon 14 have proved that the scrolls are indeed that old.

It is hard to overestimate the significance of the DSS for biblical studies. The scrolls probably constitute the single most important manuscript find in history. There have been other important finds, such as the Nag Hammadi manuscripts found in the desert sands of Egypt, but no other find has had more importance for understanding the Bible and the world of Jesus and his earliest followers.

Interest in the Bible and Christian origins rose sharply once the DSS were brought to light.

Understandably, interest in the Bible and Christian origins rose sharply once the DSS were brought to light. Scholars and clergy started talking about findings and implications, books about the scrolls rolled off the presses with increasing frequency, and the public was eager to get in on the discoveries. Crowds flocked to see the scrolls on display in Jerusalem and in traveling showcases around the world.

Tourists at Qumran. Photo: Abraham Sobkowski.

The exact number of surviving scrolls is not known. This is primarily because of the fragmentary condition of many scrolls, with the result that sometimes we do not know which fragments belong to which document. It is also because one or two (or more) scrolls that were never photographed or transcribed are probably in private hands. Thus they exist, but few people know their whereabouts or details. Overall the best estimate is that there are approximately 900 scrolls in existence, of which some 220 are Bible scrolls.

Of course, sensational claims—often media driven—began to

circulate soon after the DSS were discovered. We were told that the scrolls contain secrets that are embarrassing to the Christian faith. Some people even claimed that the Vatican tried to suppress the scrolls. Indeed, all sorts of conspiracy theories have been advanced:

- Important scrolls are missing, perhaps hidden away.
- Jesus was an Essene and once belonged to the community that produced the DSS.
- The shocking truth about Jesus and Christian origins is imbedded within the scrolls but is being kept from the world due to fears of widespread unrest.

And so it goes. What are we to make of all this? What do we really learn from the scrolls, and why do they matter?

How the Scrolls Help Us Understand the Bible

The DSS help us better understand the Bible and the world of Jesus in at least nine ways:

1. The DSS are a big help in our study of ancient writing and the science of making scrolls. Before the discovery of the DSS, we had almost no written materials from Israel dating to the time of Jesus. Now we have an entire library, with some of the scrolls remarkably well preserved (e.g., the Great Isaiah Scroll).

2. The DSS are a big help in confirming the text of the Hebrew portion of Scripture, which Christians call the Old

Evidence from the DSS indicates that the Hebrew manuscripts on which our OT translations are based were well preserved and carefully copied through the centuries.

Testament. What we have found is that the Hebrew manuscripts on which our OT translations are based were well preserved and carefully copied through the centuries, for they bear close resemblance to the OT manuscripts found at Qumran.

3. The DSS enable scholars of Aramaic and Hebrew to study these languages as they were used in the time of Jesus. This is quite important, for Jesus spoke Aramaic, and the Hebrew that was used in his time was not exactly the same as the Hebrew found in the OT.

4. Among the DSS we have found a great number of new writings, many of which we call apocryphal and pseudepigraphal. These resemble the books of the OT in content and purpose but were written in later times and falsely attributed to famous biblical figures such as Moses or Enoch in order to make the books seem important.

5. The DSS assist us in our study of the various religious and nonreligious groups among the Jewish people in the time of Jesus. The NT writings tell us about Pharisees and Sadducees, and the Jewish historian Josephus describes these and the Essenes as well, but the scrolls give us a different perspective. And if the scrolls really did belong to the Essenes, we can learn a lot more about this mysterious group.

6. The DSS give us a great many examples of how Scripture was interpreted 2,000 years ago. In some cases we find OT prophecies interpreted the same way they are interpreted

in the NT. At other times we find very different interpretations. Examination of the scrolls helps us understand the different interpretative approaches.

7. The DSS help us understand better what was happening in the century or so before the time of Jesus and the founding of the Church. This is important information if we are to understand how Jesus' contemporaries viewed the

Sermon on the Mount by Gustave Doré.

condition of their country and its pressing needs.

8. The DSS help us understand much better the teachings and beliefs of the Jewish people in the time of Jesus. The more we understand these things,

The DSS help us understand better what was happening in the century or so before the time of Jesus and the founding of the Church.

the more we can grasp the reception and rejection of Jesus as Messiah.

9. The DSS provide excellent information for understanding the Jewish background of Jesus, his first followers, and many of the writings that make up the NT.

While some of these topics are too technical to explore in depth in an introductory book such as this, we will cover relevant issues closely enough to provide readers with a better grasp of the world in which Jesus lived and taught, the world in which his movement took shape, struggled to survive, flourished, and in three centuries swept the Roman Empire.[1]

Note

1. For general orientation, including major questions and issues, see E. M. Cook, *Solving the Mysteries of the Dead Sea Scrolls: New Light on the Bible* (Grand Rapids: Zondervan, 1994); J. A. Fitzmyer, *Responses to 101 Questions on the Dead Sea Scrolls* (New York: Paulist, 1992); E. M. Schuller, *The Dead Sea Scrolls: What Have We Learned?* (Louisville: Westminster John Knox Press, 2006).

Chapter 4
The Dead Sea Region

The Dead Sea is a somewhat prominent feature in the Bible. It is first mentioned in the OT in Genesis 14:3, where it is called the "Salt Sea" and is said to be situated in the Valley of Siddim. We are also told that the cities of Sodom and Gomorrah were located in the vicinity of the Dead Sea (cf. 13:10–13), though archaeologists have not yet discovered their elusive ruins.

In the book of Numbers, the Dead Sea is said to delineate the eastern boundary of the promised land: "Then the border will go down to the Jordan and end at the Dead Sea" (Num 34:12). For obvious reasons the Dead Sea is commonly called the "Salt Sea," as for instance some translations read in v. 12 and elsewhere (e.g., Num 34:3; Deut 3:17; Josh 3:16; 12:3; 15:2,5; 18:19). It is also called the "Sea of the Arabah" (Deut 3:17; 4:49; Josh 3:16; 12:3; and 2 Kgs 14:25), while in Ezekiel 47:18; Joel 2:20; and Zechariah 14:8, it is called "the eastern sea" (Joel adds that the area is "dry and desolate").

One of the best-known sites on the Dead Sea is En-Gedi

En-Gedi. Photo: Ester Inbar.

("Spring of the Kid"), an oasis which is mentioned along with "the City of Salt" (Josh 15:62). En-Gedi is the place where David sought refuge when fleeing from Saul (1 Sam 23:29; 24:1). In OT times it was a place of vineyards and date palms (Song 1:14; Josephus, *Jewish Antiquities* 9.7).

The Dead Sea Outside the Bible

Josephus Flavius, the first-century Jewish historian and survivor of the great Jewish war with Rome (AD 66–70), called the Dead Sea the "Lake of Sodom" (*Antiquities* 5.81). The late first-century book 2 Esdras 5:7 called it the "Sea of Sodom." It is sometimes called this in the Talmud (tractate *Shabbath* 108b), a sixth-century compilation of Jewish law and lore.

The Dead Sea has also been called a "lake of Asphalt" (Pliny the Elder, *Hist. Nat.* 5.15.15; and many times in the writings of Josephus), evidently because of the ash and chunks of tar and bitumen that sometimes float to the surface (Josephus, *War* 4.479, 483

> *Josephus called the Dead Sea the "Lake of Sodom" (Antiquities 5.81).*

"all burned up"). So far as we know, this body of water was first called the "Dead Sea" by Pausanias (*Perigesis* 5.7, 4–5), a second-century Greek author and geographer who described people and places as he traveled abroad. Previous to him, early Greek writers knew of the Dead Sea (e.g., Aristotle, *Meteorology* 2.3, 39; Strabo 5.2.42). Of special interest is a lengthy description Josephus provides in which he calls the Dead Sea "bitter and unfruitful." I have included the text below:

Josephus: The Dead Sea Is Bitter and Unfruitful

The nature of the lake Asphalt is also worth describing. It is, as I have said already, bitter and unfruitful. It

is so light or thick that it bears up the heaviest things that are thrown into it; nor is it easy for anyone to make things sink therein to the bottom, if he had a mind so to do. Accordingly, when Vespasian went to see it, he commanded that some who could not swim, should have their hands tied behind them, and be thrown into the deep, when it so happened that they all swam as if a wind had forced them upwards. Moreover, the change of the color of this lake is wonderful, for it changes its appearance thrice every day; and as the rays of the sun fall differently upon it, the light is variously reflected. However, it casts up black clods of bitumen in many parts of it; these swim at the top of the water, and resemble both in shape and bigness headless bulls; and when the laborers that belong to the lake come to it, and catch hold of it as it hangs together, they draw it into their ships; but when the ship is full, it is not easy to cut off the rest, for it is so tenacious as to make the ship hang upon its clods. . . . This bitumen is not only useful for the caulking of ships, but for the cure of men's bodies: accordingly it is mixed in a great many medicines. The length of this lake is five hundred and eighty furlongs, where it is extended as far as Zoar, in Arabia; and its breadth is a hundred and fifty. The country of Sodom borders upon it. It was of old a most happy land both for the fruits it bore and the riches of its cities, although it be now all burned up. (*War* 4.476–83)

Geography and Composition of the Dead Sea

The Dead Sea is about 13 miles east of Jerusalem and is situated some 1,300 feet below sea level. It is part of a geographic formation known as the Great Rift Valley, which extends from southern Turkey in the north, south through the Red Sea, and on into eastern Africa. At one time the Dead Sea was 45 miles north to south and nine miles east to west at its widest, giving it a shoreline of about 124 miles and a surface area of about 300 square miles. In recent years the Sea has lost more than 30 feet of depth due to evaporation and the diversion of the south-flowing water of the Jordan River.

The Dead Sea is about 13 miles east of Jerusalem and is situated some 1,300 feet below sea level.

The air temperature of this region typically ranges from a low of 10 degrees Celsius (40 degrees Fahrenheit) to a high of 45 degrees Celsius (113 degrees Fahrenheit), though sometimes even higher temperatures are reached.

About 25 percent of the Dead Sea is salt and other chemicals and minerals, making it about 10 times saltier than the

Hyraxes at the Dead Sea. Photo: Mike Bannert.

Ibex at the Dead Sea.

ocean. In all it is estimated that more than 40 billion tons of salts and minerals are in the lake and its deposits. Many of these are being extracted today for commercial use. The water feels oily and is so dense that people effortlessly float

The Dead Sea is about 10 times saltier than the ocean.

on its surface. Indeed, one early writer (Solinus, *Collections* 35.2) claimed that he had heard that even bulls and camels can float on the Dead Sea!

Animals that live in the Dead Sea region include goats, the small deerlike ibex whose skin was sometimes used for the leather scrolls, and hyraxes, which are mentioned in Proverbs 30:26 (RSV: "badgers"; KJV: "conies").

Qumran, where many of the caves containing the scrolls were found, is situated on the northwest shore of the Dead Sea. Machaerus, Herod's fortress where John the Baptist was imprisoned and executed, is located on the eastern side of the Dead Sea, which today is in Jordan. Through ancient times and on into the Middle Ages, a variety of outposts and farming communities existed along the shores of this most interesting lake. And it is fitting, perhaps, that on the shore of this mineral-rich sea that preserves whatever is thrown into it, a collection of ancient scrolls successfully rode out the centuries intact, awaiting discovery in modern times.

The Shrine of the Book at the Israel Museum in Jerusalem where a number of the Dead Sea Scrolls are housed. Its unique design reflects the shape of the lids on the jars in which the scrolls were contained.
Photo: Berthold Werner.

Part II
The Science of the Scrolls

Chapter 5
The Science of Dating the Scrolls

When the first Dead Sea Scrolls (DSS) came to light, opinions as to their authenticity and date of origin varied. Some thought they hailed from medieval times; others thought they dated to a time before Jesus. This represents a discrepancy of a thousand years!

It wasn't long before other problems became apparent. Many of the scrolls were in fragments. How were they to be reassembled? There really was no such thing as a scientific approach to these kinds of problems back then. Believe it or not, in the 1950s the scroll team and their assistants used scotch tape to piece together the fragments! A number of years

Believe it or not, in the 1950s the scroll team and their assistants used scotch tape to piece together the fragments!

ago, I attended a scrolls display in the United States and noticed a dozen brown fuzz balls alongside the scrolls. What could these be, I wondered. On closer examination I realized that they were balled-up pieces of scotch tape. They had yellowed with age, and brown scroll leather fuzz was clinging to the adhesive. You will be relieved to know that this tape was carefully removed from the scrolls in the early 1990s. These sticky balls of tape are now themselves museum pieces, bearing witness to the inauspicious beginnings of the science of restoring and preserving the DSS.

In old photographs you will notice scholars smoking cigarettes while poring over the scrolls, sometimes with dangerously long extensions of ash hanging from the smoldering end. On top of that, many of the scrolls were laid out on tables that were sitting in direct sunlight! Others were treated with oil in hopes that this would make the letters more visible. These oil-treated scrolls have darkened over time, making it harder than ever to make out the writing. To say the least, many of the DSS are in noticeably poorer condition today than they were when they were discovered.

A manuscript from the Dead Sea Scrolls as currently preserved at the Citadel in Amman, Jordan. Photo: Dale Gillard.

And finally, during the reorganization of the scrolls team in the early 1990s, it was discovered that a few scroll fragments had simply disappeared! Did someone take souvenirs? Were fragments just innocently lost? The answer is not clear.

Many of the DSS are in noticeably poorer condition today than they were when they were discovered.

Along the way an impressive set of science techniques were developed that has greatly aided scrolls research. These include paleography, carbon-14 testing, highly technical image analysis, DNA testing, and new approaches to restoration and preservation of ancient documents. Other disciplines, such as archaeology and numismatics (the study of coins), have also been of great help in assessing the scrolls.

Our focus in this chapter is the origin of the DSS. Solid answers on this issue will help us assess the true significance of the scrolls and their implications for biblical studies. So how old are the scrolls? Let's put science to the test.

The Date of the Scrolls

As touched on above, when the DSS were first discovered, some scholars thought they dated back no more than a thousand years. Others suggested they were penned in the first century AD, perhaps by early Jewish Christians. A few even thought they dated back to a time well before Jesus. Without precise scientific methods for dating ancient manuscripts, scholars were unable to resolve the matter. Thus it was necessary to develop and apply sound methods for dating the scrolls. Fortunately, modern science and technology were developing new ways of dating objects, and biblical scholars were learning how to date manuscripts on the basis of handwriting style. Archaeology also made important contributions. Combined, these disciplines made it possible to date most of the scrolls to a time frame of about a half century or so. Here is how they did it:

Ostraca found at Masada. Photo: heatkernel.

Paleography

Paleography (from the Greek, meaning "ancient writing") is the study of handwriting.[1] Scholars gather handwriting samples found on ancient rolls of leather, papyrus, or pieces of pottery (called ostraca) and carefully compare the variances in style. Helpfully, ancient documents such as business papers and official decrees often include a notation about the date of their composition. Scholars note the changing styles of writing over time on the dated documents and then compare these with documents that are typically undated, such as Scripture and other literary works. By this method scholars can determine, within a half century or so, the date of composition for an undated document. Harvard University professor Frank Moore Cross pioneered the application of this method to the DSS. Subsequent study has only confirmed his brilliant conclusions. Cross found that most of the DSS were written in the last half of the first century BC and the beginning of the first century AD. This gives a date range of roughly 50 BC to AD 50 for the majority of the documents. He also determined that a goodly number of the scrolls were written 50 to 100 years earlier than this, and a few were written earlier still. Clearly his studies refuted any idea that the scrolls hailed from the medieval era.

Frank Moore Cross's paleographical studies date the DSS as follows:

Period	Number of Scrolls
250–150 BC	21
200–150 BC	20
150–50 BC	224
75–1 BC	5
50 BC–AD 68	418

Carbon-14

Around the time the first DSS were coming to light, scientists developed a new method for measuring the age of anything—plant or animal—that had once been alive. This method is popularly known as carbon 14 dating.[2]

Briefly, here is how it works: carbon 14 (aka C14) atoms are absorbed by plant life during photosynthesis. Animals and humans then eat the plants and in turn absorb the C14. When a living organism dies, it stops absorbing C14 since it is no longer building things like bone tissue. At this point the existing carbon14 atoms begin converting (via radioactive decay) to nitrogen 14 atoms. This conversion takes place at a steady rate over time. Scientists have learned what this rate is, enabling them to measure the amount of carbon conversion that has taken place and thus determine how long the organism has been dead (i.e., ceased absorbing carbon 14). When scientists complete this dating method, they arrive at a year "BP," that is, Before Present. Thus if the data indicates that a given organic object ceased absorbing carbon 14 and began radiological decay 2,000 years ago, scientists date the object 2000 BP.

Linen wrapping found with scroll fragments.

This new science was applied to the scrolls in 1950. Well, actually it was applied to a linen wrapping found in one of the jars containing scrolls. Keep in mind that linen is a fabric made from the fibers of the flax plant, which is of course an organic being that once absorbed C14 as it grew. The dating range for the linen wrapping came to as old as 167 BC and as recent as AD 233. The middle point was the first 20–30 years of the new era, which coincides with Jesus' adulthood and early ministry. The scientist who conducted the study settled on the date AD 33 for himself, the commonly accepted date for Christ's crucifixion and resurrection. In 1956 a piece of wood from the Qumran ruins was tested, yielding a dating range of 70 BC to AD 90. The correlation with the date of the linen cloth is obvious and impressive, giving us confidence that we've landed in the right date range.

Over the years C14 testing has improved in accuracy and in its present form is called Accelerator Mass Spectrometry (AMS) testing. The dating results of this method are more precise and tend to narrow the date range even more.

However, some of the tests of Qumran materials have yielded surprising results. Some items have tested to a much greater age than expected; others, to a much more recent date. Scholars now recognize why that happens. Some scrolls have been contaminated, either through contact with older scrolls (with debris from older scrolls becoming attached to the newer scroll) or through contact with modern materials, such as the oils that the original scrolls team used to soften the leather and make the writing more legible.

Despite problems such as these, scholars and scientists are satisfied that the Qumran scrolls really do date from the third, second, and first centuries BC and from the first half of the first century AD. These results agree with the paleographical analysis discussed above. When two or more distinct dating methods arrive at the same conclusion, that conclusion is well founded.

When two or more distinct dating methods arrive at the same conclusion, that conclusion is well founded.

A Comparison of Paleographic and AMS Dates

Scroll	Paleographical Date	AMS Date
1QIsa[a]	125–100 BC	202–114 BC
1QpHab	AD 1–50	88–2 BC
1QS	100–50 BC	116 BC– AD 50
1QapGen	30 BC– AD 30	47 BC– AD 48
4Q521	125–75 BC	39 BC– AD 66
11QTemple	30 BC– AD 30	53 BC– AD 21

Coins

The study of coins, or numismatics, also helps us date the DSS. More than 160 coins, minted by those who ruled over Israel from 223 to 4 BC, have been found at Qumran (see text box). Another 180 coins hail from a later era. These were issued under Archelaus, Roman governors, and Agrippa I, grandson of Herod the Great, who ruled or administered Israel from 4 BC to AD 44.

Tabulation of Coins Found at Qumran

Ruler(s)	Period	No. of Coins
Antiochus III–VII	223–129 BC	8
John Hyrcanus	134–104 BC	10
Alexander Jannaeus	103–76 BC	128
Aristobulus II	76–63 BC	1
Mattathias Antigonus	40–37 BC	6
Herod the Great	37–4 BC	15

In addition to these coins, three buried jugs were unearthed, containing a total of 561 Tyrian shekels (coins acceptable for use at the temple in Jerusalem). These coins date to the first century BC, with the latest dating to 9/8 BC, which is shortly before Jesus' birth. It is assumed that these jugs were buried for safekeeping shortly after the date of the most recent coins. Why this coin hoard was never recovered and used by later members of the Qumran community is unclear. It is also inferred that the Qumran compound was abandoned temporarily, for why bury money if you're leaving permanently? Thus it seems that this hoard was buried just before the turn of the new era (BC to AD) and then inadvertently forgotten when the Qumran site was reinhabited shortly thereafter.

The large number of coins minted by those who ruled Israel before the new era and the large number of Tyrian shekels, which also date to the time before Jesus, provide compelling evidence that Qumran was occupied and active throughout the first century BC and perhaps a few decades earlier.

But do the coins help us discover when the community was destroyed?

More than 70 coins minted during the Jewish rebellion (AD 66–70) have also been found (39 in a cloth bag and 33 in a basin). These coins bear legends reading "year two" and "year three," that is, the second and third years of the Jewish rebellion. This translates to the years 67 and 68. No "year four" (69) or "year five" (70) coins have been found. Because Josephus (*War* 4.449, 486) tells us that General

Half shekel reading "Year 2." Photo: CNG Coins (www.cngcoins.com).

Vespasian occupied Jericho in June 68, many have inferred that the not-too-distant Qumran compound must have been destroyed at about the same time. This would explain the absence of "year four" and "year five" coins at Qumran. If Vespasian had already destroyed the community, no one was there to collect new coins. This conclusion could be correct, for Josephus also says that Vespasian visited the Dead Sea and tested its reputation for buoyancy by throwing people who could not swim into the lake (*War* 4.476–77). It would be natural to assume that Vespasian's troops destroyed the compound at Qumran when they visited the Sea.

A coin showing Antiochus V. Photo: CNG Coins (www.cngcoins.com).

Although the proposed AD 68 date for the destruction of the Qumran compound is plausible, the discovery of a few coins dating to 72 and 73 (three apparently minted in honor of Vespasian himself, who was acclaimed emperor in 69) suggests that the destruction may have occurred in 73 or 74 instead. At this time General Silva, acting under Emperor Vespasian's orders, marched on Masada, some 30 miles south of Qumran. Perhaps he destroyed Qumran at this time as well.

I incline to the later date because we know Roman troops marched on Masada in 73, and it is probable that to do so they set forth from Jericho and marched south along the western shore of the Dead Sea. Along the way Silva would have encountered Qumran and then Ein Feshka, about two miles south of Qumran. Some men of Qumran seemingly resisted, and thus the compound was destroyed. Evidence of battle is seen in the many Roman arrowheads found in the ruins of Qumran. Nearby Ein Feshka, however, had been evacuated by this time, and so it was not destroyed.

I might add that if Vespasian attacked and destroyed Qumran when he visited the Dead Sea in 68, it is surprising that Josephus said nothing about it. After all, Josephus provides us with lengthy descriptions of the men of Qumran and their beliefs. I should think that

Masada.

their destruction at the hands of Vespasian, the Roman who liberated and exalted Josephus to high station, would be emphasized in Josephus's writings since Josephus owed a debt of gratitude to Vespasian. His silence on the matter of Qumran's destruction likely indicates that Josephus knew nothing of it. He knew of Masada's capture, of course, for Masada was a key fortress, and its overthrow was General Silva's main objective. Josephus learned of the siege and capture of Masada and so narrated it. But of the destruction of the small and comparatively insignificant compound at Qumran, he probably knew nothing because Silva himself would have thought it hardly worth noting.

Although certainty in this matter is beyond reach, the numismatic evidence, taken together with the account provided by Josephus, suggests that the compound at Qumran came to

The numismatic evidence, taken together with the account provided by Josephus, suggests that the compound at Qumran came to an end in AD 73.

an end in AD 73. This means that no Qumran scrolls could have been produced later than this date. The dates of the Qumran community, ranging from 120 or so BC to AD 73, matches very well the dating of the scrolls by means of paleography and carbon 14/AMS testing. With this many dating techniques reaching similar conclusions, we have a strong case for assigning a date to the Qumran community.

Pottery

Pottery provides one more way of ascertaining the age of the DSS.[4] The pottery found in the ruins at Qumran and in some of the other caves in which scrolls were found is of the same type as pottery produced in Israel in the first century BC and first century AD. Moreover, the clay that was used

Qumran Pottery. Courtesy of the Israel Antiquities Authority. Photo: Mariana Salzberg.

to make the jars found in the scroll caves is the same clay that was used to make the bowls, lamps, and other utensils found in the Qumran ruins. Thus evidence from pottery not only helps establish the time line of the scrolls, as already suggested by the methods reviewed above; it also provides evidence that the scroll caves were linked to the compound at Qumran.

General Archaeological Evidences

Archaeology in a more general sense also helps us date the DSS. The nature of the ruins at Qumran plus the indications of destruction by Roman forces helps fix the site within the larger known context of that period. In other words, the kind of buildings and incidental artifacts plus the involvement o Roman soldiers in the site's destruction fit nicely with wha we would expect to find of a dissident religious community ir first-century Israel.

Conclusion

Taken as a whole, the evidence firmly shows that most of the DSS were produced a century or so before the time of Jesus' public activities and the founding of the Christian Church. Theories that the scrolls were writ-

Most of the DSS were produced a century or so before the time of Jesus' public activities and the founding of the Christian Church.

ten by Christians, opponents of Christians, or were written ir the Middle Ages do not square with the evidence provided b four different approaches to dating.

The DSS are ancient pre-Christian documents that tell u much about the world of Jesus and his earliest followers. Bu while the great age of the scrolls is a tremendous asset to ou studies, it is also a problem in itself. After all, they were or the brink of total ruin when they were found, and early mis handling only worsened their condition. So how do scholar preserve them? We turn to this question next.

Notes

1. For more on this topic, see F. M. Cross, "Paleography," in L. H. Schiffman and J. C. VanderKam (eds.), *Encyclopedia of the Dead Sea Scrolls* (2 vols., Oxford: Oxford University Press, 2000), 2:629–34.

2. For more on this topic, see G. Doudna, "Dating the Scrolls on the Basis of Radiocarbon Analysis," in P. W. Flint and J. C. VanderKam (eds.), *The Dead Sea Scrolls After Fifty Years: A Compre hensive Assessment* (2 vols., Leiden: Brill, 1998–99) 1:430–71.

3. For more on the study of coins, see Y. Meshorer, "Numismatics," in Schiffman and VanderKam (eds.), *Encyclopedia of the Dead Sea Scrolls*, 2:619–20.

4. For more on this topic, see J. Magness, "Pottery," in Schiffman and VanderKam (eds.), *Encyclopedia of the Dead Sea Scrolls*, 2:681–86.

Photo: Mikeyphotog

Chapter 6
Restoring and Preserving the Scrolls

Some 900 Dead Sea Scrolls (DSS) have been found, but only a handful of them are in any sense "well preserved."

Scrolls That Are Well Preserved

Isaiah[a] (1QIsa[a])

Isaiah[b] (1QIsa[b])

Genesis Apocryphon (1QapGen)

Rule of the Community (1QS)

Rule of the Congregation (1QSa)

Rule of the Blessings (1QSb)

War Scroll (1QM)

Hymns Scroll (1QH)

Commentary on Habakkuk (1QpHab)

Psalms Scroll (11QPs[a])

Temple Scroll (11Q19)

But even these well-preserved scrolls have suffered damage and deterioration, extensively so in the cases of Isaiah[b] and the Genesis Apocryphon. As for the many other scrolls, not only were many of them in pieces when first discovered (sometimes very tiny fragments that required laborious reconstruction and restoration), scholars were alarmed to discover that in the few decades after their recovery from the caves, the scrolls deteriorated quite noticeably. Noting this, scholars realized the pressing need to learn how to take better care of the scrolls plus preserve their images (via photography, for instance) so as to provide guarantee against the eventual ruin of the scrolls, whether at the hands of time or catastrophe. In this chapter we survey four facets of the work done to restore and preserve the scrolls.

In the few decades after their recovery from the caves, the scrolls deteriorated quite noticeably.

Reconstruction

The primary task of reconstruction is to put together as many pieces of a scroll as possible.[1] This can be enormously difficult not only because of the great number of fragments that must be pieced together

but because scholars are not always sure whether a given collection of fragments really belong to the same scroll. DNA testing has helped alleviate the latter difficultly because it is possible to test the various fragments to see if they come from the same hide. If two fragments come from the same animal hide, they belong to the same scroll. However, DNA testing is expensive, and it is not feasible to test all of the fragments. Besides, most scrolls of any length are made of two or more different pieces of leather. Since these pieces are not always from the same animal, it is always possible that two fragments from different hides belong together on the same scroll after all.

Even when we are confident that the fragments that belong to a given document have been properly identified and segregated, we are often unsure how the fragments relate to one another. If we are unable to place the fragments in the right order and thus create coherent sentences and passages, the context is lost. If the context is lost, then we probably cannot recover what the document originally meant. This obviously diminishes a document's value for scholarship.

Fragments from Enoch.

Moreover, even when we are reasonably confident that we have most of the fragments in the proper sequence and many of the fragments preserve lines of text and sometimes whole sentences, the gaps can still leave us uncertain of the original purpose and perspective. For example, in the case of the Prayer of Enosh (4Q369), scholars are not sure if the document is a late prophecy about a future descendant of David, perhaps the Messiah, or an earlier prophecy that looked forward not to the Messiah but to the historical King David. We encounter some very interesting words and phrases, such as "first born son" and "prince and ruler" who will enjoy the "protection of the angel of intercession." Is this the Messiah or a poetic reference to King David? Either option seems possible. We are unsure which to choose because most of the context is missing.

Fitting the fragments together can be difficult because they shrink over time as the leather dries. Thus scrolls that have been torn or otherwise damaged and now survive as fragments cannot always be reassembled with certainty simply because the pieces don't fit together as they once did. Imagine the frustration of trying to reassemble a puzzle if the size and shape of many pieces had changed, no longer permitting a proper fit.

Remember, too, that many fragments were recovered by Bedouin, not professional archaeologists. The Bedouin rarely tried to keep the fragments grouped together and segregated as found. And of course, no Bedouin took notes about which fragments were taken from where. As a result scholars are in some cases unsure which cave a given scroll or fragment came from. Further complicating the situation, over the centuries many of the fragments were scattered by birds and animals which made nests of fragments from different scrolls! This means that a small heap of fragments that happen to be found together might not all come from the same scroll.

And of course reconstruction becomes difficult in cases where we are missing many pieces of a scroll (or perhaps most of the scroll), or where the document was previously unknown to us, meaning we have no parallel text with which to make comparison. A colleague once put it to me this way: Imagine trying to assemble a thousand-piece puzzle that is missing 800 pieces. Oh, and you no longer have the lid of the box with the picture to guide your efforts!

Imagine trying to assemble a thousand-piece puzzle that is missing 800 pieces. Oh, and you no longer have the lid of the box with the picture to guide your efforts!

Scholars have made significant progress in identifying fragments that belong together by coming up with ways of making proper joins (matching fragment pieces). Now that images of the fragments are available digitally, scholars are able to manipulate the fragments from the convenience of their personal offices, moving fragments here and there with the aid of computer programs. This allows them to explore new joins and thus possibly recover more text without bothering to handle the ancient materials themselves.

The restoration of one scroll was especially interesting. The Copper Scroll (3Q15) is made of thin copper foil on which

Hebrew script has been "typed" with metal tools. Over time the copper completely oxidized, making it impossible to unroll the scroll. It took years before technicians figured out how to cut the scroll in strips without damaging the words and without causing the fragile oxidized copper foil to crumble.[2] More on this topic in chapter 13.

Finally, reconstruction of the scrolls took an interesting turn in 1991 when Martin G. Abegg Jr. was able to reassemble unpublished scroll texts from an index that was first compiled in 1957 and then later supplemented by Joseph Fitzmyer and others. This index listed words in the context of sentences or phrases. Using his computer Abegg was able to piece together these sentences and phrases into complete scroll fragments. This effort in effect ended the lack of access to the unpublished scroll fragments that had frustrated scholars for years.

Conservation

The scrolls survived for two millennia in the arid Dead Sea region, hidden away in caves, some in jars, protected from the harmful rays of the sun. When recovered from the caves, the scrolls were taken to the Palestine Archaeological Museum (later named the Rockefeller Museum), where the environment was less fitting for preservation. The scrolls were exposed

Rockefeller Museum. Photo: Talmoryair.

to humidity, sunlight, tobacco smoke, oils, adhesive tape, and various cleaning agents. In a few years' time the scrolls suffered more deterioration than they had in centuries. Something would have to be done, or future generations would be left with little more than dust and debris.

Shortly after being recovered from the caves, the scrolls were exposed to humidity, sunlight, tobacco smoke, oils, adhesive tape, and various cleaning agents.

A laboratory has been created by the Israel Antiquities Authority, housed in the Rockefeller Museum, whose purpose is to apply newer and better methods of conservation.[3] The leather and papyrus documents have been properly cleaned and are now kept in environmentally controlled storage rooms. In addition to this, careful records are kept for each document, noting the nature of previous damage and what remedial steps have been taken. In some ways these are similar to medical records.

Greater care is now taken in how the DSS are displayed. The manner in which they are mounted (usually involving silk and Japanese paper) as well as the type and intensity of lighting used to display them have been standardized according to the most current technology. Long gone are the haphazard days of holding scroll fragments up against a window for a better view, or traveling about with a scroll in a shoe box.

Ongoing studies will lead to even better methods of conservation. Ultimately the aging and deterioration of these ancient materials cannot be halted, but with care the natural process can be greatly slowed.

Photography and Imaging

Another form of conservation is found in photographing and making digital images of the DSS.[4] This conserves the current state of the scrolls in digital format and makes it possible to disseminate them to scholars and students around the world for ongoing research.

The first major set of photographs were taken and housed in the Palestine Archaeological Museum. The lighting of this early photography was not optimal, with the result that it was often difficult to distinguish letters from blotches, holes, shadows, darkened areas of the leather or other marks. These features are especially problematic because most of the early photographs are black-and-white and many were photographed only once and with only a single light source.

Habakkuk Commentary, poorly photographed.

The photographs taken by John Trever in 1948 are excellent (in color and in black-and-white) and are regarded as classics.[5] Today the most important photographs have been taken by brothers Bruce and Kenneth Zuckerman. The Zuckermans and others have taken new photographs, usually employing three ranges of exposure: "visible light color; high resolution, visible light, black and white; and black-and-white infrared."[6] The results of this work are markedly improved images and in some cases the recovery of text that simply could not be seen by the naked eye.

In addition to film-based photography, scholars and technicians are producing electronic images of the scrolls. These images include X-ray, narrow-band infrared, and computer-imaging. The latter opens up a whole range of possibilities, including manipulation of images for shading and contrast, magnification (zooming), and for moving fragments for the purpose of finding joins.

As computer-related photography improves, all aspects concerning the reconstruction, study, and preservation of the scrolls will be enhanced.[7]

Preservation

Several institutions around the world house the scrolls or their images. Besides facilitating research, these institutions are concerned to preserve the scrolls and the images that have been made over the years.[8]

The Rockefeller Museum in east Jerusalem houses most of the fragmentary scrolls from Qumran Cave 4 and most of the materials recovered from Murabba'at, Wadi ed-Daliyeh, Khirbet Mird, and Wadi Seiyal. The museum is equipped with a laboratory whose specific purpose is to facilitate the preservation of the scrolls.

The Shrine of the Book, now part of the Israel Museum in west Jerusalem, houses the seven major scrolls from Cave 1, as well as documents and various artifacts from Masada and Wadi Seiyal. Some of these are on display for public viewing.

The Shrine of the Book. Photo: Deror Avi.

The National Archaeological Museum in Amman, Jordan, houses the Copper Scroll (3Q15) and a number of fragmentary scrolls from Caves 1 and 4. The most notable of these are the Genesis Apocryphon (1QapGen) and the second commentary on Isaiah (4QpIsa[b]).

The Ancient Biblical Manuscript Center (ABMC) in Claremont, California, whose mission is preservation and research, serves as an archive for photographs, negatives, and images of the DSS, biblical manuscripts, and other primary documents related to the Bible (such as books of the Apocrypha and Pseudepigrapha). These documents are held in a climate-controlled vault. Back-up copies of these images are stored in Tahoe City, California. Through inter-library loan the ABMC provides images of specific manuscripts upon request. The ABMC's collection of DSS images is particularly rich as a result of its Dead Sea Scroll Inventory Project initiated in 1988.[9]

The Israel Antiquities Authority, working in conjunction with the Shrine of the Book and the Rockefeller Museum, has initiated a major project in which all of the scrolls and fragments will be digitally photographed. The two-year project is being directed by Greg Bearman, formerly of NASA's Jet Propulsion Laboratory, Pasadena, California. These digital images will be available on the internet.

Finally, negatives (on microfiche or microfilm) are held at several locations, including the Israel Antiquities Authority in Jerusalem; at the ABMC in Claremont, California; at the Huntington Library in San Marino, California; at Oxford University in England; at Hebrew Union College in Cincinnati, Ohio; and at the Dead Sea Scrolls Institute of Trinity Western University, in Langley, British Columbia, Canada.

In view of all of these efforts to recover, restore, photograph, and preserve these ancient scrolls, what do we actually have? We begin exploring the actual content in chapter 8. First, however, we need to take a closer look at the historical context in which the scrolls and the Qumran community were embedded.

Notes

1. For more on this topic, see A. Steudel, "Scroll Reconstruction," in L. H. Schiffman and J. C. VanderKam (eds.), *Encyclopedia of the Dead Sea Scrolls* (2 vols., Oxford: Oxford University Press, 2000), 2:842–44.

2. On this interesting task, see A. Wolters, "Copper Scroll," in Schiffman and VanderKam (eds.), *Encyclopedia of the Dead Sea Scrolls*, 1:144–48.

3. On this topic, see E. Libman and E. Boyd-Alkalay, "Conservation," in Schiffman and VanderKam (eds.), *Encyclopedia of the Dead Sea Scrolls*, 1:140–42.

4. On this topic, see B. and K. Zuckerman, "Photography and Computer Imaging," in Schiffman and VanderKam (eds.), *Encyclopedia of the Dead Sea Scrolls*, 2:669–75.

5. J. C. Trever and W. H. Brownlee, *The Dead Sea Scrolls of St. Mark's Monastery. I. The Isaiah Scroll and the Habakkuk Commentary* (New Haven: American Schools of Oriental Research, 1950); idem, *The Dead Sea Scrolls of St. Mark's Monastery. II. Plates and Transcription of the Manual of Discipline* (New Haven: American Schools of Oriental Research, 1951). Photographs of all three scrolls were later reprinted together, in J. C. Trever, *Scrolls from Qumrân*

Cave I (Jerusalem: Shrine of the Book, 1974). For the first published photographs of the other scrolls from Cave 1, see E. L. Sukenik, *The Dead Sea Scrolls of the Hebrew University* (Jerusalem: Magnes Press, 1955).

5. B. and K. Zuckerman, "Photography and Computer Imaging," 571.

7. Published images of the Dead Sea Scrolls are available in the following works: E. Tov and S. Pfann (eds.), *The Dead Sea Scrolls on Microfiche: A Comprehensive Facsimile Edition of the Texts from the Judean Desert* (Leiden: Brill, 1993); S. Reed and M. Lundberg (eds.), *An Inventory List of Photographs* (Leiden: Brill, 1993); S. Pfann and E. Tov (eds.), *Companion Volume* (Leiden: Brill, 1995); G. Brooke and H. Bond (eds.), *The Allegro Qumran Photograph Collection* (Leiden: Brill, 1996).

8. On this topic, see Brooke, Schiffman, and VanderKam, "Scrolls Research," in Schiffman and VanderKam (eds.), *Encyclopedia of the Dead Sea Scrolls*, 2:844–51; A. Roitman, *The Bible in the Shrine of the Book: From the Dead Sea Scrolls to the Aleppo Codex* (Catalogue 511; Jerusalem: Israel Museum, 2006); idem, "Shrine of the Book," in Schiffman and VanderKam (eds.), *Encyclopedia of the Dead Sea Scrolls*, 2:874–75.

9. One should consult S. A. Reed, *The Dead Sea Scrolls Catalogue: Documents, Photographs and Museum Inventory Numbers,* M. . Lundberg (ed.), with M. B. Phelps; Society of Biblical Literature Resources for Biblical Study 32; Atlanta: Scholars Press, 1994).

Part III
Historical Context
of the Scrolls

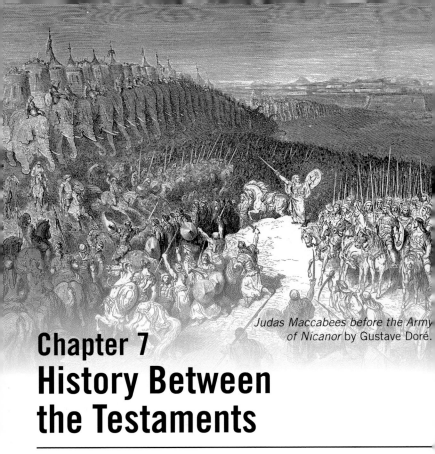

Judas Maccabees before the Army of Nicanor by Gustave Doré.

Chapter 7
History Between the Testaments

Since the Dead Sea Scrolls (DSS) were found hidden in caves, an obvious question is, Who put them there? Who were these people, and what were they doing in the wilderness with hundreds of scrolls? Were they members of the Essene religious sect, as is most commonly said? These are difficult questions, and scholars give different answers.

Among the most plausible reconstructions of the origin and identity of the Qumran community is the hypothesis that it was founded by someone whom the DSS call the Teacher of Righteousness. Due to his criticisms of the religious establishment in Jerusalem, this teacher was opposed by Jewish high priest John Hyrcanus (ruled 134–104 BC) or perhaps the priest-king Jannaeus (ruled 103–76 BC). One of these high priests (we're not sure which one) is called the Wicked Priest in the scrolls (cf. 1QpHab 8:8–13; 9:9–12).

Some have suggested that the Teacher of Righteousness was Onias the Righteous, a pious man remembered for his answered prayer (Josephus, *Antiquities* 14.22). But this identification is beset with difficulties and has not won many followers.

MAGAZINE

134508 / 7E0 / 085171

Mr L Hardwick
18 Stourhead Close
Farnborough
Hampshire
GU14 7HF

085171

C02/ C0216

EXCLUSIVE OFFER
FOR SAGA
MAGAZINE READERS

Harry Riley
1890-1935

Elsie MacNab
1900-1946

Bette Riley
1925-1992

Hugh Riley
1926-2006

findmypast

It has also been suggested that the Wicked Priest was Jonathan (who ruled 160–142 BC), the younger brother of Judas Maccabeus and Simon. In any case, it is likely that *Wicked Priest* had become a technical

Coins minted for John Hyrcanus, who may have opposed the Essene Teacher of Righteousness. Photo: CNG Coins.

term that referred to more than one of the compromising Hasmonean high priests. The Teacher of Righteousness probably came to be viewed as a title of office even if originally the title referred to a lone historical figure. Likewise, the Wicked Priest apparently came to be understood as the title of the opposing office and thus was not restricted to a single historical person.

These are just some of the problems in trying to identify the Essenes, their leaders, and their enemies. Most of the references to historical figures are veiled, making assured identification very difficult.

I believe that the men who wrote or collected the scrolls found at Qumran were Essenes. We will explore Essene beliefs and customs closely in chapters 14–17. To set the larger context for the formation of the Qumran community and Essene worldview, we must first survey Israel's history, specifically the period of time usually called "Intertestamental" history. As the name suggests, the Intertestamental period took place between the end of the OT era (c. 400 BC) and the beginning of the NT era (c. 50 AD).[1] Let's review some of the religious and political conditions that helped foster the formation and growth of groups such as the Essenes.

I believe that the men who wrote or collected the scrolls found at Qumran were Essenes.

End of the Old Testament Era

In 600–586 BC the dynasty of King David and the kingdom of Israel came to an end at the hands of Nebuchadnezzar, king of the Babylonian Empire (2 Kgs 24–25). Jerusalem was captured, and her legendary temple, built by King Solomon, was

The rebuilt temple, depicted here, was not as impressive as Solomon's temple. Photo: Ariely.

destroyed. The people were forced into exile, as had been foretold by Israel's great prophets. While in exile the Jewish people faced the threat of extinction and pressure to forsake their religion (see the books of Daniel and Esther).

For almost a century the people of Israel were without a home. In time the Babylonian Empire itself was swallowed up by the Persians. Then in the fifth century Cyrus, king of the Persian Empire (559–530 BC), decreed that the Jewish people could return to their homeland and rebuild Jerusalem and the temple (see the books of Ezra and Nehemiah). They did just that, rebuilding the walls of Jerusalem and erecting a new temple, though it was not as grand as the one built by Solomon. Ezra the scribe read the Law of Moses to the people, and those who did not know Hebrew had it translated to them in Aramaic (Neh 8:1–8), the language that had become common among the Jews. Thus the picture we have is of a wayward nation that had forgotten God and thus had been humbled and almost destroyed but had then been restored to a portion of its land.

The Intertestamental Era

In the fifth and fourth centuries BC the Persians and the Greeks fought many battles, vying for supremacy of the known world. In 490 the Persians attacked Athens but were repulsed at the famous Battle of Marathon. In 480 King Leonidas and a force of 300 Spartans fought the Persians at Thermopylae.

A coin showing Artaxerxes II.
Photo: Marie-Lan Nguyen.

One of the greatest single battles came as a result of an intrafamily struggle for the Persian throne. Upon the death of Darius II (ruled 424–404 BC), tensions rose between his surviving sons Artaxerxes II and Cyrus. After his enthronement Artaxerxes exiled his younger brother Cyrus to Asia Minor (modern Turkey) and made him governor. Artaxerxes assigned Cyrus the task of dealing with the troublesome Greeks. This maneuver backfired when Cyrus gained the confidence of the Greeks. He employed several of their generals to raise an army, ostensibly to deal with some rebellious factions in his jurisdiction but in reality aimed at overthrowing Artaxerxes. The Greek generals raised a force of some 10,000 heavily armed mercenary troops, who formed the famous and much-feared phalanx battle formation, and another 3,000 archers, slingers, and cavalry. In 401 BC this formidable force landed in Asia Minor and began an eastward march (famously referred to as the *anabasis*, a Greek word meaning "going up or going inland").

Cyrus's Greek force of perhaps 13,000 had come to take the battle to 350,000 Persians!

Soon Artaxerxes learned what his brother was doing and decided to march west and engage him rather than await his assault on Susa, the Persian capital. Artaxerxes summoned virtually his entire army, along with as many reserves and raw recruits as could be mustered. Historians estimate that his Persian army numbered about 350,000. Thus Cyrus's Greek force of perhaps 13,000 had come to take the battle to 350,000 Persians!

In the summer of 401, the two armies clashed at Cunaxa. In the first charge the Greek phalanx mowed down some 30,000 Persians. Panicked, the army of Artaxerxes fled in all directions. Even Artaxerxes himself ran for his life.

Only the rash action of Cyrus saved the day for Artaxerxes. In his eagerness to overtake his hated older brother, the younger would-be-king outrode his body guard, exposing himself to danger. Inevitably he was killed. When the Greeks learned that their paymaster was dead, they turned west and marched back to Greece, abandoning their victory.

Alexander swallowed up the whole of the Persian Empire and regions beyond, earning the name Alexander the Great. *The Family of Darius before Alexander* by Ricci.

Two generations later a young Macedonia prince, tutored by the learned philosopher Aristotle, read the story of the march of the 10,000 Greek mercenaries employed by Cyrus. He was impressed by their fighting skills, their courage, and their amazing odds-defying victory at Cunaxa. The young lad, Alexander III (born in 356 BC), was son of Philip II, king of Macedonia. Alexander dreamed of doing something as valiant as the Greeks. When Philip was assassinated (336 BC), 19-year-old Alexander got his chance. He consolidated control over Macedonia and Greece to the south and then began his conquest of the Persian Empire. He defeated the Persian king Darius III in 331. Darius fled but was assassinated the following year. When Alexander found his body in a dry riverbed, he wept for the murdered monarch.

In five years time Alexander swallowed up the whole of the Persian Empire and regions beyond, earning the name Alexander the Great. Alexander was now master of Persia, the western parts of India, all of Egypt, Asia Minor, Thrace, Macedonia, Greece, and, of course, the land of Israel.

In 323 BC, Alexander suddenly became ill and died. Was he poisoned? His principal generals fought for control of his vast empire. The two most powerful "successors" (known in the Greek as the diadochi) were Seleucus (358–281 BC) and Ptolemy (367–282 BC). Seleucus gained control of Syria and southern Asia Minor, establishing his base of power to the north of Israel. Ptolemy had mastery over Egypt, north Africa, Cyprus, two small regions of southern Asia Minor, and Israel.

Seleucus founded the Seleucid dynasty, whose regal names also included Antiochus, Demetrius, and Alexander. Ptolemy founded the Ptolemaic dynasty. Between 323 and 198 BC the Seleucids and Ptolemies fought five major wars, often with Israel as part of the contested territory. In 198 the Seleucids won a decisive victory and gained control over Israel. In later years the Seleucid kingdom (eventually called Syria) was sometimes divided with two rulers claiming the throne simultaneously (as will be noticed in the text box). The Ptolemy kings sometimes ruled jointly (as will also be noticed in the text box).

The Maccabean Revolt

Seleucid Rulers of Syria in Hasmonean Times	
Antiochus IV Epiphanes	(175–163 BC)
Antiochus V Eupator	(163–162 BC)
Demetrius I Soter	(162–150 BC)
Alexander Balas	(150–145 BC)
Demetrius II Nicator	(145–139 BC, 129–125 BC)
Antiochus VI Epiphanes	(145–142 BC)
Antiochus VII Sidetes	(139–129 BC)
Antiochus VIII Grypus	(125–96 BC)
Antiochus IX Philopator	(116–95 BC)
Demetrius III Eukairos	(95–88 BC)

In 175 BC Antiochus IV became king of the Seleucid Empire. Desiring to reunite Alexander's vast but fractured empire, he attacked Egypt in 170–169 and again in 168. During these campaigns he was frustrated by the lack of support his Jewish subjects showed him. He was also deeply offended by their refusal to allow him to offer sacrifice on the altar in Jerusalem. This would soon come back to haunt the Jews. When Antiochus defeated Ptolemaic Egypt in 168, a Roman ambassador met him on the road to Alexandria and congratulated him on his victory but then ordered him to return home or else face war with Rome. Humiliated, the proud tyrant complied.

Antiochus then took out his vengeance on his Jewish subjects, issuing a series of decrees that effectively outlawed the observance of the Jewish faith. Scrolls of the Law of Moses were burned; Jews were commanded to eat pork, a food they regarded as unclean; circumcision was banned; Jewish priests were ordered to sacrifice to Zeus and even Antiochus himself, as if he were a god. Failure to comply with these decrees meant death.

Antiochus IV styled himself as the manifestation of deity (Epiphanes), but the Jews referred to him as a madman (epimanes).
Photo: CNG Coins.

Understandably the Jews despised Antiochus IV, whose regal name (throne name) was *Epiphanes*, a Greek word meaning "manifestation," as in *manifestation of divinity*. Accordingly, the legend on some of the king's coins read: "(A coin) of Antiochus God, Manifested Conqueror." Ever fond of wordplay, the Jews rightly referred to the tyrant as Antiochus *Epimanes*, which in Greek meant "Antiochus the madman."

The books of Maccabees narrate the history of this period and came to be part of the OT Apocrypha. These books, 2 and 4 Maccabees especially, report that the Jewish people who clung to Israel's historic faith were severely persecuted. For instance, one can read about the torture and execution of the righteous elder Eleazar (2 Maccabees 6) and the graphic account of a mother and her seven sons, all of whom stood fast under pressure to forsake God even when it cost them their lives (2 Maccabees 7).

By now the Jewish people had had enough. In 167 BC one priest, Mattathias of the family of Hasmoneus, struck down the king's officer and a young Jewish man being trained in offering sacrifice to Zeus. The zealous priest and his sons Judah Maccabeus, Jonathan, and Simon summoned the faithful to join them in the wilderness. Revolt was underway.

Ptolemaic Rulers of Egypt in Hasmonean Times
Ptolemy VI Philometor (185–145 BC)
Ptolemy VII Neos Philometor (145 BC)
Ptolemy VIII Euergetes II (182–116 BC)
Ptolemy IX Soter II (142–80 BC)
Ptolemy X Alexander I (140–88 BC)
Ptolemy XI Alexander II (99–80 BC)

The sons of Mattathias garnered much support among the Jews and defeated one Greek general after another. Finally, boastful Antiochus became ill and died. The Jewish people had won the war, seemingly by the hand of God himself. Steadily they regained more and more of their historic land, winning recognition from Rome and Egypt and eventually from the Seleucid kingdom itself.

The sons of Mattathias founded what was known as the Hasmonean dynasty. At first they served as high priests, but in time they began to call themselves kings. Not all Jews were happy with this development. Some feared that the mixing of offices (political and priestly) would lead to corruption and compromise of their religion. Among the discontented were the priests who eventually established the Qumran community.

Rise of the Essenes

One of the reasons the Essenes were not happy with the high priests of the Hasmonean dynasty was that they were not descendants of the family of Zadok. Zadok had served as high priest under David and Solomon. This link to Israel's famed royal family helped make Zadokite lineage the traditional lineage for priests, and the Essenes stressed tradition. Also, the Essenes were not happy that the Hasmoneans had merged the kingly role with the priestly role. The Essenes, as demonstrated in the scrolls, firmly believed that these of-

Essene opposition to the Hasmonean high priest eventually led to a sharp falling out between the two groups, with the result that the founders of the Essenes withdrew from Jerusalem.

fices should be kept separate and distinct. Essene opposition to the Hasmonean high priest eventually led to a sharp falling out between the two groups, with the result that the founders of the Essenes withdrew from Jerusalem. In their writings the Essenes refer to one of the Jerusalem high priests as the Wicked Priest. He is said to have robbed the poor and persecuted at least one of the founders of the Essene community. Perhaps this was in reference to John Hyrcanus, who ruled Israel from 134 to 104 BC. In any case, the Essenes originated as a purist movement in response to corruption of the priesthood in Jerusalem.

Demise of the Hasmoneans and the Rise of the Herodians

Alexander Jannaeus, a Hasmonean king of Judah, died in 76 BC. He was succeeded by his widow Shelamzion Alexandra, who managed to keep the small kingdom of Israel at peace for a decade. However, things began to unravel after she died in 67 BC. Her surviving sons, Aristobulus II and Hyrcanus II, squabbled over succession. Initially Aristobulus prevailed, ruling from 67 to 63. Because he was so unpopular, his brother and many of the leading citizens of Jerusalem asked Rome to intervene. The land-hungry Romans were happy to oblige.

General Pompey marched into Jerusalem in 63 and removed Aristobulus from office. He rewarded Hyrcanus by installing him as high priest. Pompey later appointed a reliable Idumean man (meaning a man from Edom) named Antipater II as governor, thus initiating the Herodian rule over Israel and ending Hasmonean rule for the time being. As a side note, Antipater II sent his young son Herod to Rome to be educated. This boy would later be known as Herod the Great.

King Herod was appointed king of the Jews by Rome. Photo: Sauber.

In 40 BC a member of the Hasmonean family rose up and for a season became Israel's ruler in defiance of the Roman will. Rome responded by placing a legion of soldiers at 25-year-old Herod's disposal, declaring him "king of the Jews" and assigning him the task of gaining his kingdom. Herod did just that, demonstrating again and again military genius, personal fighting skills, and sometimes just plain good luck. In 37 Herod defeated Antigonus, who had temporarily reestablished Hasmonean rule over Israel, and became king of the Jews in reality.

Herod's reign was lengthy and noteworthy. He famously rebuilt Jerusalem, dismantling the second temple and erecting a magnificent replacement. He also enlarged the temple precincts, equipping it with a series of

Herod's reign was lengthy and noteworthy. He famously rebuilt Jerusalem, dismantling the second temple and erecting a magnificent replacement.

The Hulda Gates, part of Herod's rebuilt temple, as they are seen today.

administrative buildings. Herod built palaces and fortresses at Hebron, Jericho, and Masada. He also built a volcano-shaped fortress called the Herodium atop a mountain and rebuilt the city and harbor of Caesarea Maritima.

Herod's building program was impressive, but his marriages and family life were a self-inflicted disaster. Historians aren't sure, but Herod may have had as many as 10 wives—and no, he was not a polygamist! His wives came one at a time, and some of them (as well as other family members) met with unfortunate "accidents" such as drowning in the family swimming pool whenever Herod grew suspicious of them.

Among the most notable executions ordered by Herod were those of his sons Alexander and Aristobulus in 7 BC and then his son Antipater III only days before his own death in 4 BC.[2] Herod believed each of these sons was involved in intrigues against his throne. It is no wonder that longtime friend and ally Caesar Augustus remarked of Herod: "I would rather be Herod's pig than his son!" To understand the force of this quip, note that in Greek "pig" [*hus*] sounds a bit like "son" [*huios*]. Since Jews would never kill and eat pigs, Augustus suggested that around Herod a pig would have greater longevity than one of his sons.[3]

After Herod's death, Rome granted three of his surviving sons portions of his kingdom. Archaelus received the southern half, consisting of Samaria and Judea. His title was "ethnarch," which in Greek means "ruler of the people." His half brother Herod Antipas received the northwest part of the kingdom, Galilee, and a region in the east (Peraea). His title was "tetrarch," which in Greek means "ruler of one quarter" (i.e., one quarter of Herod's kingdom). Herod Philip (or simply Philip) received the northeast part of the kingdom, which was made up of Gaulanitis, Batanaea, Auranitis, and Trachonitis. This region also amounted to about one quarter of Herod's kingdom, so Philip too was given the title "tetrarch."

Demise of the Herodians and the Jewish State

Because he was unable to maintain order, in AD 6 Archaelus was replaced by a Roman governor. Philip died in 34, and Antipas was removed in 39. In 41 Agrippa I, grandson of Herod the Great, was granted the whole kingdom and became the new "king of the Jews." In 44 he died a painful death ("eaten of worms") that is recounted in the book of Acts (12:20–23) and in Josephus (*Antiquities* 19.343–50).

A coin depicting Agrippa I.
Photo: CNG Coins.

Upon the death of Agrippa I, Rome recognized his young son Agrippa II as the new king but nevertheless appointed a Roman governor over the whole kingdom. The real power lay with these governors, and they administered Israel until the great revolt in 66. This revolt was put down in 70 (and the Masada stronghold was finally overthrown in 74). When the dust settled, Roman governors continued to administer Israel.

In AD 115, during the reign of the great Spanish emperor Trajan, the Jewish people in northern Africa revolted (there may have been uprisings in Israel at this time also). This second revolt was finally put down in 117. In 132, during the reign of the great architect and emperor Hadrian, the Jews in Israel (mostly in Judea) revolted yet again. The leader of the revolt was one Simon ben Kosibah, whose correspondence was found in one of the caves of Murabba'at. Simon's nickname was Bar Kokhba, meaning "son of the star," almost certainly in allusion to Numbers 24:17, a passage widely regarded as foretelling the coming of the Messiah. It seems that many Jews who didn't believe in Jesus as Messiah placed their hopes in Bar Kokhba instead. It was a futile hope.

It seems that many Jews who didn't believe in Jesus as Messiah placed their hopes in Bar Kokhba instead. It was a futile hope.

Rome put down this third revolt in 135, killing Simon and officially ending the Jewish state. Jews were no longer allowed to live in Jerusalem (though in time they were allowed back), and the city's name was changed. The Romans built a new temple dedicated to Zeus (or Jupiter, as the Romans called this deity) in the same place where Herod's magnificent temple once stood. The Jewish state was not restored until 1947–48, the very year of the discovery of the first cave containing the DSS. The obscure Jewish sect, called Essenes by those who wrote about them, suddenly reentered history and gained a level of fame and notoriety none of their contemporaries would ever have imagined possible.

Notes

1. For a lively, reader-friendly overview of Old Testament and intertestamental history, see J. R. Howard, *QuickSource Guide to Understanding Jesus* (Holman QuickSource; Nashville: Holman Reference, 2009), 20–80. For a more in-depth study, see L. L. Grabbe, *Judaism from Cyrus to Hadrian* (2 vols., Minneapolis: Fortress, 1992).

2. See Josephus, *War* 1.664; *Jewish Antiquities* 16.394 and 17.187 respectively.

3. This cynical comment is reported by Macrobius, *Saturnalia* 2.4.11.

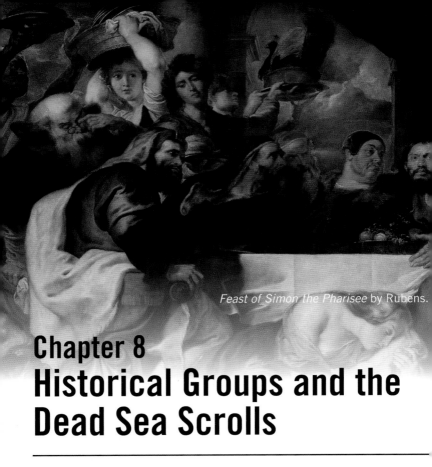

Feast of Simon the Pharisee by Rubens.

Chapter 8
Historical Groups and the Dead Sea Scrolls

Just like any other community in history, the Qumran community that wrote and/or collected the Dead Sea Scrolls (DSS) was shaped by the people and events of their era. In the previous chapter we looked at the broad sweep of events in Israel before and shortly after the time of Christ. In this chapter and the two that follow, we take a closer look at the people and parties of this time frame, roughly 200 BC to AD 100. Better acquaintance with these folks will help us understand more accurately how the men of the scrolls fit into the times.

The Hasmonean and Herodian Rulers

The Hasmonean rulers were major factors in prompting the Essenes to form as a group and separate themselves from the temple establishment in Jerusalem, this despite the fact that the Hasmoneans were inheritors of the Maccabean revolt that sought to free Israel from foreign *The Essenes saw the Hasmonean rulers as compromisers and false priests.*

rule and pagan influence. The Essenes saw the Hasmonean rulers as compromisers and false priests. In fact, the harsh epithet "Wicked Priest," which appears in the Essene commentary on the prophet Habakkuk (1QpHab), is a reference to one of the Hasmonean high priests.

The Hasmonean Rulers

Mattathias (167–166 BC)

Judas Maccabeus, son of Mattathias (166–160 BC)

Jonathan, son of Mattathias (160–142 BC)

Simon, son of Mattathias (142–134 BC)

John Hyrcanus I, son of Simon (134–104 BC)

Aristobulus I, son of John Hyrcanus I (104–103 BC)

Alexander Jannaeus, brother of Aristobulus I (103–76 BC)

Shelamzion Alexandra, wife of Jannaeus (76–67 BC)

Aristobulus II, son of Jannaeus (67–63 BC)

Hyrcanus II, son of Jannaeus (63–40 BC; died 30 BC)

Antigonus Mattathias, son of Aristobulus II (40–37 BC)

The Herodian rulers replaced the Hasmonean dynasty late in the first century BC. From the Essene point of view the Herodians just picked up where the Hasmoneans had left off. The crimes and religious disgraces of the Herodians played an important role in shaping the worldview and eschatological (end-time) thinking of the Essenes. This was especially caused by the close ties Herod the Great and his sons forged with the pagan Roman Empire. For the Essenes, such an unholy alliance was proof that the end was near.

A few of the Herodians played roles in the life of Jesus and the early Church. Herod the Great sought to slay the infant Jesus because it was said that Jesus was "born king of the Jews" (Matt 2:1–18).[1] Herod's notorious tendency to execute allies and family members, especially his wife and sons, provides a grim backdrop to this story.

Herod Antipas and Herod Philip, both sons of Herod the Great, come into play as well. We see this first in the life and ministry of John the Baptist, who criticized Antipas for dismissing his wife and taking up with Herodias, the former wife of Philip. Antipas arrested John because of his criticisms and later, through the machinations of Herodias and her daughter, executed the prophet. Antipas also played a brief role in the final days of Jesus, when he finally met the famous Galilean prophet and healer (Luke 23:6–9; see also 13:31–33). Ironically, a man named Manaen, who grew up with Herod Antipas, became a Christian and was a leader in the Church at Antioch (Acts 13:1).

The grandson and great grandson of Herod the Great make brief appearances in the story of the early Church. King Herod Agrippa I persecuted the Church, killing James the brother of John and imprisoning Peter (Acts 12:1–3). Later, the arrogant Agrippa was struck by "an angel of the Lord" and died a lingering, painful death (Acts 12:20–23; Josephus, *Antiquities* 19.343).

The Herodian Rulers

Herod the Great — king of all Israel (37–4 BC)

Archelaus — ethnarch of Samaria and Judea (4 BC– AD 6)

Antipas — tetrarch of Galilee and Peraea (4 BC– AD 39)

Philip — tetrarch of Gaulanitis etc. (4 BC– AD 34)

Agrippa I — tetrarch of Galilee and Peraea (AD 39–41)

Agrippa I — king of all Israel (AD 41–44)

Agrippa II — king of all Israel (AD 49–93)

Roman Rulers

In the time of Roman governor Festus, the apostle Paul had the opportunity to meet King Agrippa II and his sister Bernice (Acts 25:22–23; 26:1–29). Hearing Paul's testimony of faith in the risen Jesus, Agrippa responded: "Are you

Hearing Paul's testimony of faith in the risen Jesus, Agrippa responded: "Are you going to persuade me to become a Christian so easily?" (Acts 26:28).

St. Paul by El Greco.

going to persuade me to become a Christian so easily?" (26:28). This response hints at both Paul's persuasiveness and the formidable obstacles to faith present among worldly rulers.

Jesus and his early followers had several personal encounters with Roman officials stationed in Israel. Jesus was interrogated by Pontius Pilate, prefect (governor) of Samaria and Judea (Mark 15:1–5). Jesus' followers encountered a variety of officials in years to come as the Christian faith spread throughout the Roman Empire.

When attacked by a mob in the temple precincts Paul was "rescued" by a Roman commander, who asked him if he was the Egyptian Jew wanted by authorities for instigating an uprising (Acts 21:26–38; for more on the Egyptian Jew, see Josephus, *War* 2.261–63; *Antiquities* 20.169–72).

When he was threatened by assassins, Paul was protected by a Roman tribune named Claudius Lysias (Acts 23:24), who delivered him safely to the governor of Israel, Felix (AD 52–60). Felix heard Paul out but declined to pass judgment (24:22–27). We are told that Felix "was accurately informed about the Way" (24:22), that is, an accurate knowledge of the Christian faith. His knowledge may have been due to his Jewish wife Drusilla, who was interested to hear what Paul had to say of the crucified and risen Jesus. Interestingly enough, Drusilla was the younger daughter of Herod Agrippa I. At one time she had been married to Azizus, king of Emesa in Syria (see Josephus, *Antiquities* 19.354–55; 20.138–44).

Because Felix did not decide Paul's case, the apostle eventually was heard by Festus (AD 60–62), who succeeded Felix (Acts 24:27). Paul welcomed the opportunity to speak to the Roman procurator, again proclaiming his faith in the

Messiah (26:1–23). When Paul finished speaking, Festus asserted: "You're out of your mind, Paul! Too much study is driving you mad!" (24).

The Roman Governors

Prefects of Samaria and Judea

Coponius	(AD 6–9)
Marcus Ambibulus	(AD 9–12)
Annius Rufus	(AD 12–15)
Valerius Gratus	(AD 15–19/25)
Pontius Pilate	(AD 19/25–37)
Marcellus	(AD 37)
Marullus	(AD 37–41)

Procurators of all Israel

Fadus	(AD 44–46)
Tiberius Alexander	(AD 46–48)
Ventidius Cumanus	(AD 48–52)
Felix	(AD 52–60)
Porcius Festus	(AD 60–62)
Albinus	(AD 62–64)
Gessius Florus	(AD 64–66)

In 62 Festus died in office. Before his successor, Albinu (62–64), could arrive, Annas the high priest convened the San hedrin and condemned to death James, the brother of Jesu and recognized leader of the Church in Jerusalem (Acts 12:17 15:13; 21:18; Gal 2:9). When Albinus arrived and learned tha James had been stoned to death, he wrote a threatening lette to Annas, telling him to discontinue such actions. King Agrip pa II then removed Annas from office and appointed Jesus son of Damnaeus, as the new high priest (Josephus, *Antiqui ties* 20.197–203).

The Romans are also mentioned in the DSS, though not ex plicitly as is the case in the NT. In the scrolls they are referre to as the Kittim (more on this below) and are presented as th principal villains who will be vanquished in a great future war when the Sons of Light battle the Sons of Darkness.

Roman Rulers During Herodian Period
Herod the Great — king of all Israel (37–4 BC)
Julius Caesar (48–44 BC)
Caesar August (31 BC– AD 14)
Tiberius (AD 14–37)
Gaius Caligula (AD 37–41)
Claudius (AD 41–54)
Nero (AD 54–68)
Galba, Otho, Vitellius (AD 68–69)
Vespasian (AD 69–79)
Titus (AD 79–81)
Domitian (AD 81–96)
Nerva (AD 96–98)
Trajan (AD 98–117)
Hadrian (AD 117–138)

Josephus on the Sadducees and Pharisees

During the time that the Essenes emerged as an organized group, two other groups also formed, more or less as political parties who had distinct and closely held religious convictions. These were the Pharisees and Sadducees. Both groups are mentioned in the Gospels and elsewhere in the NT. The Pharisees are particularly prominent, being mentioned some 100 times; the Sadducees merit a little more than a dozen references. Both groups are also mentioned in the writings of Josephus. After singing the praises of the Essenes, this is what Josephus says about the Pharisees and Sadducees:

> But then as to the two other orders at first mentioned: the Pharisees are those who are esteemed most skillful in the exact explication of their laws, and hold the position as first sect. These ascribe all to fate [or provi-

dence], and to God, and yet allow, that to act what is right, or the contrary, is principally in the power of men, although fate does cooperate in every action. They say that all souls are incorruptible; but that the souls of good men are only removed into other bodies,—but that the souls of bad men are subject to eternal punishment. But the Sadducees are those that compose the second order, and take away fate entirely, and suppose that God is not concerned in our doing or not doing what is evil; and they say, that to act what is good, or what is evil, is at men's own choice, and that the one or the other belongs so to every one, that they may act as they please. They also take away the belief of the immortal duration of the soul, and the punishments and rewards in Hades. Moreover, the Pharisees are friendly to one another, and are for the exercise of concord

Josephus.

and regard for the public. But the behavior of the Sadducees one towards another is in some degree wild; and their conversation with those that are of their own party is as barbarous as if they were strangers to them. And this is what I had to say concerning the philosophic sects among the Jews. (*War* 2.162–66)

About 15 years later, Josephus says more about the Pharisees and Sadducees, again in the context of a discussion on the Essenes:

The Jews had for a great while three sects of philosophy peculiar to themselves; the sect of the Essenes, and the sect of the Sadducees, and the third sort of opinions was that of those called Pharisees; of which sects although I have already spoken in the second book of the *Jewish War*, yet will I a little touch upon them now.

Now, for the Pharisees, they live meanly, and despise delicacies in diet; and they follow the conduct of reason; and what that prescribes to them as good for them, they do; and they think they ought earnestly to strive to observe reason's dictates for practice. They also pay a respect to such as are [advanced] in years; nor are they so bold as to contradict them in anything which they have introduced; and, when they determine that all things are done by fate, they do not take away the freedom from men of acting as they think fit; since their notion is, that it has pleased God to make a temperament, whereby what he wills is done, but so

Head of a Pharisee by Munkácsy.

that the will of men can act virtuously or viciously. They also believe that souls have an immortal vigor in them, and that under the earth there will be rewards or punishments, according as they have lived virtuously or viciously in this life; and the latter are to be detained in an everlasting prison, but that the former shall have power to revive and live again; on account of which doctrines, they are able greatly to persuade the body of the people; and whatsoever they do about divine worship, prayers, and sacrifices, they perform them according to their direction; insomuch that the cities gave great attestations to them on account of their entire virtuous conduct, both in the actions of their lives and their discourses also.

But the doctrine of the Sadducees is this: That souls die with the bodies; nor do they regard the observation of anything besides what the law enjoins them; for they think it an instance of virtue to dispute with those teachers of philosophy whom they frequent; but this doctrine is received but by a few, yet by those still of the greatest dignity; but they are able to do almost nothing of themselves; for when they become magistrates, as they are unwillingly and by force sometimes obliged to be, they addict themselves to the notions of the Pharisees, because the multitude would not otherwise bear them.[2] (*Antiquities* 18.11–17)

The Pharisees in the Bible

From what Josephus says, the Pharisees appear to have been strict in their adherence to the Law, careful in what they ate, and firm in their belief of bodily resurrection. This fits the NT data exactly. Compared to the Sadducees, the Pharisees are "more lenient in matters of punishment" (Josephus, *Antiquities* 13.294). Although Josephus has presented the Pharisees in philosophical dress, his description does agree in broad outline with what we are told about them in the NT.

> *From what Josephus says, the Pharisees appear to have been strict in their adherence to the Law, careful in what they ate, and firm in their belief of bodily resurrection. This fits the New Testament data exactly.*

In the Gospels the Pharisees often ask Jesus loaded questions or express disapproval of his behavior. For instance, they objected to Jesus' associating with "sinners and tax collectors" (e.g., Mark 2:16). They faulted Jesus for permitting his disciples to do on the Sabbath "what is not lawful to do" (e.g., v. 24). They were especially critical of Jesus for healing people on the Sabbath (Mark 3:1–7; John 9:13–16). They faulted Jesus for permitting his disciples to eat with unwashed hands and thus defile themselves (Mark 7:1–5).

Paul's declaration that he was on trial for the hope of the resurrection (Acts 23:6–9) created a sharp division between the Pharisees and the Sadducees who served on the Council (or Sanhedrin) because the Pharisees believed in resurrection while the Sadducees did not.

The apostle Paul mentions his former life as a Pharisee (Acts 26:5), describing it this way in two of his letters:

> If anyone else thinks he has grounds for confidence in the flesh, I have more: circumcised the eighth day; of the nation of Israel, of the tribe of Benjamin, a Hebrew born of Hebrews; as to the law, a Pharisee; as to zeal, persecuting the church; as to the righteousness that is in the law, blameless. (Phil 3:4–6)

Paul described himself as a Hebrew born of Hebrews. *Paul* by Rublev.

> For you have heard about my former way of life in Judaism: I persecuted God's church to an extreme degree and tried to destroy it; and I advanced in Judaism beyond many contemporaries among my people, because I was extremely zealous for the traditions of my ancestors. (Gal 1:13–14)

Paul described his life as a Pharisee in terms and images that cohere with everything we know about the Pharisees from extrabiblical sources. A sampling of his descriptions of his life as a Pharisee includes:

- zeal
- extreme zealotry
- commitment to the traditions of his fathers
- emphasis on righteousness that is in the law
- belief that he was blameless by observing the law

The Pharisees in the Dead Sea Scrolls

Do the DSS refer to the Pharisees?[3] This is an interesting and difficult question. If the Pharisees are referenced, it is never explicitly, for they are never mentioned by name. But scholars do think the Pharisees are indirectly referenced in the scrolls. I am inclined to agree. The Pharisees may be alluded to in three ways.

Pharisee by M. Bihn & J. Bealings.

First, the Pharisees may be mentioned in an allegorical interpretation of Scripture that appears in the DSS. In an interpretation of Isaiah 7:17, in which the prophet mentions that "Ephraim separated from Judah," the Damascus Document (CD) applies "Ephraim" to those who backslid (in contrast to those who "held fast") and were handed over to the sword (CD 7:11–13; see also 13:23–14:3). Scholars think the scroll author portrayed "Ephraim" as the Pharisees and those who "held fast" as the Essenes, the men of the Qumran community. Thus the Essenes were critical of the Pharisees.

Second, the DSS may include mocking allusions to the Pharisees, such as the way they studied Scripture. The scrolls speak critically of those who "seek after smooth things," looking "for ways to break the law" (CD 1:18–19). Pharisees saw themselves as searching[4] for life in Scripture, seeking the way in which they should "walk" (Hebrew: *halak*, to "walk"). It is to this idea that the scrolls make mocking reference when they refer to those who seek after the "smooth things" (Hebrew: *halaq*, "smooth"). In other words, the DSS are mocking those who make a show of searching out God's path (*halak*) while choosing instead the easy paths (*halaq*).

Third, one of the scrolls may have the Pharisees in mind when it critiques a specific legal interpretation on divorce. We know what the Pharisees believed about divorce because they asked Jesus his opinion (Mark 10:2–9). The Pharisees apparently interpreted Deut 24:1–4 quite expansively, permitting divorce on almost any grounds and thus permitting remarriage as well (which was probably the real motive for getting divorced in the first place; see Matt 5:27–37). Jesus refuted the Pharisees by appealing to Genesis 1:27 ("He created them male and female") and 2:24 ("This is why a man leaves his father and mother and bonds with his wife, and they become one flesh"). The men of Qumran held the same view as Jesus and even cited the same passages from Genesis in order to claim that the Shoddy-Wall-Builders commit fornication when they divorce and remarry (see CD 4:19–5:5; 4Q416 frag. 2, column iii, line 20–column iv, line 5). Who were these Shoddy-Wall-Builders? Probably the Pharisees. After all, the Shoddy-Wall-Builders held a loose view on divorce just as the Pharisees did, and the men of Qumran used the same argument Jesus used to show that this loose view was unbiblical. So you have a common stance (loose views on divorce) and a common refutation (appeal to Genesis), which suggests a common group is in view (i.e., that the Pharisees were the subject of Jesus' rebuke and that of the Essenes as well).

The Dead Sea Scrolls may include mocking allusions to the Pharisees, such as the way they studied Scripture.

The Sadducees

As for the Sadducees, Josephus says that they were far more open to the pleasures of life, were harsh in their judgments against those who broke the law, did not believe in life after death (either bodily resurrection or immortality of the soul), and thus did not believe in heaven or hell.

Though less frequently than the Pharisees, the Sadducees do make several appearances in the NT.[5] The most important appearance in the Gospels is in the passage where they asked Jesus about the woman widowed seven times: "In the resurrection, when they rise, whose wife will she be?" (Mark 12:23). The evangelist Mark introduces the episode by noting that the Sadducees "say there is no resurrection" (v. 18).

In the first century many of the ruling priests, including the high priests, were affiliated with the Sadducees.

The Sadducean rejection of the resurrection is what lay behind the dissension with the Pharisees in the Council, mentioned above (Acts 23:6–8). The evangelist Luke, who wrote the book of Acts, rightly sums up Sadducean views: "The Sadducees say there is no resurrection, and no angel or spirit, but the Pharisees affirm them all" (v. 8).

In the first century many of the ruling priests, including the high priests, were affiliated with the Sadducees (Acts 5:17). Josephus remarks that Annas, who served as high priest for only a few months in AD 62 and was the son of Annas the high priest mentioned in the NT, "followed the school of the Sadducees, who are indeed more heartless than any of the other Jews" (*Antiquities* 20.199).

The Sadducees in the Scrolls

Some scholars think the DSS (especially in a few of the commentaries, or *pesharim*) allude to the Sadducees when it refers to Manasseh. For instance, we are told in the commentary on Nahum that the "meaning of 'Amon' is Manasseh, and 'the streams' are the nobles of Manasseh" (4QpNah frags. 3–4, column iii, line 9, commenting on Nah 3:8). Later, we hear of the "wicked of . . . a divisive group who ally themselves to Manasseh" (ibid., column iv, line 1); and again: "This refers to Manasseh in the Last Days, for his kingdom shall be brought low in Israel" (ibid., column iv, line 3, commenting on Nah 3:10). The "divisive group" mentioned above could very naturally refer to the powerful Sadducees, with whom the Essenes disagreed on so many vital points.

However, some scholars have suggested that the authors

of the DSS may have been friendly rather than hostile to the Sadducees. They suggest that some of the laws found in the scrolls reflect the Sadducean legal interpretation of the Law of Moses. It has also been suggested that the one dozen or so occurrences of the epithet "sons of Zadok" (CD 4:3; 1QS 5:2; 1QSa 1:2, 24; 1QSb 3:22; 4Q174 1:17) point to a Sadducean origin of the Qumran community. Almost no one today agrees with this hypothesis. The Essenes almost certainly viewed both the Pharisees and the Sadducees negatively, whether or not the scrolls say so explicitly.

> *The Essenes almost certainly viewed both the Pharisees and the Sadducees negatively, whether or not the scrolls say so explicitly.*

The Herodians

Three times in the Gospels we encounter a group called the "Herodians" (Greek: *Herodianoi*). On one occasion they joined forces with the Pharisees and asked Jesus whether it is lawful to pay taxes to Caesar (Matt 22:15–22; Mark 12:13–17). On another occasion some Herodians conferred with the Pharisees and together explored ways to destroy Jesus (Mark 3:6). Nowhere else in the NT do we hear of a party called the Herodians. So who were they?

> *It has been suggested that the Herodians were likely a Jewish party that supported Herodian rule over Israel, which would mean that these were Jews who supported Roman rule in Israel.*

It has been suggested that the Herodians were a Jewish party that supported Herodian rule over Israel, which would mean that these were Jews who supported Roman rule in Israel. The Pharisees generally were not sympathetic either to Herodian rulers or the Roman Empire. Perhaps this is the point the evangelists were trying to make: that in their deadly opposition to Jesus, even two diametrically opposed parties (Roman-supporting Herodians and Roman-opposing Pharisees) found enough common cause to lay down their mutual dislike for one another.

The Professionals

Who were the power brokers among the Jews of this era? In the NT Gospels and the book of Acts, it is clear that they are the high priests, ruling priests (i.e., chief priests), elders, and scribes. Most of these were affiliated with either the Pharisees or the Sadducees. Many of the ruling priests belonged to or at least leaned toward the politically savvy Sadducees, while other priests identified with the Pharisees. So also in the case of the scribes, who would have been equivalent to modern lawyers, accountants, clerks, and notaries public.

High priests played prominent roles in persecuting Jesus and His early followers. *Christ before Caiaphas* by Stom.

High priests played prominent roles in the lives of Jesus and the early Church. When seized in the garden of Gethsemane, Jesus was taken to Annas, a former high priest (John 18:13, 24). Annas was also present when the Sanhedrin threatened Peter and other apostles in the early days of the Christian movement (Acts 4:6). After appearing before Annas, Jesus was sent to Caiaphas, son-in-law to Annas (Matt 26:57; John 11:49; 18:13,24). Caiaphas was also present at the aforementioned meeting of the Sanhedrin (Acts 4:6). He also may have been the high priest who questioned Stephen (7:1) and is probably the high priest from whom Saul of Tarsus (later the apostle Paul) received letters authorizing him to take action against the Christians of Damascus (9:1). Josephus tells us that five of Annas's sons went on to serve as high priests, a line of succession unparalleled in Israel's history (*Antiquities* 20.198).

Ananias, son of Nebebaeus, ordered guards to strike Paul when he was brought before the Sanhedrin (Acts 23:2). Paul apologized for speaking against Ananias. "'I did not know, brothers,' said Paul, 'that it was the high priest. For it is written, You must not speak evil of a ruler of your people'" (v. 5).

Despite Ananias's villainy, Paul quoted Exodus 22:28 and thus acknowledged that even a crooked high priest must be honored by virtue of his office.

The high priesthood of the New Testament period was dominated by a few aristocratic families. The high priesthood of this period was dominated by a few aristocratic families: those of Boethus, Phiabi, and Annas. Only the latter is mentioned in the NT; all three are mentioned in the later literature of the rabbis. We also hear of other ruling priests who apparently never reached the lofty office of high priest. These include John and Alexander "of the high-priestly family" (Acts 4:6) and one Sceva, whose seven sons were well-known exorcists (19:14).

In the Gospels and Acts we also hear of ruling priests who often appear in the company of elders and scribes. These men opposed Jesus in Jerusalem and succeeded in having him condemned and executed.

All high priests were ruling priests, but not all ruling priests became high priests. Some ruling priests served as "captain of the temple guard," others as "captains of the treasury," and others as "back-up high priest" (in the event that the high priest died or was disqualified on the eve of offering a sacrifice that only the high priest could offer).

Elders were prominent laymen, some of whom were probably members of the Sanhedrin, the Jewish council that functioned more or less as a court and legislative assembly.

In the scrolls we find many references to priests, high priests, elders, and even a few references to ruling priests and scribes. In other words, all of the terminology in the NT that relates to the professionals of Jewish society, particularly concerning the temple and the Sanhedrin, is also found in the DSS. This demonstrates the pertinence of the DSS in biblical studies, plus it affirms that the scrolls originated from the same era as Jesus. Do the scrolls mention by name any historical figures? To this question we shall turn in the next chapter.

Israel's High Priests Appointed by Herodians and Roman Governors

Ananel (37–36 BC)

Aristobulus (35 BC)

Jesus, son of Phiabi (?)

Simon, son of Boethus (?)

Matthias, son of Theophilus (?)

Joseph, son of Ellem (?)

Joazar, son of Boethus (4 BC)

Eleazar, son of Boethus (4 BC–?)

Jesus, son of See (?)

Annas, son of Sethi (AD 6–15)

Ishmael, son of Phiabi (AD 15–16)

Eleazar, son of Annas (AD 16–17)

Simon, son of Camithus (AD 17–18)

Joseph, called Caiaphas (AD 18–37)

Jonathan, son of Annas (AD 37)

Theophilus, son of Annas (AD 37–41)

Simon Cantheras, son of Boethus (AD 41–?)

Matthias, son of Annas (?)

Elionaeus, son of Cantheras (?)

Josephus, son of Camei (?– AD 47)

Ananias, son of Nebebaeus (AD 47–59)

Ishmael, son of Phiabi (AD 59–61)

Joseph Cabi, son of high priest Simon (AD 61–62)

Annas, son of Annas (AD 62)

Jesus, son of Damnaeus (AD 62–63)

Jesus, son of Gamaliel (AD 63–64)

Matthias, son of Theophilus (AD 65–66)

Phannias, son of Samuel (AD 67–?), appointed by the rebels

Notes

1. The wise men's description of Jesus as the one "born King of the Jews" (Matt 2:2) would not be well received by Herod the Great, who was an Idumean at birth, not a Jew, and became "King of the Jews" by decree of the Roman senate. In contrast, Jesus was of the family of King David.

2. The translation is based on W. Whiston, *The Works of Flavius Josephus* (2 vols., Philadelphia: Lippincott, Grambo, 1850; reprinted by Thomas Nelson, 1998). For a more recent translation, with Greek text, see H. St. J. Thackeray, et al., *Josephus* (10 vols., London: Heinemann; Cambridge, MA: Harvard University Press, 1926–65).

3. For a succinct description of the Pharisees, especially in relation to the Dead Sea Scrolls, see A. I. Baumgarten, "Pharisees," in L. H. Schiffman and J. C. VanderKam (eds.), *Encyclopedia of the Dead Sea Scrolls* (2 vols., Oxford: Oxford University Press, 2000), 2:657–63.

4. The Hebrew verb for "search" is *darash*, from which the noun *midrash* is derived. Apparently the Pharisees referred to their study of Scripture as "midrash," or searching of Scripture for additional law and knowledge (see John 7:52). The later rabbis continued to use this language. Indeed, the rabbinic commentary on Scripture is called midrash.

5. For a succinct description of the Sadducees, especially in relation to the Dead Sea Scrolls, see E. Main, "Sadducees," in Schiffman and VanderKam (eds.), *Encyclopedia of the Dead Sea Scrolls*, 2:812–16.

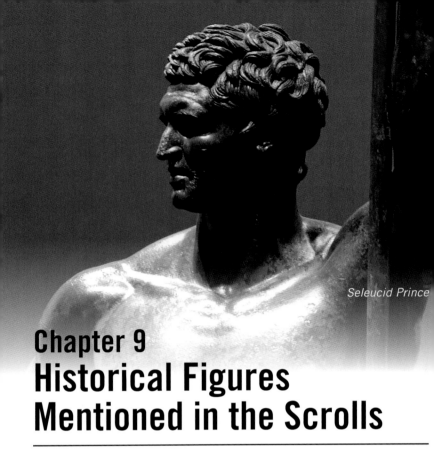
Seleucid Prince

Chapter 9
Historical Figures Mentioned in the Scrolls

A few historical figures are mentioned by name or by veiled reference in the Dead Sea Scrolls (DSS). These references cohere with the events that took place in Israel and nearby nations from about 140 BC to the beginning of the new era. This information, together with what we are told by early writers such as Philo, Pliny, and Josephus, encourages us to identify the authors of the DSS with the people who lived at Qumran, who are called Essenes. In this chapter we take a brief look at some of the historically significant figures who play a role in the DSS.

Seleucid and Ptolemaic Rulers

Some of the Greek kings of Syria (the Seleucids or Antiochids) and Egypt (the Ptolemies) are mentioned by name in the DSS. Why is this? One theory is that there were no widely recognized nicknames for foreign rulers as there were for Jewish rulers (such as Wicked Priest, Lion of Wrath, and the like). Thus perhaps the authors used specific names of foreign rulers when they wished to speak of the groups the rulers represented. In this case the named leader embodies and represents his entire people group.

As recounted above, the Maccabean revolt launched by the priest Mattathias of the Hasmonean family was a reaction to the oppressive decrees of Antiochus IV Epiphanes, who thought he could transform the Jewish faith into a religion more to his liking. One of the DSS, a commentary on Habakkuk, refers to this ruler and one of his descendants:

The Maccabean revolt launched by the priest Mattathias of the Hasmonean family was a reaction to the oppressive decrees of Antiochus IV Epiphanes, who thought he could transform the Jewish faith into a religion more to his liking. *Maccabean Revolt* by Doré.

"Wherever the lion goes to enter, there also goes the whelp [without fear" (Nah 2:11b). This refers to Deme]trius, king of Greece, who sought to enter Jerusalem through the counsel of the Flattery-Seekers; Jerusalem...[never fell into the] power of the kings of Greece from Antiochus until the appearance of the rulers of the Kittim; but afterwards it will be trampled [by the Gentiles]. (4Q169 frags. 3–4, column i, lines 1–4, partially restored)

Although it is much debated, I think this commentary was written in the 80s or 70s BC, years before Roman General Pompey's infamous arrival in Jerusalem in 63 BC. Aware of Rome's reputation in the eastern Mediterranean world and sensitive to their hunger for expansion, the author of this commentary anticipated a future conquest of Jerusalem at the hands of the Romans (obliquely referred to as the "Kittim"). Whereas the Greek rulers of Syria, from Antiochus IV (175–163 BC) to Demetrius III (95–88 BC),[1] had failed to take Jerusalem, the mighty Roman Empire would succeed in doing so. The author simply saw the writing on the wall.

The Flattery-Seekers (or Seekers of Smooth Things) are probably the Pharisees, who attempted to overthrow Alexander Jannaeus, the Hasmonean ruler of Israel. They failed, and Jannaeus exacted terrible retribution upon them. This incident seems to be recounted in the Damascus Document:

> They did not separate from the people, but arrogantly threw off all restraint, living by wicked customs, of which God had said, "Their wine is venom of snakes, the cruel poison of vipers" (Deut 32:33). "The snakes" are the kings of the Gentiles, and "their wine" is their customs and "the poison of vipers" is the chief of the kings of Greece, who comes to wreak vengeance on them. But the "Shoddy-Wall-Builders" and "Whitewashers" understood none of these things, for one who deals in mere wind, a spewer of lies, had spewed on them, one on whose entire company God's anger had burned hot. (CD 8:8–13)

Jesus prophesied the fall of Jerusalem. *Fall of Jerusalem* by Hayez.

What I find interesting is the prophecy of a coming capture of Jerusalem. This did not take place in the first century BC, as the commentator evidently anticipated, but it did take place in the first century AD, as Jesus of Nazareth prophesied (Mark 13:2; Luke 19:41–44).

The name "Ptolemy," the dynastic name of the Greek rulers of Egypt, occurs three times in a fragment of 4Q578 (frag. 1, lines 2–4), but we are unable to make out what is being said. In any event, reference to the Seleucid and Ptolemaic rulers fixes the DSS and the Qumran community in a known point of time.[2]

Hasmonean Rulers

In our survey of Intertestamental Israel, we mentioned people such as Simon, Alexandra, and Aristobulus. Some of these names appear in the scrolls.[3] In a list of names in a very fragmentary scroll, we find "[Yona]than, Simon" (4Q245 frag. 1, column i, line 10), which could refer to Jonathan and his younger brother Simon. These sons of Mattathias were Hasmoneans who ruled Israel 160–142 BC and 142–134 BC respectively. We may also have reference to Simon and his son John Hyrcanus I (ruled 134–104 BC) in another fragmentary scroll (4Q339, frag. 1, line 9), this time in a list of false prophets. So much for the hope that the Hasmoneans would restore Israel to God!

However, in another fragmentary scroll we find a psalm of praise in honor of King Alexander Jannaeus (whose Hebrew name and title were "King Jonathan"). A portion of the psalm reads as follows:

> Awake, O Holy One,
> for Jonathan, the king,
> and all the congregation of Your people
> Israel
> that is (dispersed) to the four
> winds of the heavens;
> let peace be on all of them
> and Your kingdom.
> May Your name be blessed. (4Q448 2:1–9)

Scholars have been surprised that a psalm in praise and prayerful support for Alexander Jannaeus would be found in the Qumran library. However, this surprise is largely based on the assumption that Jannaeus is the Lion of Wrath mentioned in the commentary on Habakkuk. Below we shall explore the possibility of a different identification.

Shelamzion Alexandra, the wife, widow, and successor to Jannaeus, is also mentioned in the scrolls, along with her feuding sons Hyrcanus II and perhaps Aristobulus:

> [1][. . . to] give him honor among the Nabate[ans . . . [2] . . . the fo]urth [day] of this tribe's service [. . . [3] . . .] that is the twentieth of the month [. . . [4] . . .] foundation, Shelamzion entered [. . .] to receive [. . . [5] . . .] Hyrcanus rebelled [against Aristobulus . . . [6] . . .] (4Q332 frag. 2, lines 1–6, partially restored)

The scroll is so fragmentary that we cannot determine what is being said. That Israel was at one time ruled by a woman is itself very interesting.[4] The name Shelamzion, which in Hebrew means "Peace of Zion," was very popular in aristocratic circles in the time of Jesus.

Time and Major Figures and Events

587 BC The capture of Jerusalem, the destruction of the Temple, and the deportation of many Jews to Babylonia. One century later Ezra was a principal figure in the return of some Jews to Jerusalem.

333–332 Alexander the Great sweeps through Israel and conquers Asia Minor, Egypt, and most of the Middle East.

323 Death of Alexander.

167 Desecration of the temple by the Seleucid ruler, Antiochus IV Epiphanes, who ruled 175–163 BC.

164–163 Judas Maccabeus (the "hammer") defeats General Lysias; Antiochus IV dies; Judas rules Judea, begins to enlarge borders; Hasmonean dynasty is founded.

160 Death of Judas; succeeded by Jonathan.

142 Death of Jonathan; succeeded by Simon.

134 Death of Simon; succeeded by John Hyrcanus I.

104 Death of John Hyrcanus I (son of Simon); succeeded by Aristobulus I.

103 Death of Aristobulus I (son of John Hyrcanus I); succeeded by Alexander Jannaeus.

78 Birth of Herod (the Great).

76 Death of Alexander Jannaeus (son of John Hyrcanus I).

67 Death of Alexandra (wife of Alexander Jannaeus).

67–63 Aristobulus II rules briefly amid dissension; people appeal to Rome.

63 Pompey enters Jerusalem, thus beginning the era of Roman dominance. Hyrcanus II (son of Alexander Jannaeus) is made high priest.

48 Julius Caesar gains mastery over Roman Empire.

44 Death of Julius Caesar; Mark Antony and young Octavian (grandnephew of Caesar) avenge Caesar's murder and establish Second Triumvirate.

40 Roman senate, at prompting of Mark Antony, declares Herod (son of Antipater II) "King of the Jews"; Parthians support Antigonus (son of Aristobulus II).

37 Herod defeats Antigonus, last of the Hasmonean rulers, and becomes king of Israel in fact; marries Mariamne (granddaughter of Hyrcanus II); during his reign he rebuilds Jerusalem and the temple; founds several cities and fortresses; and marries and divorces/murders 10 wives.

31 Octavian defeats Mark Antony and Cleopatra at Actium; becomes Roman emperor; changes name to Augustus, forgives Herod for siding with Mark Antony; confirms his royal title.

20 Birth of Herod Antipas.

6 or 5 Birth of Jesus.

4 Death of Herod the Great; kingdom divided between three surviving sons.

AD 6 Archelaus (son of Herod the Great) is deposed.

6–15 Annas (or Ananus) is appointed high priest.

14 Death of Augustus; succeeded by stepson Tiberius.

18 Joseph bar Caiaphas (son-in-law of Annas) is appointed high priest.

19 or 25 Pontius Pilate is appointed prefect (governor) of Samaria and Judea.

30 or 33 Jesus is crucified.

34 Death of Herod Philip (son of Herod the Great).

36 Pilate massacres Samaritans at foot of Mount Gerizim.

37 Pilate and Joseph Caiaphas are removed from office; death of Tiberius; succeeded by Gaius Caligula; the birth of Josephus.

39 Caligula banishes Herod Antipas (son of Herod the Great) to Gaul; succeeded by Agrippa I (son of Aristobulus and Bernice, grandson of Herod the Great).

41 Agrippa I named king of Israel; death of Caligula; succeeded by Claudius.

44 Death of Agrippa I.

c. 50 Death of Philo of Alexandria, who describes the Essenes.

54 Death of Claudius; succeeded by Nero.

62 Ananus (son of Annas) becomes high priest, without Roman approval puts to death James the brother of Jesus; Roman governor Albinus removes Ananus from office.

66 The Jewish revolt begins.

68 Death of Nero; succeeded by Galba.

68–69 Brief reigns of Galba, Otho, and Vitellius.

69 General Vespasian, commander of the Roman forces against the Jews, is proclaimed emperor.

70 Jerusalem is captured by Titus (son of Vespasian); temple is badly damaged by fire; it is later demolished.

73–74 General Silva destroys Qumran compound, besieges, and captures Masada.

c. 78 Josephus publishes *The Jewish War*, in Aramaic, then in Greek.

79 Death of Vespasian; succeeded by his son Titus; death of Pliny the Elder, who describes the Essenes.

81 Death of Titus; succeeded by Domitian (brother of Titus).

c. 93 Death of Agrippa II (son of Agrippa I), after ruling portions of Israel beginning in 49 (cf. Acts 25:13–26:32); Bernice was his sister.

96 Death of Domitian; succeeded by Nerva, respected senator.

98 Death of Nerva; succeeded by adopted son Trajan; death of Josephus(?), who describes the Essenes.

115 Jewish revolt in North Africa.

117 Jewish revolt put down; death of Trajan; succeeded by adopted son Hadrian.

132–135 The great Jewish revolt led by Simon ben Kosiba, dubbed "bar Kokhba," whose letters were found at Murabba'at; defeated by Hadrian.

138 Death of Hadrian.

Notes

1. For more on the Seleucids, see I. M. Gafni, "Antiochus IV Epiphanes," and U. Rappaport, "Seleucids," in L. H. Schiffman and J. C. VanderKam (eds.), *Encyclopedia of the Dead Sea Scrolls* (2 vols., Oxford: Oxford University Press, 2000), 1:29 and 2:861–63, respectively.

2. For more discussion, see G. Bohak, "Ptolemies," in Schiffman and VanderKam (eds.), *Encyclopedia of the Dead Sea Scrolls*, 2:720–21.

3. See I. M. Gafni, "Hasmoneans," in Schiffman and VanderKam (eds.), *Encyclopedia of the Dead Sea Scrolls*, 1:329–33.

4. See T. Ilan, "Shelamzion Alexandra," in Schiffman and VanderKam (eds.), *Encyclopedia of the Dead Sea Scrolls*, 2:872–74.

fortresses and build siege ramps, which is how General Silva and his troops overcame Masada in AD 74. The commentator believes the fourth prophecy (1:16a) refers to the standards of the Roman army, standards that bore images which Jews found repellant. In the fifth prophecy (1:16b) the author finds reference to Roman taxes, particularly the yearly tribute. Recall that Jesus was asked about the lawfulness of Jews paying the Roman tribute (Mark 12:13–17). Finally, the commentator believes the sixth prophecy (Hab 1:17) refers to the pitiless violence of Roman warfare.

The Kittim are also mentioned in many other scrolls (4QpNah, 4Q285, 4Q332, 4Q554, 11Q14). The contest between the Messiah and the Kittim, described in 4Q285, is of particular interest and will be discussed below.

General Silva and his troops overcame Masada in AD 74. Photo: Grauesel.

The Lion of Wrath, said by the scrolls to be the fulfillment of the prophecy in Nahum 2:11–12, was for years taken to be a reference to Alexander Jannaeus (or King Jonathan), especially bearing in mind his harsh revenge upon the Pharisees who allied themselves with Demetrius III (as is perhaps alluded to in 4QpNah frags. 3–4, column i, lines 6–8).[2] Recently, however, it has been persuasively argued that the Lion of Wrath was instead a Nebuchadnezzar-style conqueror, probably the Roman

The Hosea Commentary.

emperor.[3] On this reading the commentary on Nahum looks to the future and the anticipated triumph of the Romans, not to the recent past in which Alexander Jannaeus had taken his revenge. Unfortunately, the commentary on Nahum is fragmentary, so certainty about this matter is probably unattainable. Here is how the key passage reads:

"Where is the lions' den, the feeding place or the cubs?" (Nahum 2:11a) This refers to . . . a dwelling for the wicked Gentiles. "Wherever the lion goes to enter, there also goes the whelp without fear" (Nah 2:11b). This refers to Demetrius, king of Greece, who sought to enter Jerusalem through the counsel of the Flattery-Seekers; but it never fell into the power of the kings of Greece from Antiochus until the appearance of the rulers of the Kittim; but afterwards it will be trampled by the Gentiles . . . . "The lion catches enough for his cubs, and strangles prey for his mates" (Nah 2:12a). This refers to . . . to the Lion of Wrath who would kill some of his nobles and the men of his party. . . . "He fills his cave with prey, his den with game" (Nah 2:12b). This refers to the Lion of Wrath . . . vengeance against the Flattery-Seekers, whom he will hang up alive. And they will become a curse, as it was in Israel in former times. (4QpNah frags. 3–4, column 1, lines 1–8, partially restored)

The epithet "Lion of Wrath" also appears in the commentary on Hosea (4QpHos frag. 2, line 2), but the context is also uncertain due to the fragmentary condition of the text.

The Wicked Priest and the **Man of the Lie** (a.k.a. "spouter of the lie," "scoffer," and "man of mockery") are taken as references to two distinct persons by some scholars, but these unflattering nicknames probably initially referred to only one person, most likely one of the Hasmonean high priests.[4] Perhaps it later came to apply to other Hasmonean high priests. The Wicked Priest or Man of the Lie, and his loyal following, the **House of Absalom**, oppose the Teacher of Righteousness, as we see in the commentary on Habakkuk:

> "For the wicked man hems in the righteous man" (Hab 1:4b). The "wicked man" refers to the Wicked Priest, and "the righteous man" is the Teacher of Righteousness. (1QpHab 1:12–13)

> "How can you look on silently, you traitors, when the wicked destroys one more righteous than he?" (Hab 1:13b). This refers to the house of Absalom and the members of their party, who kept quiet when the Teacher of Righteousness was rebuked, and they did not help him against the Man of the Lie, who had rejected the Law in the presence of their entire company. (1QpHab 5:8–12)

The Damascus Document warns that the Man of Mockery preaches lies to Israel.

According to the Damascus Document the Man of Mockery preached lies to Israel:

They are the ones who depart from the proper way. That is the time of which it was written, "Like a rebellious cow, so rebelled Israel" (Hos 4:16). When the Man of Mockery appeared, who sprayed on Israel lying waters, "he led them to wander in the trackless wasteland" (Ps 107:40; Job 12:24). He brought down the lofty heights of old, turned aside from paths of righteousness. (CD 1:13–16)

In the commentary on Psalm 37, we learn that the Wicked Priest spied on and attempted to murder the Teacher of Righteousness:

"The wicked man observes the righteous man and seeks to kill him. But the Lord will not leave him in his power and will not condemn him when he comes to trial" (Ps 37:32–33). This refers to the wicked priest who observes the Teacher of Righteousness and seeks to kill him. (4Q171 frags. 3–10, column iv, lines 7–8)

In the following passage from the commentary on Habakkuk, we catch a glimpse of the event that probably brought the Qumran community into existence.

"Look, traitors, and see, and be shocked, for the Lord is doing something in your time that you would not believe it if told" (Hab 1:5). This passage refers to the traitors with the Man of the Lie, because they did not listen to the words of the Teacher of Righteousness from the mouth of God. It also refers to the traitors to the New Covenant, because they did not believe in God's covenant and desecrated his holy name; and finally, it refers to the traitors in the Last Days. They are the cruel Israelites who will not believe when they hear everything that is to come upon the latter generation that will be spoken by the Priest in whose heart God

has put the ability to explain all the words of his servants the prophets, through whom God has foretold
everything that is to come upon his people and the
Gentiles. (1QpHab 1:16–2:10)

The Man of the Lie, identified as the Wicked Priest earlier in the commentary, did not listen to the teaching of the
Teacher of Righteousness, whose words came from the very
mouth of God. The commentator says Habakkuk's prophecy
also refers to "traitors to the New Covenant," the Covenant
that is spelled out in the DSS, especially in the Rule of the
Community (1QS).

One should note how the commentary becomes eschatological in its orientation. The commentator says that Habakkuk's prophecy "refers to the traitors in the Last Days." God's
truth, especially as it pertains to the Last Days, has been spoken by the Teacher of Righteousness, who in 1QpHab 2:7–8 is
identified as "the Priest in whose heart God has put the ability
to explain all the words of his servants the prophets, through
whom God has foretold everything that is to come upon his
people and the Gentiles."

From this commen-
tary we may infer that
the Qumran community
was founded by a ruling
priest, perhaps one who
had even been a mainline
high priest but was de-
posed for his criticism of
the establishment priest-
hood in Jerusalem. This
priest's followers regarded him as the Teacher of
Righteousness, a man opposed by a Wicked Priest, who spout-
ed lies to Israel and scoffed at the teaching of God's faithful
representative.

> *We may infer that the
> Qumran community was
> founded by a ruling priest,
> perhaps one who had
> even been a mainline high
> priest but was deposed
> for his criticism of the
> establishment priesthood
> in Jerusalem.*

Qumran. Photo:Sobkowski.

Shoddy Wall Builders, White-Washers, and Flattery-Seekers stood in opposition to the Teacher of Righteousness and his loyal followers. Possibly these epithets were interchangeable, referring to one group rather than three. It seems that this group of opponents sought middle ground between the Teacher or Righteousness and his archenemy the Wicked Priest. Thus they are not of the same foul stripe as the Kittim, the Wicked Priest, and others. Nevertheless, because of their lack of support for the Teacher, they, too, became his enemies.

Commenting on the meaning of Deuteronomy 32:33 and explaining the meaning of "snakes" and "the poison of vipers," the author of the Damascus Document says the following about the faithless:

> "The snakes" are the kings of the Gentiles, and "their wine" is their customs and "the poison of vipers" is the chief of the kings of Greece, who comes to wreak vengeance on them. But the "Shoddy-Wall-Builders" and "White-Washers" understood none of these things, for one who deals in mere wind, a spouter of lies, had spewed on them, one on whose entire company God's anger had burned hot. (CD 8:10–13)

The Flattery-Seekers (or Seekers of Smooth Things) appear in three of the commentaries found among the scrolls: the third commentary on Isaiah (4QpIsa^c), the commentary on Nahum (4QpNah), and the commentary on selected verses from the Prophets and the Psalms (4Q177).

In the first reference to the Flattery Seekers in the commentary on Nahum, we are told of their appeal to Demetrius, king of Greece (4QpNah frags. 3–4, column i, lines 1–3). This same incident is described by Josephus (*War* 1.92–98; *Antiquities* 13.377–83). Judging by this they were probably Pharisees or at least supporters of the Pharisaic party.[5]

Ephraim and Manasseh are other epithets that bear brief mention. "Ephraim" refers to blacksliders and apostates of Israel (CD 7:13; 4Q167 frag. 10, line 1), while "Manasseh" is said to join itself to a divisive group (4QpNah frags. 3–4, column

At its core, the Essene outlook included the expectation that God's Messiah would come and set things right. The DSS help demonstrate that Messianic hope was widespread in the century before Jesus was born in Bethlehem.

iv, line 1). Elsewhere we hear of the "wicked of Ephraim and Manasseh" (4Q171 frags. 1–2, column ii, lines 17–18).[6]

The Branch of David and **Prince of the Congregation** are both ways in which the DSS reference the Messiah. At its core, the Essene outlook included the expectation that God's Messiah would come and set things right. The DSS help demonstrate that Messianic hope was widespread in the century before Jesus was born in Bethlehem.

Notes

1. For discussion of the Sons of Light and the Sons of Darkness, see J. Duhaime, "Light and Darkness," in L. H. Schiffman and J. C. VanderKam (eds.), *Encyclopedia of the Dead Sea Scrolls* (2 vols., Oxford: Oxford University Press, 2000), 1:495–96.

2. This is the view in H. Eshel, "Alexander Jannaeus," in Schiffman and VanderKam (eds.), *Encyclopedia of the Dead Sea Scrolls*, 1:16–18.

3. See G. L. Doudna, *4Q Pesher Nahum: A Critical Edition* (London and New York: Sheffield Academic Press, 2001). This is a lengthy, technical work.

4. See T. H. Lim, "Wicked Priest," in Schiffman and VanderKam (eds.), *Encyclopedia of the Dead Sea Scrolls*, 2:973–76.

5. For more discussion of these sobriquets and the question of identity, see A. I. Baumgarten, "Seekers After Smooth Things," in Schiffman and VanderKam (eds.), *Encyclopedia of the Dead Sea Scrolls*, 2:857–59.

6. For more discussion of these sobriquets, see H. Eshel, "Ephraim and Manasseh," in Schiffman and VanderKam (eds.), *Encyclopedia of the Dead Sea Scrolls*, 1:253–54.

Photo: James Byrum

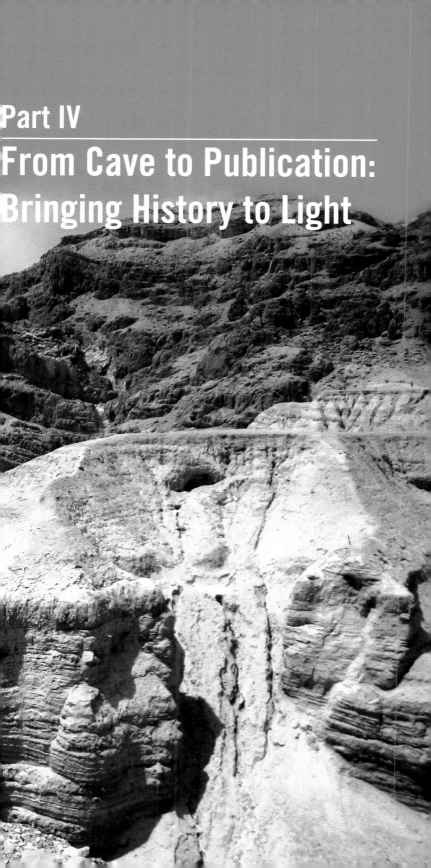

Part IV

From Cave to Publication: Bringing History to Light

Chapter 11
The Scrolls, Cave by Cave

A surprising variety of documents have been found among the Dead Sea Scrolls (DSS).[1] We have more than 200 Bible scrolls, more than one dozen formal commentaries on Scripture (mostly on Psalms and the writings of the prophets), a variety of extracanonical psalms and hymns, visions, calendars, instructions on how to apply the laws of Moses, extracanonical biblical-like narratives, paraphrases of Scripture, and more.

In this chapter we review the contents of the scrolls in inventory fashion, cave by cave. However, we begin not with a discovery found in a cave but a discovery found in a dusty synagogue closet.

Cairo Genizah

As mentioned in chapter 2, the first documents relating to the DSS were not found in the vicinity of the Dead Sea; they were instead found in the genizah of the old Ben-Ezra Synagogue in Cairo, Egypt. Nor were these documents as old as those found in the Dead Sea region. The Cairo synagogue documents date back to the medieval era, ranging from the 800s to the 1200s and beyond.

The documents were found in the Cairo synagogue in 1896

Scholar Solomon Schechter studies the scrolls from the Cairo Genizah. Photo: Syndics of Cambridge University Library (Cambridge University Library, T-S NS 176.2).

or 1897. Those that are relevant to the DSS include portions of Sirach (CSir), an Aramaic portion of the Testament of Levi (CTLevi ar), and the Damascus Document (CD). The Damascus Document was published in 1910 under the title *Fragments of a Zadokite Work.*[2] Later, when the scrolls in the Dead Sea region were discovered, scholars realized that the so-called "Zadokite Work" found in Cairo was in reality the Damascus Document of the Essene sect at Qumran. The version found at Cairo was a later copy of the Qumran document.

The Qumran Caves

The 11 Qumran caves are numbered according to the order of their discovery. The first was discovered in the spring of 1947 (perhaps earlier); the last in 1956. The scrolls are referred to by cave number and document number. For example, 4Q521 means document 521 from Cave 4 of Qumran. Documents found elsewhere have different sigla. For example, CD means the Damascus Document (D) from the Cairo synagogue genizah (C).

> *The scrolls are referred to by cave number and document number. For example, 4Q521 means document 521 from Cave 4 of Qumran.*

We have seen how the scrolls are named. How about individual texts within the scrolls? Qumran texts are usually cited using Arabic numerals by column and line number. For example, 1QS 9:3–6 means the Serek ("Rule") document from Qumran, discovered in Cave 1, column 9 of the scroll, lines 3 to 6 of the column. Notice that this is not the same thing as saying chapter 9, verses 3 to 6.

The above nomenclature works well for scrolls that are whole or nearly so, but because most scrolls are fragmentary, they are cited in a different way. For instance, 4QpNah 3–4 i 6 indicates that we are speaking about fragments 3 and 4 (Arabic numerals), column i (lowercase Roman numerals), line 6 (Arabic numerals). Setting the two methods side by side helps you see the different approaches:

Fragmentary scrolls are cited in a different way. For instance, 4QpNah 3–4 i 6 indicates that we are speaking about fragments 3 and 4, column i, line 6.

1QS 9:3–6 for a whole or nearly whole scroll

4QpNah 3–4 i 6 for scroll fragments

Now for the cave-by-cave inventory of the discoveries at the Qumran site. This will serve as a handy reference and will help you see how the discoveries unfolded sequentially as one cave after another was searched and cleared.

Cave 1 at Qumran. Photo: Hoysameg.

Qumran, Cave 1. To the best of our knowledge, Cave 1 was discovered sometime early in 1947. Some 77 or 78 scrolls were found in this cave. These are: 1Q1–72, 1QIsaiah^a, 1QpHabakkuk, 1QapGen (two scrolls that were never numbered, though the 1Q20 fragment belongs to it), 1Q28^a, 1Q28^b (appendixes to 1QS, another otherwise unnumbered scroll), 1QM, and 1QH. Broken down by category:

- 1Q1–12 and 1QIsaiah^a are Bible scrolls (1QIsaiah^b = 1Q8).
- 1Q13 is a phylactery (Bible verses worn on one's arm or head), which comprises several quotations of Scripture.
- 1Q14–16 and 1QpHab are pesharim (commentaries) on Micah, Habakkuk, Zephaniah, and Psalms.
- 1Q17–18 are copies of the pseudepigraphon Jubilees, known from other manuscripts.
- 1Q19–27 comprise various pseudepigraphal texts, some of them previously known (such as 1Q21 = Aramaic Testament of Levi, and 1Q23–24 = Enochic Book of Giants).
- 1Q28 and 1QS and 1Q28a–b comprise Cave 1's Rule of the Community and appendixes.
- 1Q29–31 comprise various liturgical texts
- 1Q32 describes the New Jerusalem, a text found in other caves.
- 1Q33 and 1QM comprise the famous War Scroll or Milhamah.
- 1Q34 and 1Q34bis comprise Festival Prayers, while 1Q35–40 are hymnic compositions.
- 1Q41–62 are unclassified Hebrew fragments.
- 1Q63–68 are unclassified Aramaic fragments.
- 1Q69–70bis are unclassified papyrus fragments.
- 1Q71–72 are small fragments of Daniel.

Qumran, Cave 2. Qumran's Cave 2, discovered in February 1952, contained approximately 33 scrolls: 2Q1–33 plus "debris in a box," which may or may not represent miniscule remains of additional scrolls. By category, Cave 2 yielded:

- 2Q1–17 represent portions of the five books of Moses, one prophet (Jeremiah), and three Writings (Psalms, Job, and two Ruth scrolls).
- 2Q18 are fragments of Sirach.
- 2Q19–20 are fragments of Jubilees.
- 2Q21–23 are other apocryphal texts.
- 2Q24 is a copy of the Aramaic New Jerusalem.
- 2Q25 is a juridical text.
- 2Q26 is the Enochic Book of Giants.
- 2Q27–33 are unclassified fragments.

Qumran, Cave 3. Cave 3, discovered in March 1952, has yielded some 15 documents: 3Q1–15, plus uninscribed fragments (3QX1–4), a leather knot (3QX4), debris in a box (3QX5), and a squeeze of Cave 3 clay (3QX6).

- 3Q1–3 are Bible scrolls representing Ezekiel, Psalms, and Lamentations.
- 3Q4 is a pesher (commentary) on Isaiah.
- 3Q5 is a fragment of Jubilees.
- 3Q7 may be a fragment of a Testament of Judah.
- 3Q15 is by far the most interesting item. It is called the Copper Plaque or the Copper Scroll.

Cave 4 at Qumran. Photo: Franco56.

Qumran, Cave 4. Cave 4, discovered in September 1952, has been described as the "mother lode." Situated just opposite the ruins at Qumran, this cave yielded up the fragments of over 500 documents, including:

Cave 4, discovered in September 1952, has been described as the "mother lode."

- Some 125 Bible scrolls
- One dozen or more pesharim
- Dozens of scrolls of apocryphal and pseudepgraphal texts
- A host of sectarian texts, including:
    - The Rule of the Community
    - The Damascus Covenant
    - Hymns
    - Calendars of one sort or another
    - Rules on purity

- ▪ MMT (Miqsat Ma'ase ha-Torah = "Some of the Works of the Law"), extant in six fragmentary copies (i.e. 4Q394–99). This is perhaps the most important sectarian document found in this cave.
- Several other texts have come to light that have great significance for understanding Jesus (e.g., 4Q246, 4Q500, 4Q521, and 4Q525). These will be discussed later in the book.

Qumran, Cave 5. Cave 5, also discovered in September 1952, yielded a number of significant items, including:

- 5Q1–7, comprising seven biblical scrolls. These are Deuteronomy, Kings, Isaiah, Amos, Psalms, and two copies of Lamentations.
- 5Q8 is a phylactery.
- 5Q9–15 are seven identified nonbiblical texts (5Q9–15), all of which have their counterparts in other caves.
- 5Q16–25 are an estimated 10 unidentified texts.

Qumran, Cave 6. Cave 6 was discovered in September or October 1952. It has yielded some interesting finds, including:

- 6Q1–7 are biblical scrolls, including Genesis, Leviticus, possibly Deuteronomy, Kings, Song of Songs, and Daniel.
- 6Q19 is in Aramaic. It is related to the book of Genesis and may even be a version of it.
- 6Q20 is also in Aramaic and is either a version of Deuteronomy or is related to it.
- 6Q21–31 and 6QX1 and 6QX2 nonbiblical texts.

Qumran, Cave 7. Cave 7, discovered in February 1955, yielded several Greek manuscripts, including:

- 7QLXXExod = 7Q1 and 7QLXXEpJer = 7Q2 (Letter of

Cave 7. Photo: Albeiro Rodas.

Jeremiah, one of the books of the OT Apocrypha). LXX = Septuagint, or Greek translation of the OT.

- Several unidentified fragments which a few scholars have tried to identify as NT writings (esp. 7Q5 as Mark 6:52). The NT identifications have won few followers among scholars. In fact, the fragments have recently been identified as belonging to the pseudepigraphal book of Enoch. Most of the fragments from cave 7 remain unidentified.

Qumran, Cave 8. Cave 8 was discovered in March and April 1955. Eight texts have been recovered:

- A few fragments of Genesis (8Q1 = Gen 17:12–19 and 18:20–25)

- Several fragments of the Psalms (8Q2 = Pss 17:5–9,14; 18:6–9,10–13)

- A phylactery with clusters of quotations from Exodus and Deuteronomy (8Q3)

- Mezuzah with Deuteronomy 10:12–11:21 (8Q4)
- A hymn (8Q5), which appears to extol God: "In your name, O Mighty One, I spread fear."

Qumran, Caves 9–10. The yield from these caves was lower than others. The findings include:

- In Cave 9 we have one unclassified papyrus fragment (9Qpap).
- In Cave 10 we have one ostracon (10QOstracon) with only two letters (*yod, shin*) at the beginning of a word or name. An ostracon is a piece of pottery on which someone has inked letters or words. The plural is ostraca.

Qumran, Cave 11. Discovered in February 1956, Cave 11 was the last of the Qumran caves to yield written materials. It produced several important finds, including nine biblical scrolls.

- 11Q1–2 are scrolls of Leviticus.
- 11Q3 is a scroll of Deuteronomy.
- 11Q4 is a fragment of Ezekiel.
- 11Q5–9 are five Psalms scrolls.
- There were also 11 identified nonbiblical scrolls (11Q10–20), including the important temple texts (11Q19–20), and five unidentified or unclassified texts (11Q21–25).

Summary

Documents have been found at other sites, such as Murabba'at and Masada, but by far and away the Qumran site has yielded the greatest number of ancient writings. The rich variety of the documents represents a gold mine for biblical scholarship. While most people automatically assume that all of the scrolls are in Hebrew, the caves yielded more than 60 writings in Aramaic. This comprises about 10 percent of the find (if we do not count the Bible scrolls). Furthermore, 19 documents from Qumran's Cave 7 are Greek. These yield rich information about political and religious realities in the era before and during the life of Christ.

The Caves and the Scrolls at a Glance

Cave No.	Bible	Non-Bible
1	17	36
2	18	15
3	3	7
4	171	431
5	8	17
6	6	24
7	–	17
8	4	1
9	–	1
10	–	–
11	9	16

Notes

1. For thumbnail sketches of the Scrolls, along with selected bibliography, see C. A. Evans, *Ancient Texts for New Testament Studies: A Guide to the Background Literature* (Peabody, MA: Hendrickson, 2005), 76–154.

2. See R. H. Charles, "Fragments of a Zadokite Work," in R. H. Charles (ed.), *The Apocrypha and Pseudepigrapha of the Old Testament* (2 vols., Oxford: Clarendon Press, 1913) 2:785–834. New editions, supplemented with the fragments found at Qumran, are now available.

Chapter 12
The First Scrolls to Be Published

In this section we survey the first Dead Sea Scrolls (DSS) that were published in the heady days of discovery and excitement (1947–1968). These early scrolls include the discoveries made at the Egyptian synagogue and the first cave at Qumran in the Dead Sea region. These documents greatly influenced the way scholars understood the Qumran community and its library.

Damascus Document

One of the most important DSS is known as the Damascus Document. The largest surviving portions are two copies from the medieval era, both of which were found in the Cairo synagogue:

- Ms A dates from the tenth century and includes 16 columns of text.
- Ms B dates from the twelfth century and is comprised of two long columns (curiously numbered 19 and 20).

Additionally, eight frag-
ments of the Damascus Document were found in Qum-
ran's Cave 4 (i.e., 4Q266–73),
a small fragment from Cave
5 (i.e., 5Q12), and five fragments of a copy from Cave 6

The earliest draft of the Damascus Document may have been composed sometime in the second century BC.

(i.e., 6Q15). The earliest draft of the Damascus Document may
have been composed sometime in the second century BC.[1]

The large fragments from Cairo were found in a genizah,
a storage room where sacred writings such as the Bible were
retired after being withdrawn from regular use due to wear
and tear. Writings that contained God's name were not to
be thrown out as trash. Normally, books stored in a genizah
would eventually be buried in a funeral-like service. But for
some reason the old books and documents stored in the
genizah at Cairo were never buried. Instead, they remained
stowed away and forgotten for centuries, finally coming to
light in the 1890s. Thus, it turned out that the first of the DSS
to be discovered in modern times was found in Egypt, not
in Israel! Later, when the caves of Qumran and other nearby
Dead Sea locations were explored, more fragmentary copies of
the Damascus Document were found.

The Damascus Document. Photo: Syndics
of Cambridge University Library (Cambridge
University Library, T-S 10K6,1r).

The Cairo version
of the Damascus Docu-
ment was published
in 1910 under the title
*Fragments of a Zadok-
ite Work.* It was called
this because it contains
many references to the
"sons of Zadok," under-
stood to be the true de-
scendants and heirs of
the famous high priest
Zadok who served dur-
ing the reigns of David
and his son Solomon.
Eventually the writing
became known as the
Damascus Document

The Ben Ezra Synagogue in Cairo. Photo: Daniel Mayer.

because it frequently mentions Damascus, whether literally or figuratively.

The Damascus Document is made up of three major sections: (1) an admonition and call for the faithful to separate from the wicked of Israel, along with a reminder of Israel's history, (2) a description of the laws by which the renewed community—priests and laity alike—were to live, and (3) rules pertaining to community life.

The Damascus Document begins with a call to listen and be reminded of how God had dealt with his people in the past:

> So listen, all you who recognize righteousness, and consider the deeds of God; for He has a suit against every mortal and He executes judgment upon all who despise Him. When in their treachery they abandoned him He turned away from Israel and from His sanctuary and gave them up to the sword; but when He remembered the covenant of the forefathers, He left a remnant to Israel and did not allow them to be totally destroyed, but in a time of wrath three hundred and ninety years when He put them into the power of Nebuchadnezzar, king of Babylon. (CD 1:1–6)

The theme of the Damascus Document revolves around renewal of the covenant.

The theme of the Damascus Document revolves around renewal of the covenant. We find some interesting allegorical (or symbolic) interpretations in which the men of Qumran identify themselves and their mission. The document (A 6:2–11) appeals to Numbers 21:18 ("The princes dug the well; The nobles of the people hollowed it out with a scepter and with their staffs") and interprets the "well" as a reference to the Law of Moses, the "diggers" as members of the Qumran community who were called to live in Damascus, and the "staff" with which the digging was done as the Teacher of Righteousness, the authoritative teacher of the Qumran community. The interpreter of the Law, said to be the "star" of the Numbers 24:17 prophecy, is again mentioned, this time as one who joins the community in Damascus (A 7:13–21). The covenant is renewed in the land of Damascus. Those who oppose it, called the Men of Mockery and Shoddy-Wall Builders, shall have no part in restored Israel (A 8:8–21; B 19:20–35).

The men of the renewed covenant, who heed the teaching of the revered Teacher of Righteousness, will be vindicated when God raises up Israel's Messiah:

> If the seed of Israel lives according to this law, they shall never know condemnation. This is the rule for those who live in camps, who live by these rules in the era of wickedness, until the appearance of the Messiah of Aaron and of Israel. (A 12:21–13:1)

> And this is the exposition of the regulations by which they shall be governed in the age of wickedness until the appearance of the Messiah of Aaron and of Israel, so that their iniquity may be atoned for. (A 14:18–19)

> But those who give heed to God are the poor of the flock [cf. Zech 11:7]: They will escape in the time of punishment, but all the rest will be handed over to the sword when the Messiah of Aaron and of Israel comes,

just as it happened during the time of the first punishment. (B 19:9–11)

Notice that the Damascus Document speaks of a "Messiah of Aaron and of Israel." Most interpreters think two figures are in view here: First, an anointed high priest, who of course must be descended from Israel's first high priest, Aaron. Second is an anointed king who would be a descendant of King David. "Messiah" is the Hebrew word for *anointed*, and the OT commonly speaks of anointed priests, kings, and prophets. More will be said about the Messiah in the DSS in chapters 26 and 27.

Language and concepts similar to that which is found in the Damascus Document also appear in other scrolls that are widely believed to be founding documents of Qumran community. We examine these next.

The Rule of the Community.

Rule of the Community

When first published, the document now known as the Rule of the Community was called the Manual of Discipline. Since the text actually calls itself the "Rule of the Community" (Hebrew: *Serek ha-Yahad*),

The Rule of the Community is something akin to a charter or constitution. It spells out rules by which members of the community must conduct themselves.

scholars are satisfied that this is the best title for the scroll. The best preserved copy (1QS) was found in Cave 1. Ten fragmentary copies (4Q255–64) were found in Cave 4, and two small fragments of another copy (5Q11) were found in Cave 5. Scholars believe that the document was composed some time around 100 BC.[2]

The Rule of the Community is something akin to a charter or constitution. In fact it follows the pattern of other charters and constitutions from late antiquity. The scroll spells out rules by which members of the community, or Yahad (from the Hebrew word meaning "one" or "unity"), must conduct themselves. The Rule is made up of six major sections: (1) introduction, (2) a ceremonial ritual for entering the community, (3) a discourse on the division of humans into two camps: one guided by a spirit of holiness and the other by a spirit of wickedness, (4) rules for the organization of the community, (5) the theological foundation of the community, and (6) a concluding hymn of praise.

There are also two appendixes to the Rule of the Community: The Rule of the Congregation (1QSa = 1Q28a) and the Rule of the Blessings (1QSb = 1Q28b). It has been plausibly suggested that the longer document, the Rule of the Community, pertains to life in the present age, while the Rule of the Congregation and the Rule of the Blessings pertain to the age to come.

The Rule of the Community begins by explaining what the writing is and what its purpose is:

A text belonging to the Instructor, who is to teach the

The men of Qumran believed that by going out into the wilderness to interpret the Law of Moses correctly, they were fulfilling the prophecy of Isaiah 40:3. Photo: A. Sobkowski.

Holy Ones how to live according to the book of the Rule of the Community. He is to teach them to seek God with all their heart and with all their soul, to do that which is good and upright before Him, just as He commanded through Moses and all His servants the prophets. He is to teach them to love everything He chose and to hate everything He rejected, to distance themselves from all evil and to hold fast to all good deeds. (1:1–5)

In a discussion that reminds NT readers of Paul's emphasis on the battle between flesh and spirit (Romans 7–8), the Rule of the Community declares:

He created humankind to rule over the world, appointing for them two spirits in which to walk until the time ordained for His visitation. These are the spirits of truth and falsehood. Upright character and fate originate with the Habitation of Light; perverse, with the Fountain of Darkness. The authority of the Prince of Light extends to the governance of all righteous people; therefore, they walk in the paths of light. Correspondingly, the authority of the Angel of Darkness embraces the governance of all wicked people, so they walk in the paths of darkness. (3:17–21)

Until now the spirits of truth and perversity have contended within the human heart. All people walk in both wisdom and foolishness. As is a person's endowment of truth and righteousness, so shall he hate perversity; conversely, in proportion to bequest in the lot of evil, one will act wickedly and abominate truth. God has appointed these spirits as equals until the time of decree and renewal. (4:23–25)

The Rule of the Community spells out the requirements for joining the community of the renewed covenant:

This is the rule for the men of the Community who volunteer to repent from all evil and to hold fast to all that He, by His good will, has commanded. They are to separate from the congregation of perverse men. They are to come together as one with respect to Law and wealth. Their discussions shall be under the oversight of the Sons of Zadok—priests and preservers of the covenant—and according to the majority rule of the men of the Community, who hold fast to the covenant. These men shall guide all decisions on matters of Law, money and judgment. They are to practice truth together with humility, charity, justice, lovingkindness and modesty in all their ways. (5:1–4)

The men of this community believed that in going out into the wilderness and interpreting the Law of Moses correctly, they were fulfilling the prophecy of Isaiah 40:3:

When such men as these come to be in Israel, conforming to these doctrines, they shall separate from the session of perverse men to go to the wilderness, there to prepare the way of truth, as it is written, "In the wilderness prepare the way of the Lord, make straight in the desert a highway for our God" (Isa 40:3). This means the expounding of the Law, decreed by God through Moses for obedience, that being defined by what has been revealed for each age, and by what the prophets have revealed by His holy spirit. (8:12–16)

The men of Qumran believed they constituted the "Way" in fulfillment of Isaiah.

The men of Qumran believed they constituted the "Way" in fulfillment of Isaiah. They expected to expound the Law of God, "until there come the Prophet and the Messiahs of Aaron and of Israel" (9:11). These eschatological figures would put everything right. It is interesting to observe that this use of Isaiah 40:3 is quite similar to its usage by early Christians, who also referred to their movement as "the Way" (see Acts 9:2; 19:9; 24:14,22). Both groups saw themselves as the fulfillment of major OT themes.

The Rule of the Congregation foresees the day when the men of reputation assemble for a great banquet (see Isa 25:6), a time when God will have begotten the Messiah among them (1QSa 2:11–12; see Ps 2:1,7). The men of reputation include the priests and the long-awaited Messiah.

The Rule of the Blessings delineates the various blessings to be pronounced on the priests and the high priest, concluding with a blessing for the royal Messiah, who will judge with fairness and exact punishment on Israel's enemies.[3] Notice the many allusions to Isaiah 11:

(These are the words of blessing) belonging to the Instructor, by which to bless the Prince of the Congregation whom God chose. . . . And He shall renew for him the Covenant of the Community, so as to establish the kingdom of His people forever, that "with righteousness he may judge the poor, and decide with equity for the meek of the earth" [Isa 11:4], walk before Him blameless in all the ways of His heart, and establish His covenant as holy in distress for those who seek Him. May the Lord lift you up to an eternal height, a mighty tower in a wall securely set on high! Thus may you be righteous by the might of your mouth, lay waste the earth with your rod! With the breath of your lips may you kill the wicked!" [Isa 11:4, modified]. May He give you "a spirit of counsel and eternal might rest upon you, the spirit of knowledge and the fear of God" [Isa 11:2]. May "righteousness be the belt around your waist, and faithfullness the belt around your loins" [Isa 11:5]. May He "make your horns iron and your hoofs bronze!" [Mic 4:13]. (1QSb 5:21–26)

Hodayot and Other Hymn Scrolls

One of the major scrolls found in Cave 1 comprises several hymns. It was given the Hebrew name Hodayot, which in English is roughly translated *Thanksgiving Hymns*. Its siglum is 1QHodayot[a] (or more simply 1QH[a]). Careful examination of the 100 or so fragments led to the identification of a second hymn scroll (1QH[b] = 1Q35). Several more fragments of these hymns have been found in Cave 4 (i.e., 4QH[a-f] = 4Q427–432). These scrolls were probably composed shortly after 100 BC.[4]

The Thanksgiving Hymns powerfully describe the frame of mind of the covenanters of Qumran. Their separation from the corrupt world, their spiritual ascents into the heavens, and their pain at being opposed and rebuffed by nonbelievers constitute the main themes of these hymns. There are 19 complete hymns plus fragments of several others. Some scholars have suggested that a few of the hymns were composed by the Teacher of Righteousness himself, for here and there we may hear echoes of the Teacher's difficulties in the face of those who oppose him:

> I give thanks to You, O Lord,
> for You have made my face to shine by Your covenant,
> and . . .
> . . . I seek You, and as an enduring dawning,
> as perfect light, You have revealed Yourself to me.
> But these Your people go astray.
> For they flatter themselves with words,
> and mediators of deceit lead them astray,
> so that they are ruined without knowledge.
> For . . . their works are deceitful,
> for good works were rejected by them.
> Neither did they esteem me;
> even when You displayed Your might through me.
> Instead, they drove me out from my land as a bird
> from its nest.

And all my friends and acquaintances have been driv-
en away from me;
they esteem me as a ruined vessel.
But they are mediators of a lie and seers of deceit.
They have plotted wickedness against me,
so as to exchange Your law, which You spoke distinctly
in my heart,
for flattering words directed to Your people.
They hold back the drink of knowledge from those
who thirst,
and for their thirst they give them vinegar to drink,
that they might observe their error,
behaving madly at their festivals and getting caught
in their nets.
But You, O God, reject every plan of Belial,
and Your counsel alone shall stand,
and the plan of Your heart shall remain for ever.
They are pretenders; they hatch the plots of Belial,
they seek You with a double heart, and are not founded in Your truth.
(1QH^a 12:6–15)

The hymnist also petitions God:

Keep Your servant from sinning against You and from
stumbling over all the words of Your will. Strengthen
. . . against the spirits of wickedness to walk in all that
You love, and despise all that You hate, and to do that
which is good in Your eyes. (1QH^a 4:35–36)

The hymnist compares himself, a mere mortal of flesh, to
kneaded clay:

By the mysteries of Your insight You assigned all these
things to make Your glory known. But what is the spirit of flesh that it might understand all these things and
obtain insight into the council of Your great wonders?
And what is one born of woman among all Your awe-
some works? He is but an edifice of dust, kneaded with
water, . . . his foundation is obscene shame . . . and a

perverted spirit ruled him. If he acts wickedly, he will become a sign for eternity and a sign to the generations, . . . to all flesh. Only by Your goodness shall a man be justified, and by the abundance of Your compassion . . . with Your splendor You glorify him, and You satisfy him with an abundance of delights; with eternal peace and long life. For You have spoken and Your word will not depart. (1QH^a 5:30–35)

Although it has been suggested that the Teacher of Righteousness thought of himself as the Suffering Servant of the Lord (see Isa 52:13–53:12), most scholars are not convinced that this is so. Chiefly he was looking forward to Messiah.

War of the Sons of Light and Sons of Darkness

This famous scroll is usually referred to as the War Scroll. Its official designation is 1QM ("M" for the Hebrew word *milhamah*, which means "war"). The original scroll comprised at least 20 columns of text. It begins with the chilling words, "For the Instructor, the Rule of the War. The first attack of the Sons of Light shall be undertaken against the forces of the Sons of Darkness, the army of Belial."

The scroll probably dates to the middle of the first century BC. The battle formations it describes resemble those of the Roman army, which is consistent with the proposed date of composition since the Jews would have witnessed firsthand the military formations used by the Roman occupiers of Israel.[5]

The War Scroll begins with the chilling words, "For the Instructor, the Rule of the War. The first attack of the Sons of Light shall be undertaken against the forces of the Sons of Darkness, the army of Belial."

The War Scroll describes the great and final eschatological battle between the Sons of Light and the Sons of Darkness. In this battle the evil Prince of Darkness (also known as Belial or Beliar, as in 2 Cor 6:15) and his corrupt minions will

Fragment from the War Scroll.

ɔe annihilated. The scroll provides detailed instructions for ɔroper battle formations for the Sons of Light. The righteous ɔriests of the Qumran community play prominent roles in the ɪnticipated eschatological battle. Only those who are ritually ɔure may participate. The scroll also contains the thanksgiv-ng hymn that is to be sung when the battle is won.

Seven fragments from Cave 4 appear to be related to the War Scroll (i.e., 4Q491–97), as well as the fragments of a text ːalled the Rule of War (i.e., 4Q285 = 11Q14). In the latter text ɪ figure is mentioned who is called the Prince of the Congrega-ːion and the Branch of David. This figure will meet the "King ɔf the Kittim" (which probably means the Roman emperor) in ɔattle and will kill him. This is a remarkable prediction, said ːo be in fulfillment of a prophecy in Isaiah, a prophecy which ʌe already saw alluded to in the Rule of the Blessings (1QSb). According to 4Q285:

> Just as it is written in the book of Isaiah the prophet, "And the thickets of the forest shall be cut down with an ax, and Lebanon with its majestic trees will fall. A shoot shall come out from the stump of Jesse and a branch shall grow out of his roots" [Isa 10:34–11:1]. This is the Branch of David. Then all forces of Belial shall be judged, and the king of the Kittim shall stand for judgment and the Leader of the community—the Branch of David—will have him put to death. Then all Israel shall come out with timbrels and dancers, and the high priest shall order them to cleanse their

bodies from the guilty blood of the corpses of the Kittim. (4Q285 frag. 5, lines 1–6, with several restorations)

If it was widely known that the Essenes expected the Messiah to kill the "king of the Kittim," then one can understand why Pontius Pilate, the Roman governor of Judea and Samaria, took interest in Jesus of Nazareth. After all, Jesus was sometimes referred to as "King of the Jews" (Mark 15:2). Thus the DSS give us the vital background for understanding some of the paranoid reactions Jesus met in his ministry.

The Great Isaiah Scroll

Arguably the most famous of the seven scrolls that first came to light in the late 1940s was the so-called Great Isaiah Scroll (i.e., 1QIsa^a). This lengthy scroll preserves virtually the entire book of Isaiah, missing only a few words and letters, usually along

> *The DSS give us the vital background for understanding some of the paranoid reactions Jesus met in his ministry.*

the bottom margin of the scroll. John Trever, a young scholar engaged in postdoctoral studies in Jerusalem in 1948, photographed and published this vital scroll. A second large scroll of Isaiah (1QIsa^b) was also found in Cave 1, but it was not as well preserved.[6]

The Great Isaiah Scroll.

Whereas Scroll "a" closely follows the Hebrew preserved in the Masoretic manuscript tradition, Scroll "b" takes liberties with the text, almost to the point that it could be regarded as a paraphrase rather than a copy of Isaiah. The fragmentary 1QIsaiah^b was edited and published by Eleazar Sukenik, one of the first scholars to see the Cave 1 scrolls.

It is difficult to exaggerate the significance of the Great Isaiah Scroll. Prior to the discovery of the DSS, the oldest complete copy of the Hebrew Bible (on which our translations of the OT are based) was the Leningrad Codex, which dated to the year AD 1008. The scrolls take us back to about 50–100 BC and, in the case of the Great Isaiah Scroll, possibly back to 150 BC. Thus the DSS enable scholars of the Hebrew OT to trace the original text back another 1,100 years or so closer to the original manuscript of Isaiah.

The amazing thing is that the Hebrew text of the Great Isaiah Scroll is almost identical to the traditional Hebrew text that translators of the Bible have been using for centuries. The Great Isaiah Scroll, as well as many of the other Bible scrolls, is an impressive testament to

The DSS enable scholars of the Hebrew Old Testament to trace the original text back another 1,100 years or so closer to the original manuscript of Isaiah.

the care with which the ancient scribes copied and passed on Scripture. More will be said about the Bible scrolls below.

Pesharim (Commentaries on Scripture)

For many scholars the most fascinating finds are the pesharim or commentaries on Scripture. Pesharim is plural; the singula *pesher* means "interpretation." Several pesharim were found in Cave 1, and more were found in Cave 4. Although isolated phrases and verses of Scripture are interpreted here and there in almost all of the scrolls, the pesharim are "running com mentaries," that is, commentaries on whole biblical books o on extended passages.[7] The pesharim found among the DSS are as follows:

- Isaiah 3Q4, 4Q161–165 (cf. 4Q500)
- Hosea 4Q166–167
- Micah 1Q14, 4Q168
- Nahum 4Q169
- Habakkuk 1QpHab
- Zephaniah 1Q15, 4Q170
- Malachi 4Q253a, 5Q10
- Psalms 1Q16, 4Q171, 4Q173
- Canticles? 4Q240

Several scrolls offer commentary on the book of Genesis (i.e., 4Q252–54 and 254a). Although the interpretations of fered in these scrolls are pesherlike, they are not considered pesharim because they are not running commentaries as such

The best-preserved pesher is on Habakkuk. This scroll pre serves 13 columns of commentary on Habakkuk 1:2–2:20 Although the pesher does not comment on all of Habakkuk (which in the Hebrew Bible ends at 3:19), the scroll evidently preserves the whole commentary. The commentary on Habak kuk never received an official scrolls number, so it is known as 1QpHab, that is, the pesher ("p") on Habakkuk, from Cave 1 of Qumran.

The discovery of the Habakkuk commentary was a sensa tion because it shows us how members of the Qumran com munity tried to relate details in Habakkuk's ancient prophe cy to contemporary events and persons. Where the prophet

Habakkuk declares that "the wicked restrict the righteous" (1:4), the writer of the pesher explains that "the 'wicked man' refers to the Wicked Priest, and 'the righteous man' is the Teacher of Righteousness" (1QpHab 1:13). The pesher later quotes Habakkuk 1:6 ("Look! I am raising up the Chaldeans, that bitter, impetuous nation.") and explains that "this refers to the Kittim, who are swift and mighty in war, annihilating many people" (1QpHab 2:10–13). In these examples we see that the interpreter is updating the prophecy of Habakkuk. The prophet is no longer speaking of the Chaldeans, who conquered Jerusalem long ago; he is instead speaking of the contemporary rise of the Kittim (the Romans). Likewise, the Qumran interpreter understands Habakkuk's mention of the wicked as a reference to the wicked high priest of his day, who opposed the Teacher of Righteousness, the leader and perhaps founder of the Qumran community. As a rule this is what pesharim do; they update the prophecies of old, applying them to events that have overtaken the men of Qumran.

> *The commentary on Habakkuk shows us how members of the Qumran community tried to relate details in Habakkuk's ancient prophecy to contemporary events and persons.*

The Genesis Apocryphon

The Genesis Apocryphon (or Secret book of Genesis) of Cave 1 is written in Aramaic and is a first-person retelling of some of the narratives of Genesis concerning the patriarchs. This imaginative retelling of Scripture is fascinating to scholars and nonscholars alike, and we learn something about how Scripture was handled in the eras before and during Jesus' ministry.[8]

The Genesis Apocryphon is an example of *implicit* commentary. Instead of commenting explicitly on the meaning of the biblical story as found in the text of Scripture, the original story is paraphrased and retold, bringing out new ideas and sometimes avoiding details in the old story that are embarrassing or theologically awkward (such as Abraham, the great patriarch of faith, fibbing to Pharaoh about the truth of his relationship with Sarah).

At the beginning of the Genesis Apocryphon, we read that Lamech suspected that the birth of his son Noah was in some way supernatural. For this reason Lamech went to his father Methuselah and asked advice. Methuselah in turn took the matter to his father Enoch for an explanation. Enoch explained that sin had taken place in the days of his father Jared involving the sons of God (Gen 6:1–3). Therefore, God was about to bring upon the earth a fearful judgment in which Noah would play a role. The Noah story is then retold with several other embellishments.

The next hero in the Genesis Apocryphon is Abraham. The document says Abraham was explicitly warned in a dream that men would try to kill him in order to take his wife. When Pharaoh learned of Sarah's beauty, he took her and tried to kill Abraham. Sarah then saved his life by claiming that Abraham was her relative. This retelling of the story alters the biblical account at key junctures in an attempt to avoid portraying Abraham as a deceiver.

Only three columns of Genesis Apocryphon are well preserved. Most of the 23 columns are in poor shape, with only a few words and phrases that can be deciphered. It has been suggested that *Book of the Patriarchs* would be a better title for this work. Recently the words *Book of the Words of Noah* have been detected through infrared image enhancement in column 5 of the scroll. What this could mean is disputed.[9]

Interpretive paraphrases such as we find in the Genesis Apocryphon help us better understand how Scripture was handled in ancient times and how various passages may re

Interpretive paraphrases such as we find in the Genesis Apocryphon help us better understand how Scripture was handled in ancient times and how various passages may relate to one another.

late to one another. Compare, for example, 1 and 2 Chronicles with the parallel stories in 1 and 2 Samuel and 1 and 2 Kings. One might also compare the way Stephen selected and paraphrased Israel's history in the speech he gave his accusers in Acts 7.

Notes

1. For more on the Damascus Document, see J. C. VanderKam and P. W. Flint, *The Meaning of the Dead Sea Scrolls: Their Significance for Understanding the Bible, Judaism, Jesus, and Christianity* (San Francisco: HarperCollins, 2002), 215–17.

2. For more on 1QS, see M. A. Knibb, *The Qumran Community* (Cambridge: Cambridge University Press, 1987), 77–144.

3. For more on 1QSa and 1QSb, see L. H. Schiffman, *The Eschatological Community of the Dead Sea Scrolls* (Society of Biblical Literature Monograph Series 38; Atlanta: Scholars Press, 1989).

4. For more on the Thanksgiving Hymns, see B. P. Kittel, *The Hymns of Qumran: Translation and Commentary* (Society of Biblical Literature Dissertaion Series 50; Chico: Scholars Press, 1981).

5. For more on the War Scroll, see Y. Yadin, *The Scroll of the War of the Sons of Light Against the Sons of Darkness* (Oxford: Oxford University Press, 1962).

6. For more on the Great Isaiah Scroll, see W. H. Brownlee, *The Meaning of the Qumrân Scrolls for the Bible: With Special Attention to the Book of Isaiah* (New York: Oxford University Press, 1964), 155–259; J. Trever, *Scrolls from Qumrân Cave I* (Jerusalem: Shrine of the Book, 1974), 13–123 (photographic plates).

7. For more on the Pesharim Scrolls, see W. H. Brownlee, *The Midrash Pesher of Habakkuk* (Society of Biblical Literature Monograph Series 24; Missoula: Scholars Press, 1979); M. P. Horgan, *Pesharim: Qumran Interpretations of Biblical Books* (Catholic Biblical Quarterly Monograph Series 8; Washington: Catholic Biblical Association, 1979).

8. For more on the Genesis Apocryphon, see J. A. Fitzmyer, *The Genesis Apocryphon of Qumran Cave I: A Commentary* (rev. ed., Rome: Pontifical Biblical Institute Press, 1971).

9. See R. C. Steiner, "The Heading of the *Book of the Words* of Noah on a Fragment of the Genesis Apocryphon: New Light on a 'Lost' Work," *Dead Sea Discoveries 2* (1995), 66–71.

Exhibit in the Shrine of the Book.
Photo: Bantosh.

Chapter 13
The Second Round of Scrolls

As more caves were discovered and the number of scrolls and fragments multiplied, scholars began to second-guess their early assumptions about the Qumran community and its extensive library. For example,

Some of the Dead Sea Scrolls also give us an idea of what many Jews outside of the Qumran community valued.

contrary to initial impressions, scholars soon recognized that not all the scrolls were products of the community. While the hundreds of scrolls from the 11 caves at Qumran give us an idea of what members of that community valued, read, and studied, some of the scrolls also give us an idea of what many Jews *outside* of the Qumran community valued.

Songs of the Sabbath Sacrifice

Ten scrolls have been identified as belonging to what are called the Songs of the Sabbath Sacrifice. Eight of these fragmentary scrolls were found in Cave 4 (4Q400–407), one was found

The Songs of the Sabbath Sacrifice.

in Cave 11 (11Q17), and one at Masada (Mas1k). These texts describe the heavenly throne room and an angelic liturgy. They are of special interest for NT study because of their numerous references to the kingdom of God, a special emphasis in Jesus' teachings.[1]

The songs, 13 in all, are liturgical in nature, composed to honor God and the Sabbath, specifically the angelic priests who some believed served in the heavenly temple. Scholars think these songs predate the founding of the Dead Sea sect. The group approved of the songs and was influenced by them.

Why 13 songs and not 52, thus covering each week of the calendar year? Good question. It has been suggested that these songs were to be repeated in four three-month cycles, which would add up to a year (4 quarters x 13 weekly songs = 52 weeks). The first song begins:

The Songs of the Sabbath Sacrifice probably predate the founding of the Qumran community.

A text belonging to the Instructor. The song accompanying the sacrifice on the first Sabbath, sung on the fourth of the first month. Praise the God of . . ., you divine beings of utter holiness; rejoice in the kingdom of his divinity. For He has established utter holiness among the eternally holy, that they might become for Him priests of the inner sanctum in His royal temple, ministers of the Presence in His glorious innermost chamber. In the congregation of all the wise divine beings. (4Q400 frag. 1, column 1, lines 1–4; in places restored)

One by one the songs are dedicated to the first 13 Sabbaths of the year. The song quoted above was dedicated to the first Sabbath. Here is the beginning of the song dedicated to the seventh Sabbath:

> A text belonging to the Instructor. The song accompanying the sacrifice on the seventh Sabbath, sung on the sixteenth of the (second) month. Praise the most high God, you who are exalted. (4Q403 frag. 1, column 1, line 30)

Another song sounds forth:

> The precepts governing the holy ones has He inscribed for them, that all the eternally holy might thereby be sanctified. He has purified the pure who belong to the light, that they may recompense all those who transgress the true Way, and make atonement for those who repent of sin, obtaining for them His good pleasure. He has given tongues of knowledge to the priests who draw near, so that from their mouths issue the teachings governing all the holy ones, together with the precepts concerning His glory. (4Q400 frag. 1, column 1, lines 15–18)

The numerous occurrences of the phrases "your kingdom" and "his kingdom" show that the idea of the "kingdom of God" was known and appreciated by the men of the Qumran community. There are many more references to the kingdom in the other scrolls. What this shows is that Jesus' emphasis on the kingdom was not unusual. It was a theme of vital interest among his Jewish contemporaries, and Jesus claimed to give authoritative teachings about it.

Jesus' emphasis on the kingdom was not unusual. It was a theme of vital interest among his Jewish contemporaries, and Jesus claimed to give authoritative teachings about it.

The Melchizedek Scroll

Published almost a decade after its recovery from Cave 11, the Melchizedek Scroll (11QMelch = 11Q13) envisions a time when the prophecy of Isaiah 61:1–3 will be fulfilled. It will be a time of God's final jubilee (Lev 25:13), when the sins and debts of his people will be forgiven. It will be a time when the mysterious Melchizedek, the king and high priest of Salem who blessed the victorious Abraham (Gen 14:18–20; cf. Ps 110:4), will make his appearance.[2] Melchizedek appears elsewhere in the scrolls (e.g., 4Q401, 4Q403, and possibly 4Q544), leading interpreters to suspect that as a biblical figure he was highly regarded at Qumran.

The remains of the Melchizedek Scroll, made up of some 16 fragments, date to about 100 BC or perhaps a little earlier. We have most of column 2 and just small pieces of columns 1 and 3. According to the author, "Melchizedek will carry out the vengeance of God's judgments, and on that day he will free them from the hand of Belial and from the hand of all the spirits of his lot" (col. ii line 13). The

The remains of the Melchizedek Scroll, made up of some 16 fragments, date to about 100 BC or perhaps a little earlier.

most intriguing feature of this scroll concerns the identity of Melchizedek. He seems to function as an angel or God's representative bringing salvation to God's elect.

Jesus' appeal to his exorcisms as proof that the kingdom of God has come upon his contemporaries (cf. Luke 11:20) coheres with the eschatological expectation of the Melchizedek Scroll and may explain, at least in part, why the author of Hebrews chose to compare Jesus with Melchizedek, the mysterious priest of God Most High (cf. Hebrews 5–7).

Vision of Amram

The priest Amram, son of Qahat (also Kohath), father of Aaron, Moses, and Miriam (Exod 6:18–20; Num 26:58–59), is the principal figure in a work preserved in five or six fragmentary copies called the *Vision of Amram* (4Q543–48). He is mentioned in other Jewish writings of late antiquity (such as

Pseudo-Philo, *Biblical Antiquities* 9:1–10) and is said to have received visions (Josephus, *Jewish Antiquities* 1.210–16). This interesting work begins as follows:

> A copy of the book "The Words of the Vision of Amram, son of Levi." It contains everything that he told his sons and everything that he commanded them on the day he died, in the 136th year, that is, the year of his death, in the one-hundred and fifty-second year of Israel's sojourn in Egypt. (4Q543 frag. 1, lines 1–4)

In his vision Amram saw two angels, one like a serpent and the other pleasant in appearance (4Q544 frag. 1, lines 10–14). They rule over humankind, struggling against one another to control human fate. We see here the moral and cosmic dualism attested elsewhere in the scrolls.[3]

There are many visions and testaments found among the Dead Sea Scrolls. Some we already knew about (such the *Book of Enoch*); others were new to us, such as the Vision of Amram.

A Letter on the Law

One of the most dramatic Qumran discoveries is the Cave 4 document called *A Halakhic Letter*, which means a letter concerned with how one should walk. In this case "walk" (from the Hebrew word *halak*) does not mean how you get around on your feet but your way of living in light of the Mosaic Law. It is also called Miqsat Ma'ase ha-Torah (4QMMT) because of the important role played by the phrase, "some of the works of the Law."[4]

One of the most dramatic Qumran discoveries is the Cave 4 document called A Halakhic Letter, *which means a letter concerned with how one should walk.*

The Letter on the Law (= 4Q394–99) appears to be an irenic letter written to the high priest of Jerusalem by the Qumran community. Perhaps it was penned by the famed Teacher of Righteousness himself at a time before the Essenes fully gave up hope for the corrupted mainstream priesthood at

Jerusalem. The letter delineates some 20 interpretations of the Mosaic Law that the author believes are important. Some of the legal interpretations include:

- Wheat produced by Gentiles may not be brought into the temple.

- The blind and deaf are to be excluded from the "purity of the Temple."

- Prohibition of dogs from entering Jerusalem.

- Purification rules for lepers.

- Impurity of human bones.

- Marriage laws pertaining to priests.

In one of the fragments, there is a reference to the contents of Scripture: "We have written to you [sing.], so that you might understand the book of Moses, and the words of the prophets, and David" (my translation; cf. Luke 24:44). The peaceful tone is evident here, too, as the author tried to woo the high priest into fidelity to the Law.

The ruling which barred the blind and deaf from entering the temple is interesting when one remembers that "the blind and the lame came to [Jesus] in the temple complex, and He healed them" (Matt 21:14). This incident in Matthew's Gospel

Jesus demonstrated a different understanding of God's Law and acceptance of marginalized persons.

apparently represents an implicit rejection of the priestly prejudice leveled against those who had physical defects. In this way Jesus demonstrated a different understanding of God's Law and acceptance of marginalized persons.

With regard to NT teaching, the most important feature of this Qumran text is its reference to a person being reckoned righteous by doing the works of the Law. How this relates to the NT teaching is discussed later in this book.

The Temple Scroll. Photo: Marion Doss.

Temple Scroll

Five fragmentary scrolls preserve substantial portions of a document called the Temple Scroll. The identification of the two largest scrolls (11QTemple[a] and 11QTemple[b] = 11Q19 and 11Q20) is certain. The other three (4Q365a, 4Q524, and 11QTemple[c] = 11Q21) are much less certain. 11QTemple[b] is a second, fragmentary copy of the Temple Scroll. There are at least three dozen fragments.[5]

The Temple Scroll is the largest single scroll from Qumran, measuring some 28 feet in length (67 cols. of text) in "Herodian" script. This style of writing dates the scroll to sometime between 30 BC and AD 70. It is believed that the original work was composed in the time of John Hyrcanus (134–105 BC), one of the Hasmoneans who ruled the Jewish people after the ouster of the Seleucids.

The Temple Scroll alters what the book of Deuteronomy says about crucifixion.

The Temple Scroll contains various laws, with the first section concerned with the temple, and the second based on Deuteronomy 12–26. Unlike Deuteronomy, the Temple Scroll gives the laws in the first person, directly by God. Of special interest is the fact that some of the laws are given slightly different readings or emphases from Deuteronomy in order to underscore the distinctive beliefs of the Qumran community.

One of the most interesting features of the Temple Scroll is its allusion to crucifixion, a cruel form of execution widely practiced in the Roman Empire. Here is what the biblical book of Deuteronomy says about hanging a criminal:

If anyone is found guilty of an offense deserving the death penalty and is executed, and you hang his body on a tree, you are not to leave his corpse on the tree overnight, but are to bury him that day, for anyone hung on a tree is under God's curse. You must not defile the land the LORD your God is giving you as an inheritance. (Deut 21:22–23)

Part of this Bible passage is quoted, paraphrased, and expanded in the Temple Scroll:

If a man is a traitor against his people and gives them up to a foreign nation, so doing evil to his people, you are to hang him on a tree until dead. On the testimony of two or three witnesses he will be put to death, and they themselves shall hang him on the tree. If a man is convicted of a capital crime and flees to the nations, cursing his people and the children of Israel, you are to hang him, also, upon a tree until dead. But you must not let their bodies remain on the tree overnight; you shall most certainly bury them that very day. (11Q19 64:7–11)

According to Deuteronomy, the criminal is first put to death (by stoning or by some other means) and is then hanged on a tree. At the end of the day, his body should be taken down and given proper burial in order to protect the purity of the land. The Temple Scroll alters the instructions. It says the criminal can be hanged while still living and remain there "until dead" (lines 8 and 10–11). The Temple Scroll still allows for the criminal to be executed first, then hanged (as in line 9), but certain types of malefactors (traitors, persons convicted of a capital crime such as murder or treason, and persons who curse God's people) are to be hanged alive.

The interpretive adjustment of Deuteronomy made in the Temple Scroll may have been prompted by the reality that crucifixion was practiced in Israel during the Roman period. Recall that the apostle Paul applied Deuteronomy 21:23 to Jesus, who was hanged alive on the cross until death overtook him (Gal 3:13). It is important to observe also that in both Deuteronomy and in the expanded version in the Temple Scroll it is required that the corpse of the criminal be taken down and buried rather than being left hanging overnight.

The Job Targum

A targum (from the Aramaic word *trgm*, which means "to translate") is an Aramaic translation/paraphrase of a book of Hebrew Scripture. Two and probably three targums have been found among the DSS:

- the lengthy 11tgJob (11Q10)

- the fragments 4QtgLeviticus (4Q156)

- the fragments 4QtgJob (4Q157)

One scholar has sought to identify 4Q550 as a targum of Isaiah, but this is doubtful. Also, 6Q19 may be a targum of Genesis, but the fragment is so small that such an identification cannot be confirmed.[6]

Targums are a type of retelling of Scripture. They can be conservative in their approach, or they can be quite interpretive and expansive.

Targums are another type of retelling of Scripture (as we saw in the Genesis Apocryphon discussed above). They can be conservative in their approach, giving readers a fairly literal Aramaic translation of Hebrew Scripture, or they can be quite interpretive and expansive, making changes here and there and adding all sorts of illustrative and imaginative material. These Aramaic paraphrases are not too different from modern English paraphrases of the Bible. Perhaps Eugene Peterson's *The Message* is a good example of a modern "targum" of the Bible.

About 15 percent of the Job Targum found in Cave 11 has survived. It offers a literal translation of the Hebrew version of Job found in today's Bible. It is estimated that the original scroll, some 23 feet in length and about five inches or so in height (from top margin to bottom margin) contained 68 columns of text. The portion that has survived corresponds to portions of Job 17:14–42:12, plus several small fragments. The scroll probably dates to 125–150 BC and is thought to be the oldest targum in existence.

Although as a translation the Job Targum is conservative, it does "adjust" the text in a few places. For example, the sovereignty of God and the righteousness of Job are enhanced to a higher degree than appears in the Hebrew text of Scripture.

The targum fragments found at Qumran are much older than the well-preserved targums we have of the OT, which date to the Middle Ages. How were the targums used? It is believed that they were read as part of the worship services held in synagogues from the time near the end of the Roman Empire on into the Middle Ages. These targums are as follows (presented according to the divisions of the Hebrew Bible):

Pentateuch
Onqelos
Pseudo-Jonathan
Fragment Targum
Neofiti

Prophets
Former Prophets
Isaiah
Jeremiah
Ezekiel
The Twelve (i.e., the Minor Prophets)

Writings
Psalms
Proverbs
Job
Song of Songs
Ruth
Lamentations
Qohelet (or Ecclesiastes)
Esther
Chronicles

The Copper Plaque

The Copper Plaque of Cave 3 (3QTreasure = 3Q15) was discovered in March 1952. Also known as the Copper Scroll, it directs the reader to several hidden treasures of gold, silver, and other valuables. This remarkable document is made up of three thin copper sheets, riveted together, measuring approximately 30 cm x 30 cm. In all, 12 columns of text have survived, making up 64 sections. No other scroll like this has ever been found.

Because the copper was completely oxidized and crumbled whenever it was handled, it was not possible to unroll it. Unwilling to accept that the scroll would never be read, scholars sought a way to cut the copper into strips without destroying any of the ancient text. Easier said than done! In 1955 and 1956 H. Wright Baker of the Manchester College of Science and Technology coated the rolled-up plaque with adhesive and then cut the plaque into 23 strips. In this way the plaque was dissected rather than unrolled. After careful cleaning, most of the Hebrew text could be read! Here is an example of what can we can make out from the Copper Plaque (3Q15 1:13–2:4):

In the plastered Reservoir of Manos, at the descent to the left, three cubits up from the bottom: silver coins totaling forty talents.

The Copper Scroll. Photo: HolyLandPhotos.org.

In the salt pit that is under the steps: forty-one talents of silver coins.

In the cave of the old Washer's Chamber, on the third terrace: sixty-five ingots of gold.

At the outset scholars debated whether the Copper Plaque tells of real treasure. After all, it describes hidden treasure that adds up to many tons! Could the spartan Qumran community be so wealthy? Perhaps it is the stuff of legend. Nevertheless, most scholars think real treasure is in view, for it is hard to explain why a legendary treasure would be described in such a dry, matter-of-fact bookkeeping style. Although it is debated, it is commonly suggested that the treasure inventoried in this plaque was not the property of members of the Qumran community but instead belonged to the Jerusalem temple. Presumably it was hidden before the advancing Roman army encircled the city in AD 69. The temple treasure interpretation is possibly supported by the mention of many temple-related items, but it is impossible to be sure of this conclusion.[7]

Other Scrolls of Interest

There are many more scrolls of great interest for Christians and NT interpreters. *The Prayer of Enosh* (4Q369) offers an imaginative version of the prayer of one of the preflood figures, Enosh, son of Seth and father of Kenan (Gen 4:26; 5:6–11). Some interpreters have

The Prayer of Enosh (4Q369) offers an imaginative version of the prayer of one of the preflood figures, Enosh, son of Seth and father of Kenan (Gen 4:26; 5:6–11).

argued that this fragmentary text is visionary, eschatological, and probably messianic (with David serving as the template for the coming Redeemer). The eschatological interpretation is perhaps supported by the reference to Enoch from "the seventh generation" (cf. Jude 14–15). The principal figure is designated "first-born son" and "prince and ruler," who perhaps is said to wear "the crown of the heaven and the glory of the clouds" (the text is only partially restored). Others disagree, arguing that the scroll is speaking about historical Israel rather than a messianic prince. Seen in this light, 4Q369 represents another example of rewritten Bible.

The much talked about *Messianic Apocalypse* (4Q521) foretells the appearance of an anointed one (Messiah) to whom heaven and earth will listen. The text goes on to say that marvelous things will take place, including the freeing of prisoners, the restoration of sight to the blind, the healing of the wounded, the resurrection of the dead, and the proclamation of good news to the poor. Linkage of the Messiah with words and phrases from Isaiah 26:19; 35:5–6; and 61:1–2 makes this text relevant for understanding Jesus' reply to the imprisoned John the Baptist (cf. Matt 11:5 = Luke 7:22), who struggled to understand how Jesus' ministry fit with Messianic expectations.

The Son of God *text contains impressive parallels with the angelic announcement found in Luke 1:32–35.*

The Aramaic *Son of God Text* (4Q246) has also attracted a great deal of attention. It foretells the coming of a "great" one who will be called "Son of God," "Son of the Most High," and will rule forever. Many interpreters have been struck by the impressive parallels with the angelic announcement found in Luke 1:32–35.

The Beatitudes text (4Q525) is a wisdom text that contains a string of beatitudes and thus offers the closest literary parallel to the beatitudes of Jesus (Matthew 5 and Luke 6). Fragment 15 is also of interest. Its warnings of burning serpents, vipers' venom, flames of death, and the "pit" may contribute to our understanding of Jewish demonology in late antiquity and perhaps shed light on this aspect of Jesus' ministry (e.g., Luke 10:19, "Look, I have given you the authority to trample on snakes and scorpions and over all the power of the enemy; nothing will ever harm you").

Other Dead-Sea Region Scrolls

Besides Qumran and its vicinity, other locations in Dead Sea region have yielded interesting finds. These sites include:

- Masada, Herod's mountain fortress and palace, where archaeologists found fragments of Scripture, apocryphal books, and even some Greek and Latin texts (including a few lines of Virgil's *Aeneid*).

- Murabba'at, where archaeologists found dozens of documents, including Scripture, papers, and letters written by Simon ben Kosibah (nicknamed Bar Kokhba, "Son of the Star"), leader of the third Jewish revolt (AD 132–135).

- Khirbet Mird, where archaeologists found Christian texts, including fragments of Matthew, Mark, John, and Acts, and a few other sites where a variety of documents (such as deeds and business papers) were found.[8]

Most of these documents date to the end of the Second Temple period (which ended with the destruction of the temple in AD 70), some date to the beginning of the second century AD, and others date from even later times. This means many of these texts originated after Christianity.

Notes

1. For more on the Songs of the Sabbath Sacrifice, see C. Newsom, *Song of the Sabbath Sacrifice* (Harvard Semitic Series 27; Atlanta: Scholars Press, 1985); J. R. Davila, *Liturgical Works* (Eerdmans Commentaries on the Dead Sea Scrolls; Grand Rapids: Eerdmans, 2000), 83–167.

2. For more of the Melchizedek Scroll, see P. J. Kobelski, *Melchizedek and Melchiresa'* (Catholic Biblical Quarterly Monograph Series 10; Washington: Catholic Biblical Association, 1981).

3. For more on the Amram Scrolls, see M. E. Stone, "Amram," in L. H. Schiffman and J. C. VanderKam (eds.), *Encyclopedia of the Dead Sea Scrolls* (2 vols., Oxford: Oxford University Press, 2000), 1:23–24.

4. For more on the Halakhic Letter, see E. Qimron and J. Strugnell, *Qumran Cave 4. V: Miqsat Ma'ase Ha-Torah* (Discoveries in the Judean Desert 10; Oxford: Clarendon Press, 1994).

5. For more on the Temple Scroll, see Y. Yadin, *The Temple Scroll: The Hidden Law of the Dead Sea Sect* (London: Random House, 1985).

6. For more on the Job Targum, see M. Sokoloff, *The Targum to Job from Qumran Cave XI* (Ramat-Gan: Bar-Ilan University Press, 1974).

7. A. Wolters, *The Copper Scroll: Overview, Text and Translation* (Sheffield: Sheffield Academic Press, 1996).

8. For a list of all documents found in the vicinity of the Dead Sea, see L. H. Schiffman and J. C. VanderKam (eds.), *Encyclopedia of the Dead Sea Scrolls* (2 vols., Oxford: Oxford University Press, 2000), 2:1013–56.

Part V

Who Were the Essenes?

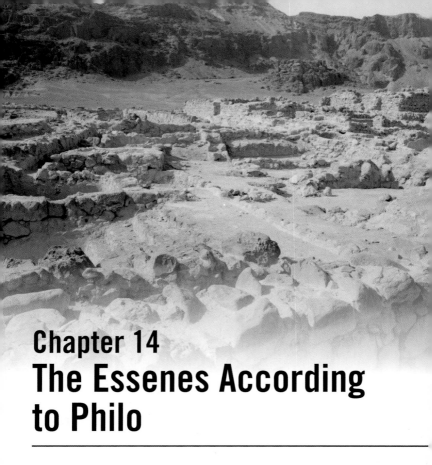

Chapter 14
The Essenes According to Philo

Evidence suggests that the Dead Sea Scrolls (DSS) were written and/or collected by a group known as Essenes, part of whose membership resided at Qumran.[1] One of the key sources for this conclusion is Philo of Alexandria (c. 20 BC to AD 50), a prolific Jewish writer. Although he was Jewish, Philo's favored language was Greek, the principal language of Alexandria. Fortunately, most of his writings have survived down to our day, but scholars dispute how they should be classified. Are they biblical interpretation, philosophy, apologetics, or even psychology? Philo's diverse writings probably reflect all of these interests, but in my judgment his chief purpose was apologetics; he wanted to show that Judaism, particularly as seen in the Scriptures of the Jewish people (the OT), provided a superior worldview to that of pagan Greeks. His allegorical "exegesis" of OT passages should be understood in this light. Philo was interested not in what actually happened in the original events recorded in Scripture but in how the biblical story could speak to thinking persons of the Greco-Roman world.

Philo carried out this purpose by interpreting the bibli-

Philo's chief purpose was apologetics; he wanted to show that Judaism, particularly as seen in the Scriptures of the Jewish people (the Old Testament), provided a superior worldview to that of pagan Greeks. *Philo* by Rembrandt.

cal stories (mostly from the Pentateuch) in ways that matched Neoplatonism, the philosophical view that what the physical senses perceive on earth is but an imperfect reflection of the true and perfect reality of heaven. Philo's approach resembles that of Stoic philosophers who allegorized Homer's epic stories the *Odyssey* and the *Iliad.* Similarly, Philo read allegorical meanings into the biblical narratives. For example, Philo said Cain (Gen 4:1–15) is to be understood as "foolish opinion," which is to be replaced by Abel, to be understood as "good conviction" (*On the Sacrifices of Abel and Cain* 5). Or again, when Abram was commanded to depart from his home country (Gen 12:1–4), the patriarch was actually commanded to escape the prison house of his physical body and turn his thoughts God-ward (*On the Migration of Abraham* 1–12).

Fortunately for all of us interested in the DSS and the question of who wrote and collected them, Philo had a lot to say about the Essenes.[2] We will quote extensive sections of his writings in order to grasp his assessment of this important religious group. To begin with, here is what he had to say in a tract titled *Quod omnis probus liber sit (Every Good Man Is Free)*:

Every Good Man Is Free—an Excerpt from Philo

Moreover Palestine and Syria too are not barren of exemplary wisdom and virtue, which countries no slight portion of that most populous nation of the Jews inhabits. There is a portion of those people called Essenes, in number something more than four thousand in my opinion, who derive their name from their piety, though not according to any accurate form of the Grecian dialect, because they are above all men devoted to the service of God, not sacrificing living animals, but studying rather to preserve their own minds in a state of holiness and purity.

These men, in the first place, live in villages, avoiding all cities on account of the habitual lawlessness of those who inhabit them, well knowing that such a moral disease is contracted from associations with wicked men, just as a real disease might be from an impure atmosphere, and that this would stamp an incurable evil on their souls. Of these men, some cultivating the earth, and others devoting themselves to those arts which are the result of peace, benefit both themselves and all those who come in contact with them, not storing up treasures of silver and of gold, nor acquiring vast sections of the earth out of a desire for ample revenues, but providing all things which are requisite for the natural purposes of life; for they alone of almost all men having been originally poor and

Philo said the Essenes did not seek gold and silver, but the "things which are requisite for the natural purposes of life."

destitute, and that too rather from their own habits and ways of life than from any real deficiency of good fortune, are nevertheless accounted very rich, judging contentment and frugality to be great abundance, as in truth they are.

Among those men you will find no makers of arrows, or javelins, or swords, or helmets, or breastplates, or shields; no makers of arms or of military engines; no one, in short, attending to any employment whatever connected with war, or even to any of those occupations even in peace which are easily perverted to wicked purposes; for they are utterly ignorant of all traffic, and of all commercial dealings, and of all navigation, but they repudiate and keep aloof from everything which can possibly afford any inducement to covetousness; and there is not a single slave among them, but they are all free, aiding one another with a reciprocal interchange of good offices; and they condemn masters, not only as unjust, inasmuch as they corrupt the very principle of equality, but likewise as impious, because they destroy the ordinances of nature, which generated them all equally, and brought them up like a mother, as if they were all legitimate brethren, not in name only, but in reality and truth.

But in their view this natural relationship of all men to one another has been thrown into disorder by designing covetousness, continually wishing to surpass others in good fortune, and which has therefore engendered alienation instead of affection, and hatred instead of friendship; and leaving the logical part of philosophy, as in no respect necessary for the acquisition of virtue, to the word-catchers, and the natural part, as being too sublime for human nature to master, to those who love to converse about high objects (except indeed so far as such a study takes in the contemplation of the existence of God and of the creation of the universe), they devote all their attention to the moral part of philosophy, using as instructors the laws of their country which it would have been impossible for the human mind to devise without divine inspiration.

Now these laws they are taught at other times, indeed, but most especially on the seventh day, for the seventh day is accounted sacred, on which they abstain from all other employments, and frequent the sacred places which are called synagogues, and there they sit according to their age in classes, the younger sitting under the elder, and listening with eager attention in becoming order.

Then one, indeed, takes up the holy volume and reads it, and another of the men of the greatest experience comes forward and explains what is not very intelligible, for a great many precepts are delivered in enigmatical modes of expression, and allegorically, as the old fashion was; and thus the people are taught piety, and holiness, and justice, and economy, and the science of regulating the state, and the knowledge of such things as are naturally good, or bad, or indifferent, and to choose what is right and to avoid what is wrong, using a threefold variety of definitions, and rules, and criteria, namely, the love of God, and the love of virtue, and the love of mankind. Accordingly, the sacred volumes present an infinite number of instances of the disposition devoted to the love of God, and of a continued and uninterrupted purity throughout the whole of life, of a careful avoidance of oaths and of falsehood, and of a strict adherence to the principle of looking on the Deity as the cause of everything which is good and of nothing which is evil. They also furnish us with many proofs of a love of virtue, such as abstinence from all covetousness of money, from ambition, from indulgence in pleasures, temperance, endurance, and also moderation, simplicity, good temper, the absence of pride, obedience to the laws, steadiness, and everything of that kind; and, lastly, they bring forward as proofs of the love of mankind, goodwill, equality beyond all power of description, and fellowship, about which it is not unreasonable to say a few words.

> *According to Philo, three guiding principles among the Essenes were: "the love of God, and the love of virtue, and the love of mankind."*

In the first place, then, there is no one who has a house so absolutely his own private property, that it does not in some sense also belong to every one: for besides that they all dwell together in companies, the house is open to all those of the same notions, who come to them from other quarters; then there is one magazine among them all; their expenses are all in common; their garments belong to them all in common; their food is common, since they all eat in messes; for there is no other people among which you can find a common use of the same house, a common adoption of one mode of living, and a common use of the same table more thoroughly established in fact than among this tribe: and is not this very natural? For whatever they, after having been working during the day, receive for their wages, that they do not retain as their own, but bring it into the common stock, and give any advantage that is to be derived from it to all who desire to avail themselves of it; and those who are sick are not neglected because they are unable to contribute to the common stock, inasmuch as the tribe have in their public stock a means of supplying their necessities and aiding their weakness, so that from their ample means they support them liberally and abundantly; and they

> *"For whatever they, after having been working during the day, receive for their wages, that they do not retain as their own, but bring it into the common stock, and give any advantage that is to be derived from it to all who desire to avail themselves of it."*

cherish respect for their elders, and honour them and care for them, just as parents are honoured and cared for by their lawful children: being supported by them in all abundance both by their personal exertions, and by innumerable contrivances.

Such diligent practisers of virtue does philosophy, unconnected with any superfluous care of examining into Greek names render men, proposing to them as necessary exercises to train them towards its attainment, all praiseworthy actions by which a freedom, which can never be enslaved, is firmly established.

And a proof of this is that, though at different times a great number of chiefs of every variety of disposition and character, have occupied their country, some of whom have endeavoured to surpass even ferocious wild beasts in cruelty, leaving no sort of inhumanity unpractised, and have never ceased to murder their subjects in whole troops, and have even torn them to pieces while living, like cooks cutting them limb from limb, till they themselves, being overtaken by the vengeance of divine justice, have at last experienced the same miseries in their turn: others again having converted their barbarous frenzy into another kind of wickedness, practising an ineffable degree of savageness, talking with the people quietly, but through the hypocrisy of a more gentle voice, betraying the ferocity

> *Said Philo, "No one, not even of those immoderately cruel tyrants, nor of the more treacherous and hypocritical oppressors was ever able to bring any real accusation against the multitude of those called Essenes or Holy."*

of their real disposition, fawning upon their victims like treacherous dogs, and becoming the causes of irremediable miseries to them, have left in all their cities monuments of their impiety, and hatred of all mankind, in the never to be forgotten miseries endured by those whom they oppressed: and yet no one, not even of those immoderately cruel tyrants, nor of the more treacherous and hypocritical oppressors was ever able to bring any real accusation against the multitude of those called Essenes or Holy. But everyone being subdued by the virtue of these men, looked up to them as free by nature, and not subject to the frown of any human being, and have celebrated their manner of messing together, and their fellowship with one another beyond all description in respect of its mutual good faith, which is an ample proof of a perfect and very happy life. (*Quod omnis probus liber sit* 75–91).

The Enviable System—an Excerpt from Philo

Philo had more to say about the Essenes in a lost work titled *A Defense of the Jews* (*Apologia pro Judaeis*). Fortunately the portion of this work in which he commented on the Essenes is quoted in a surviving book entitled *Preparation for the Gospel*, which was written by the early church historian named Eusebius. In the excerpt below Philo demonstrates high esteem for the "enviable system" of the Essenes:

But our lawgiver trained an innumerable body of his pupils to partake in those things, who are called Essenes, being, as I imagine, honoured with this appellation because of their exceeding holiness.

And they dwell in many cities of Judaea, and in many villages, and in great and populous communities. And this sect of them is not an hereditary of family connexion; for family ties are not spoken of with reference to acts voluntarily performed; but it is adopted because of their admiration for virtue and love of gentleness and humanity.

At all events, there are no children among the Essenes, no, nor any youths or persons only just entering upon manhood; since the dispositions of all such persons are unstable and liable to change, from the imperfections incident to their age, but they are all full-grown men, and even already declining towards old age, such as are no longer carried away by the impetuosity of their bodily passions, and are not under the influence of the appetites, but such as enjoy a genuine freedom, the only true and real liberty. And a proof of this is to be found in their life of perfect freedom; no one among them ventures at all to acquire any property whatever of his own, neither house, nor slave, nor farm, nor flocks and herds, nor any thing of any sort which can be looked upon as the fountain or provision of riches; but they bring them together into the middle as a common stock, and enjoy one common general benefit from it all.

"No one among them ventures at all to acquire any property whatever of his own."

And they all dwell in the same place, making clubs, and societies, and combinations, and unions with one another, and doing every thing throughout their whole lives with reference to the general advantage; but the different members of this body have different employments in which they occupy themselves, and labour without hesitation and without cessation, making no mention of either cold, or heat, or any changes of weather or temperature as an excuse for desisting from their tasks. But before the sun rises they betake themselves to their daily work, and they do not quit it till some time after it has set, when they return home rejoicing no less than those who have been exercising themselves in gymnastic contests; for they imagine that whatever they devote themselves to as a practice

is a sort of gymnastic exercise of more advantage to life, and more pleasant both to soul and body, and of more enduring benefit and equability, than mere athletic labours, inasmuch as such toil does not cease to be practised with delight when the age of vigour of body is passed; for there are some of them who are devoted to the practice of agriculture, being skillful in such things as pertain to the sowing and cultivation of lands; others again are shepherds, or cowherds, and experienced in the management of every kind of animal; some are cunning in what relates to swarms of bees; others again are artisans and handicraftsmen, in order to guard against suffering from the want of anything of which there is at times an actual need; and these men omit and delay nothing, which is requisite for the innocent supply of the necessaries of life.

Rope found at Qumran. The Essenes valued hard work, considering it an act of worship.

Accordingly, each of these men, who differ so widely in their respective employments, when they have received their wages give them up to one person who is appointed as the universal steward and general manager; and he, when he has received the money, immediately goes and purchases what is necessary and furnishes them with food in abundance, and all other things of which the life of mankind stands in need.

And those who live together and eat at the same table are day after day contented with the same things, being lovers of frugality and moderation, and averse to all sumptuousness and extravagance as a disease of both mind and body.

And not only are their tables in common but also their dress; for in the winter there are thick cloaks found, and in the summer light cheap mantles, so that whoever wants one is at liberty without restraint to go and take whichever kind he chooses; since what belongs to one belongs to all, and on the other hand whatever belongs to the whole body belongs to each individual.

And again, if any one of them is sick he is cured from the common resources, being attended to by the general care and anxiety of the whole body. Accordingly the old men, even if they happen to be childless, as if they were not only the fathers of many children but were even also particularly happy in an affectionate offspring, are accustomed to end their lives in a most happy and prosperous and carefully attended old age, being looked upon by such a number of people as worthy of so much honour and provident regard that they think themselves bound to care for them even more from inclination than from any tie of natural affection.

"If any one of them is sick he is cured from the common resources, being attended to by the general care and anxiety of the whole body."

Again, perceiving with more than ordinary acuteness and accuracy, what is alone or at least above all other things calculated to dissolve such associations, they repudiate marriage; and at the same time they practise continence in an eminent degree; for no one of the Essenes ever marries a wife. . . . This now is the enviable system of life of these Essenes, so that not only private individuals but even mighty kings, admiring the men, venerate their sect, and increase their dignity and majesty in a still higher degree by their approbation and by the honours which they confer on them. (*Praeparatio Evangelica* 8.11.1–14, 18)

What Philo tells us coheres at several points with things we find in the DSS, thus helping build the case for the Essenes as authors and collectors of the scrolls found at Qumran.[3] In the next two chapters we review what Josephus and two Greco-Roman writers tell us about the Essenes and then make a few observations about how this bears on the findings at Qumran.

Notes

1. For a concise summary of the evidence, see T. S. Beall, "Essenes," in L. H. Schiffman and J. C. VanderKam (eds.), *Encyclopedia of the Dead Sea Scrolls* (2 vols., Oxford: Oxford University Press, 2000), 1:262–69.

2. The translations are based on C. D. Yonge, *The Works of Philo Judaeus* (4 vols., London: Henry G. Bohn, 1854–55; reprinted by Hendrickson Publishers, 1993). For a more recent translation, with Greek text, see F. H. Colson et al., *Philo* (12 vols., London: Heinemann; Cambridge, MA; Harvard University Press, 1929–53).

3. Philo also mentions the Essenes briefly in his tract "On the Contemplative Life," 1.

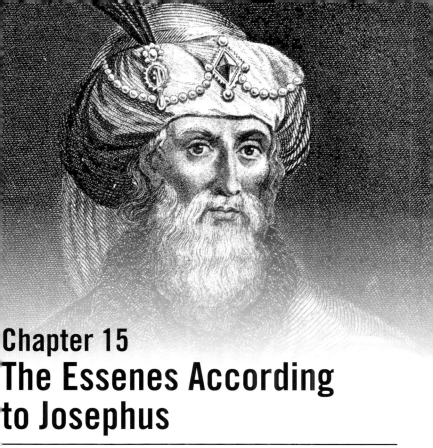

Chapter 15
The Essenes According to Josephus

The writings of Josephus provide invaluable information concerning history, politics, religious ideas, Jewish sects, and biblical interpretation. Born in the year of Gaius Caligula's accession (AD 37 or 38), young Joseph ben Matthias studied Jewish law, contemplated which sect he would join (Pharisees, Sadducees, or Essenes), and visited the Roman capital as part of an official delegation.

When the first war with Rome broke out, Josephus (as he later called himself) assumed command of Galilee. Besieged at Jotapata for 47 days, he surrendered to the Romans and prophesied that Titus Flavius Vespasianus, the commander of the Roman forces in Israel, would someday become the Roman emperor. When his prediction came to pass in 69, Vespasianus (commonly known as Vespasian) remembered Josephus favorably and made him part of his advisory council.

Shortly after the war ended in 70, Josephus went to Rome and was granted Roman citizenship. At this time he took the name "Flavius" to honor his benefactor. In the late 70s he wrote *Jewish War* (seven books). An earlier version of this work, written in Aramaic, was sent to the Jews of Mesopotamia to discourage them from revolt. In the mid-90s he completed the *Jewish Antiquities* (20 books). Shortly after 100 he published his *Life* (an appendix to *Antiquities*) and *Against Apion* (two books).

Woodcut of Josephus writing.

Josephus died in the early years of the second century. All of his writings, with the exception of the aforementioned earlier draft of *Jewish War*, were originally published in Greek. Greek was not his mother tongue, but it was the language of the Empire, and he could with some difficulty (and some assistance) write and speak it (*Ag. Ap.* 1.50).

Again we are fortunate, for like his older contemporary Philo of Alexandria, Josephus tells us many things about the Essenes.[1] We will quote what he says in two long passages. The first comes from his *Jewish War*, which he composed and circulated around AD 75.

A Severer Discipline—an Excerpt from Josephus

For there are three philosophical sects among the Jews. The followers of the first of whom are the Pharisees; of the second the Sadducees; and the third sect, who have a reputation for a severer discipline, called Essenes. These last are Jews by birth, and seem to have a greater affection for one another than the other sects have. These Essenes reject pleasures as an evil,

"Essenes reject pleasures as an evil, but esteem continence, and the conquest over our passions, to be virtue."

but esteem continence, and the conquest over our passions, to be virtue. They neglect marriage, but choose out other persons' children, while they are pliable, and fit for learning; and esteem them to be of their kindred, and form them according to their own manners. They do not absolutely deny the fitness of marriage, and the succession of mankind thereby continued; but they guard against the lascivious behavior of women, and are persuaded that none of them preserve their fidelity to one man.

These men are despisers of riches, and so very communicative as raises our admiration. Nor is there any one to be found among them who has more than another; for it is a law among them, that those who come to them must let what they have be common to the whole order—insomuch, that among them all there is no appearance of poverty or excess of riches, but every one's possessions are intermingled with every other's possessions: and so there is, as it were, one patrimony among all the brethren. They think that oil is a defilement; and if any one of them be anointed without his own approbation, it is wiped off his body; for they think to be sweaty is a good thing, as they do also to be clothed in white garments. They also have stewards appointed to take care of their common affairs, who every one of them have no separate business for any, but what is for the use of them all.

"Nor is there any one to be found among them who has more than another; for it is a law among them, that those who come to them must let what they have be common to the whole order."

They have no certain city but many of them dwell in every city; and if any of their sect come from other places, what they have lies open for them, just as if it were their own; and they go into such as they never knew before, as if they had been ever so long acquainted with them. For which reason they carry nothing with them when they travel into remote parts, though still they take their weapons with them, for fear of thieves. Accordingly there is, in every city where they live, one appointed particularly to take care of strangers, and to provide garments and other necessaries for them. But the habit and management of their bodies is such as children use who are in fear of their masters. Nor do they allow of the change of garments, or of shoes, till they be first entirely torn to pieces or worn out by time. Nor do they either buy or sell anything to one another; but every one of them gives what he has to him that wants it, and receives from him again in lieu of it what may be convenient for himself; and although there be no requital made, they are fully allowed to take what they want of whomsoever they please.

And as for their piety towards God, it is very extraordinary; for before sunrise they speak not a word about profane matters, but put up certain prayers which they have received from their forefathers, as if they made a supplication for its rising. After this every one of them are sent away by their curators, to exercise some of those arts wherein they are skilled, in which they labor with great diligence till the fifth hour. After which they assemble themselves together again into one place; and when they have clothed themselves in white veils, they then bathe their bodies in cold water. And after this purification is over, they every one meet together in an apartment of their own, into which it is not permitted to any of another sect to enter; while they go, after a pure manner, into the dining room; as into a certain holy temple, and quietly set themselves down; upon which the bak-

A sandal found at Qumran. Josephus wrote that the Essenes do not "allow for the change of garments, or of shoes, till they be first entirely torn to pieces or worn out by time."

er lays them loaves in order; the cook also brings a single place of one sort of food, and sets it before every one of them; but a priest says grace before eating; and it is unlawful for any one to taste of the food before grace be said. The same priest, when he has dined, says grace again after eating; and when they begin, and when they end, they praise God, as he that bestows their food upon them; after which they lay aside their (white) garments, and get to their labors again till the evening; then they return home to supper, after the same manner; and if there be any strangers there, they set down with them. Nor is there ever any clamor or disturbance to pollute their house, but they give every one leave to speak in their turn; which silence thus kept in their house, appears to foreigners like some tremendous mystery; the cause of which is that perpetual sobriety they exercise, and the same settled measure of meat and drink that is allotted to them, and that such as is abundantly sufficient for them.

And truly, as for other things, they do nothing but according to the injunctions of their curators; only these two things are done among them at every one's own free will, which are, to assist those that want it, and to show mercy; for they are permitted of their own accord to afford succor to such as deserve it, when they stand in need of it, and to bestow food on those that are in distress; but they cannot give any thing to their kindred without the curators. They dispense their anger after a just manner, and restrain their passion. They are eminent for fidelity, and are the ministers of peace; whatsoever they say also is firmer than an oath; but swearing is avoided by them, and they esteem it worse than perjury; for they say, that he who cannot be believed without (swearing by) God, is already condemned. They also take great pains in studying the writings of the ancients, and choose out of them what is most for the advantage of their soul and body; and they inquire after such roots and

> *"Swearing is avoided by them, and they esteem it worse than perjury; for they say, that he who cannot be believed without (swearing by) God, is already condemned."*

medicinal stones as may cure their distempers.

But now, if any one has a mind to come over to their sect, he is not immediately admitted, but he is prescribed the same method of living which they use, for a year, while he continues excluded; and they give him a small hatchet, and the fore-mentioned girdle, and the white garment. And when he has given evidence, during that time, that he can observe their continence, he approaches nearer to their way of living, and is made partaker of the waters of purification; yet is he not even now admitted to live with them; for after this demonstration of his fortitude, his temper is tried two more years, and if he appear to be worthy, they then admit him into their society. And before he is allowed to touch their common food, he is obliged to take tremendous oaths; that, in the first place, he will exercise piety towards God; and then, that he will observe justice towards men; and that he will do no harm to any one, either of his own accord, or by the command of others; that he will always hate the wicked, and be assistant to the righteous; that he will ever show fidelity to all men, and especially to those in authority, because no one obtains the government without God's assistance; and that if he be in authority, he will at no time whatever abuse his authority, nor endeavor to outshine his subjects, either in his garments, or any other finery; that he will be perpetually a lover of truth, and propose to himself to reprove those that tell lies; that he will keep his hands clear from theft, and his soul from unlawful gains; and that he will neither conceal anything from those of his own sect, nor discover any of their doctrines to others, no, not though any one should compel him so to do at the hazard of his life. Moreover, he swears to communicate their doctrines to no one any otherwise than as he received them himself; that he will abstain from robbery, and will equally preserve the books belonging to their sect, and the means of the angels. These are the oaths by which they secure their proselytes to themselves.

But for those that are caught in any heinous sins,

they cast them out of their society; and he who is thus separated from them, does often die after a miserable manner; for as is bound by the oath he has taken, and by the customs he has been engaged in, he is not at liberty to partake of that food that he meets with elsewhere, but is forced to east grass, and to famish his body with hunger till he perish; for which reason they receive many of them again when they are at their last gasp, out of compassion to them, as thinking the miseries they have endured till they come to the very brink of death, to be a sufficient punishment for the sins they had been guilty of.

> *"What they most of all honor, after God himself, is the name of their legislator (Moses); whom, if any one blaspheme, he is punished capitally."*

But in the judgments they exercise they are most accurate and just; nor do they pass sentence by the votes of a court that is fewer than a hundred. And as to what is once determined by that number, it is unalterable. What they most of all honor, after God himself, is the name of their legislator (Moses); whom, if any one blaspheme, he is punished capitally. They also think it a good thing to obey their elders, and the major part. Accordingly, if ten of them be sitting together no one of them will speak while the other nine are against it. They also avoid spitting the midst of them, or on the right side. Moreover, they are stricter than any other of the Jews in resting from their labors on the seventh day; for they not only get their food ready the day before, that they may not be obliged to kindle a fire on that day, but they will not remove any vessel out of its place, nor go to stool thereon. Nay, on the other days they dig a small pit, a foot deep, with a paddle (which kind of hatchet is given them when they are first admitted among them); and covering themselves round with their garment, that they may not affront the divine rays of light, they ease themselves into that pit, after which they put the earth that was dug out again into the pit; and even this they do only in the more lonely places, which they choose out for this purpose; and although this easement of the body be natural, yet it is a rule with them to wash themselves after it, as if it were a defilement to them.

Now after the time of their preparatory trial is over, they are parted into four classes; and so far are the juniors inferior to the seniors, that if the seniors should be touched by the juniors, they must wash themselves, as if they had intermixed themselves with the company of a foreigner. They are long-lived also; insomuch that many of them live above a hundred years, by means of the simplicity of their diet; nay, as I think, by means of the regular course of life they observe also. They condemn the miseries of life, and are above pain, by the generosity of their mind. And as for death, if it will be for their glory, they esteem it better than living always; and indeed our war with the Romans gave abundant evidence what great souls they had in their trials, wherein, although they were tortured and distorted, burnt and torn to pieces, and went through all kinds of instruments of torment, that they might be forced either to blaspheme their legislator, or to eat what was forbidden them, yet could they not be made to do either of them, no, nor once to flatter their tormentors, or to shed a tear; but they smiled in their very pains, and laughed those to scorn who inflicted the torments upon them, and resigned up their souls with great alacrity, as expecting to receive them again.

Plates found in what was probably the dining hall at Qumran. Josephus reported that the Essenes were long-lived due to the simplicity of their diet.

For their doctrine is this: That bodies are corruptible, and that the matter they are made of is not permanent; but that the souls are immortal, and continue

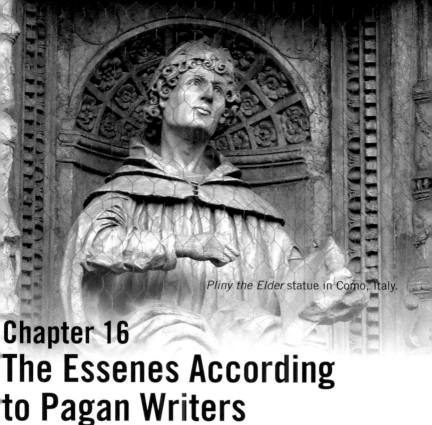

Pliny the Elder statue in Como, Italy.

Chapter 16
The Essenes According to Pagan Writers

That Jewish writers such as Philo and Josephus wrote about a Jewish sect called the Essenes is no surprise given their familiarity with Jewish national and religious life. However, that non-Jewish writers mentioned the Essenes demonstrates that this group's presence was substantial enough to merit attention on a broader scale. In this chapter we focus on two pagan authors who left behind helpful comments on the Essenes.

Pliny the Elder on the Essenes

One of these writers was a Roman aristocrat known as Pliny the Elder or Gaius Plinius Secundus (AD 23–79). Pliny was the uncle of Pliny the Younger, who is famous for having written a brief report about early Christians living in the province of Bithynia. Pliny the Elder was a military man, a Roman equestrian, commander of the fleet at Misenum, and author of the 37-book *Naturalis Historia*, an encyclopedic anthology of all natural subjects studied in late antiquity. Of special interest for biblical scholars is his description of Palestine and the Essenes.[1] Writing sometime in the late 70s, Pliny says:

On the west side of the Dead Sea, but out of range of the noxious (waters) of the coast, is the solitary tribe of the Essenes, which is remarkable beyond all the other tribes in the whole world, as it has no women and has renounced all sexual desire, has no money, and has only palm trees for company. Day by day the throng of refugees is recruited to an equal number by numerous accessions of persons tired of life and driven there by the waves of fortune to adopt their manners. Thus through thousands of ages (incredible to relate) a race in which no one is born lives on forever: so prolific for their advantage is other men's weariness of life!

Lying below the Essenes was formerly the town of Engedi, second only to Jerusalem in the fertility of its land and in its groves of palm trees, but now, like Jerusalem, a heap of ashes. Next comes Masada, a fortress on a rock, itself not far from the Dead Sea. (*Nat. Hist.* 5.73).[2]

Pliny's description of the Essenes and local geography is on the whole very accurate and well informed. He is given to some myth, however, in his assertion that the Essene community has survived "through thousands of ages." It may have seemed that way to him, writing sometime in the 70s. The Essene community, however, survived hardly more than two hundred years.

Pliny the Elder includes important information on the Essenes in his 37-volume work, *Naturalis Historia*.

Dio Chrysostom on the Essenes

A Greek writer who knew of the Essenes was Dio Chrysostom (d. circa AD 120). He is not to be confused with church father John Chrysostom. Dio was a rhetorician, orator, Stoic philosopher, and author of numerous speeches compiled as *Discourses*. According to his biographer, Synesius, Dio "praises the Essenes, a very blessed city lying beside the Dead Water in the interior of Palestine, in the same location of Sodom" (Synesius, *Vita Dionis* 3.2). Dio's reference to the "blessed city" is a bit odd, but his geographical references, including the odd sobriquet "Dead Water" (Greek: *hudor nekron*) for the Dead Sea, are accurate.

The Scrolls and the Various Testimonies About the Essenes

The parallels between the Dead Sea Scrolls and what Jewish writers Philo and Josephus and Greco-Roman writers Pliny and Dio say about the Essenes are numerous and significant. Comparison is important, for if the Essenes that these writers talked about are indeed the same people who wrote and collected the scrolls found in and near Qumran, we are in a position to know a great deal more about the purpose and perspectives of the DSS. How close are the parallels between descriptions given of the Essenes and the worldview described in the DSS?

If the Essenes that these writers talked about are indeed the same people who wrote and collected the scrolls found in and near Qumran, we are in a position to know a great deal more about the purpose and perspectives of the DSS.

Parallels between the Essenes and content of the DSS:

Sacrifices: The Essenes offered no sacrifices in Jerusalem (Philo, *Every Good Man Is Free* 75; Josephus, *Antiquities* 18.19). The DSS bear this out. The Damascus Document says that none of those who follow the Teacher of Righteousness and have entered the (Renewed) Covenant "shall enter the sanctuary to light up (God's) altar in vain"

(6:11–12; cf. 11:17–21). Instead, their righteous deeds and prayers will effect atonement (1QS 9:3–5).

Encampment: The Essenes establish themselves in "camps" and in the wilderness (Philo, *Every Good Man Is Free* 76; *On the Contemplative Life* 18–23; Josephus, *Antiquities* 18.124). According to the Community Rule scroll, the men of the Renewed Covenant were in the wilderness, in fulfillment of Isaiah 40:3 (1QS 8:13–15; CD 7:6–7).

Membership: Essene membership was made up of those who freely joined them (Philo, *A Defense of the Jews* 8.11.2–3; Josephus, *War* 2.120; Pliny the Elder, *Nat. Hist.* 5.73). This is emphasized in the DSS (CD 15:5–6; 1QS 1:11–13; 5:7–11; 6:13–14).

Initiation: The Essenes required a period of initiation before newcomers could become full members (Josephus, *War* 2.137–42). This same requirement is found in the DSS (1QS 6:13–16). Josephus said new members had to take an oath (*War* 2.139), a requirement also named in the DSS (CD 15:7–11; 1QS 5:8–9).

Communal Living: We are told that the Essenes shared their wealth, holding all things in common (Philo, *Every Good Man Is Free* 76–78, 84–86; *A Defense of the Jews* 8.11.4–5, 10–13; Josephus, *War* 2.122, 127; *Antiquities* 18.20). This point is emphasized in the DSS (CD 4:17; 1QS 1:11–13; 5:1–2; 6:13–23; 9:21–24; 10:18–19).

Austerity: The Essenes shunned pleasure (Josephus, *War* 2.120). Likewise, the DSS are critical of any desire for pleasure (1QS 4:9–11).

Modesty in Dress: The Essenes were very frugal, replacing clothing only when worn out (Josephus, *War* 2.126). The DSS warn members not to expose themselves when their clothing is so worn that it's full of holes (1QS 7:13–14).

Slavery: There were to be no slaves among the Essenes (Philo, *Every Good Man Is Free* 79; On the Contemplative Life 70–72; Josephus, *Antiquities* 18.21), a point perhaps also implied in the Damascus Document (12:10–11).

Sabbath Observance: The Essenes were unusually strict in their Sabbath observance (Philo, *Every Good Man Is Free* 81–84; *On the Contemplative Life* 30–33; Josephus, *War* 2.147). The same strictness is seen in the Damascus Document (6:18; 10:14–11:18; 12:3–6).

Morning Devotions: The Essenes prayed at dawn (Philo, *On the Contemplative Life* 89; Josephus, *War* 2.128). The DSS also indicate this practice (1QS 10:1–3).

Immersion Rites: The Essenes practiced ritual immersion for purification (Josephus, *War* 2.129). This is indicated in the DSS also (1QS 3:4–5).

Regimentation: The Essenes were highly regimented in seating arrangements (Philo, *Every Good Man Is Free* 81; *On the Contemplative Life* 30; Josephus, *War* 2.150). This is much emphasized in the DSS (CD 14:3–6; 1QS 6:8–9; 1QSa 2:11–22).

Authoritative Teacher: The Essenes recognized the interpretation of Scripture by a revered teacher (Philo, *Every Good Man Is Free* 82; *On the Contemplative Life* 31, 75–79; Josephus, *War* 2.159). According to the DSS, the Qumran community was led by someone called the Teacher of Righteousness (CD 13:2–4; 1QS 6:6–7).

Prophecy: The Essenes were known for their prophetic, predictive skills (Josephus, *War* 2.159). The same emphasis appears in the DSS. For instance, there are many futuristic interpretations of Scripture, especially in the commentaries called the pesharim (e.g., 1QpHab 7:4–5).

Secrecy: The Essenes required their distinctive teaching, including names of angels, to be hidden from outsiders (Josephus, *War* 2.142). This too is taught in the DSS (1QS 9:16–18; 1QM 9:14–16). Only members of the community could share in the essential teachings.

Sovereignty of God: The Essenes believed that human history, past and future, is determined by God (Josephus, *Antiquities* 18.18). This perspective is attested in the DSS (1QS 3:15–16).

Food Laws: The Essenes held to very strict food laws, including vegetarianism (Philo, *On the Contemplative Life* 73–74, 81–82). This is emphasized in the DSS (1QS 6:4–6; 1QSa 2:17–22).

Blessing the Meal: Before Essenes ate their meals, the priest blessed the food (Josephus, *War* 2.131). This is taught in the DSS (1QS 6:4–5).

Oil: While the majority of Jews valued oil for anointing and other purposes, the Essenes regarded it as defiling (Josephus, *War* 2.123); so also in the DSS (CD 12:15–17).

Spitting: The Essenes frowned upon spitting (Josephus, *War* 2.147), which is expressly forbidden in the DSS (1QS 7:13).

Male-Only Community: The Essenes comprised a male-only community (Philo, *A Defense of the Jews* 8.11.14–17; Josephus, *War* 2.120–21; *Antiquities* 18.21; Pliny the Elder, *Nat. Hist.* 5.73). The male orientation is apparent in the DSS (e.g., CD 7:6–9) and excavations of the cemetery at Qumran reveal many male skeletons and very few female skeletons, suggesting that the Qumran community was a community of males. Women, moreover, were viewed as inherently promiscuous (4Q184 1:13–14).

What Do the Parallels Mean?

These parallels are numerous and impressive, suggesting the Qumran community should be identified as Essene. But there are discrepancies also. For example, Josephus (*War* 2.120–21) insists that the Essenes were unmarried, yet there

These parallels are numerous and impressive, suggesting the Qumran community should be identified as Essene.

are rules and regulations for married members in the scroll known as the Damascus Document (4:19–5:2; 16:10–12). This implies that at least some members of the Qumran community were married. Rather than assuming this proves Qumran was not an Essene community, we may be right to suggest that Josephus was not aware that though the majority of Essenes were celibate, some few were in fact married.

Josephus (*War* 2.145) also claims that the Essenes passed sentence in a court numbering 100, yet the DSS give us the impression that 10 members were sufficient for rendering judgments (CD 10:4–7; cf. 4Q334 frags. 2–4, col. 1, lines 3–4). Furthermore, as noted above, Philo (*Every Good Man Is Free* 79) and Josephus (*Antiquities* 18.21) assert that there were no slaves among the Essenes, something possibly supported in the Damascus Document (12:10–11). However, in the fuller context of this discussion, possessing slaves seems presupposed (CD 11:12). Here again, what is said by the first-century Jewish writers seems out of step with the actual rules and regulations found in the DSS themselves.

There are also elements that are prominent in the scrolls but go unmentioned in Philo and Josephus, our major sources for information about the Essene way of life. For example, both Philo and Josephus are silent about the authoritative figure called the Teacher of Righteousness (CD 1:11; 20:1; 1QpHab 1:13; 8:3; 9:9) and the use of the solar calendar instead of the lunar calendar (e.g., 11Q5 27:6). What are we to make of these and other discrepancies? Do they suggest that the authors and collectors of the DSS were not Essene after all?

Many of the discrepancies involve the Damascus Document, which could indicate that in the passage of time policies and practices among the Essenes had evolved. What Philo and Josephus describe in the first century AD at points mismatches the practices envisioned in the Damascus Document, which was originally composed some 150 years earlier and thus reflects an earlier stage of Essene thought and way of life. We must also bear in mind that given the secretive nature of the Essenes, not all of their beliefs and practices were necessarily accurately understood by non-Essene Jews such as Philo and Josephus, let alone pagan outsiders such as Pliny and Dio Chrysostom. The non-Essene writers may simply have been mistaken about some of the details of the Essene way of life.[3]

Taken as a whole, the parallels between what non-Essene authors say about the Essenes and what we actually find in the scrolls themselves strongly suggest that the inhabitants of Qumran were indeed Essenes. The manner of life evidenced by the site's ruins and the DSS themselves match very closely the things we learn about the Essences from Josephus and others. This does not mean

When all evidence is considered, it seems clear that the Essenes, who were said to live in an austere community beside the "Dead Water," were indeed the people who inhabited the Qumran community.

that all Essenes lived near the Dead Sea or that every Essene community was the same. It is only natural that each specific Essene group would differ somewhat from the next. When all evidence is considered, it seems clear that the Essenes, who were said to live in an austere community beside the "Dead Water," were indeed the people who inhabited the Qumran community.

Notes

1. Pliny's source was probably Marcus Vipsanius Agrippa, the governor of Syria and friend of Herod the Great. Agrippa produced a map of Herod's Israel.

2. Translation based on H. Rackham, *Pliny the Elder: Naturalis Historia* (London: Heinemann; Cambridge, MA: Harvard University Press, 1949). The testimony of Pliny is paraphrased by third-century Solinus, in his *Collections* 35.1–12; and, very briefly, in

Martianus Capella, *On the Marriage of Philology and Mercury* 6.679. Rackham translates the opening line as "noxious exhalations." The Latin text simply reads "noxious" (nocent). In context, it is clear that Pliny is referring to the undrinkable water of the Dead Sea, not to fumes.

3. For more parallels, with more detailed documentation, see L. H. Feldman, "Josephus Flavius," and G. E. Sterling, "Philo Judaeus," in L. H. Schiffman and J. C. VanderKam (eds.), *Encyclopedia of the Dead Sea Scrolls* (2 vols., Oxford: Oxford University Press, 2000), 1:427–31 and 2:663–69, respectively.

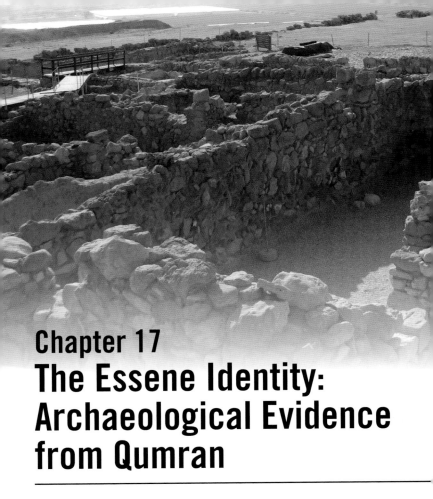

Chapter 17
The Essene Identity: Archaeological Evidence from Qumran

The archaeology of the ruins at Qumran, the nearby cemetery, and the nearby caves in which scrolls and pottery were found, supports the conclusion that the Qumran community was in fact an Essene community. In this chapter we outline several evidences for this conclusion.

What Was the Compound, and Who Lived There?[1]

Not everyone thinks Essenes lived at Qumran, and not everyone thinks the ruins found on the plateau on the north bank of Wadi Qumran belonged to the men who wrote and gathered the scrolls found in the nearby caves. Let's review the alternate theories, as summarized by respected scrolls scholar and antiquities curator Magen Broshi:

Commercial Warehouse: Alan Crown and Lena Cansdale have suggested that the ruins at Qumran belonged to a commercial warehouse, situated along a major trade route.[2] Broshi counters by noting that there were no major trade routes within easy reach of Qumran, nor is there any evidence (such as a quay) to indicate commerce across the Dead Sea. Moreover, there are no large storage rooms or adequate living quarters for large numbers of travelers or transportation crews.

The Wadi Qumran.

Villa Rustica: Robert Donceel and Pauline Donceel-Voute have proposed that the ruins at Qumran are of a *villa rustica*, that is, a simple villa for winter vacations and visits.[3] But Broshi rightly asks why anyone would build a villa in an inhospitable setting whose salty, sandy soil cannot support the sort of vegetation needed to make such an establishment viable (let alone beautiful). The walls of the buildings are made of undressed stone. They are not plastered. There is no evidence of any art, mosaics, or decorative features, as are always found in homes and villas belonging to affluent persons. Moreover, there is very little evidence of the presence of women, which is hard to explain if the ruins are those of a villa.

> *There is no evidence of any art, mosaics, or decorative features, as are always found in homes and villas belonging to affluent persons.*

Fortress: Norman Golb argues against any connection whatsoever between the caves that contained scrolls and the ruins of Qumran. He suggests that the ruins are of a fortress and that the nearby cemetery contains the remains of 1,200 men who defended the fortress against a Roman attack during the Jewish revolt of AD 66–70.[4] As for the scrolls in the nearby caves, he suggests they were brought to the wilderness by people from Jerusalem and have no connection to Qumran.

Broshi rightly objects to this proposal, for the walls of the ruins are narrow, weak, and made of ill-fitted stones. That's not the sort of thing used to build fortresses. Moreover, the entrances are not designed for defense. Such a fortress would be easy to attack and overwhelm. Even so, a frontal attack would not even be necessary to destroy the compound, for the community's water supply was undefended and thus could have been cut off by invaders without difficulty. As for the 1,200 graves, it is extremely doubtful that the Roman army would have bothered to bury so many of their defeated

Chemical analysis shows that the ink used to write the Dead Sea Scrolls was produced from materials that are native to the Dead Sea region.

foes. There is no evidence that they did this with any of the other Jewish forces they defeated throughout the Revolt. As to the proposal that the scrolls were linked to Jerusalem rather than Qumran, it is nothing but speculation. No evidence links the scrolls to Jerusalem, and one cannot help but wonder why anyone would think that the scrolls would be safer out in the wilderness than they would be behind the massive walls of Jerusalem.

Furthermore, chemical analysis shows that the ink used to write the Dead Sea Scroll was produced from materials that are native to the Dead Sea region.[5] This strongly tells against Golb's theory that the scrolls were produced in Jerusalem or elsewhere and then taken to the Dead Sea caves shortly before the Roman army besieged Jerusalem.

Fortified Farming Estate: Yizhar Hirschfeld suggests that the ruins are the remains of a fortified country estate, whose primary purpose was farming.[6] Broshi raises the same objections raised against the proposals of the Donceels and Golb, noting that the environment of Qumran could scarcely support a thriving farm and that the structure scarcely qualifies as "fortified."

Country House: Jean-Baptiste Humbert proposes that the ruins began as a country house and then later became a compound for the Essenes. He points to similarities in the architectural design of the Qumran ruins and the designs of other structures that archaeologists believe were country houses.[7] Broshi raises the same objections raised against the similar proposals of the Donceels and Hirschfeld. The general architectural similarities between the Qumran site and known country houses do not provide sufficient support for concluding that Qumran represents a country house. Furthermore, this theory does not take into account other important lines, which we review below.

Assessing These Alternative Views: Broshi rightly underscores the failure of all five alternate theories to account for three major lines of evidence and argumentation:

First, they fail to account for the presence of the large library in the nearby caves. To assert that these caves are merely coincidental to the Qumran site begs the question, for several of them have been dug into the same marl mudstone plateau on which the Qumran ruins are situated and are no more than a few dozen meters' distance from the ruins. Archaeologically speaking, the caves and the Qumran site are essentially atop one another.

Second, how do the alternate theories account for 10 immersion pools for ritual purity? Surely one, at most two, would be sufficient for the inhabitants of a villa or a small fortress. That Qumran contains 10 such structures strongly suggests a significant population of religious devotees.

The presence of 10 immersion pools at Qumran indicates the importance the community placed on ritual purity. Photo: Teqoah.

Third, if Qumran was a villa or country house, how do we account for the adjacent cemetery, which holds 1,200 graves? This question is also problematic for Golb's fortress theory, for surely there were not 1,200 defenders present at one time? The ruins indicate that the site could hardly have accommodated one-tenth that number. And, of course, the ruins give no indication of fortification and military orientation.

Broshi has concluded that at most only a few of the residents at Qumran lived in the compound proper. Excavations and surveys, especially those of Hanan Eshel and Magen Broshi himself in 1995–96, discovered many caves in the vicinity of the ruins, some of them man-made, and most of them containing pottery. They concluded that it was in caves such as these that most of the men who resided at Qumran actually lived. This seems well supported by available evidence and the simple, self-denying lifestyle of the Essenes.

Ostraca and Inkwells

While excavating on the Qumran plateau near the community ruins in 1996, a team headed by archaeologist James Strange discovered two pieces of an ostracon, on which several lines of Hebrew could just barely be made out. It appears to be a receipt or a list of property certain named individuals gave to others. The phrases "in year two" and "on the second year" appear on the ostracon. These may refer to the rebels' reckoning of the calendar after the Jewish Revolt that began in AD 66. Thus "year two" may refer to the second year of the revolt, which

Inkpot found at Qumran.

was AD 67. Although it is hotly debated, some scholars think they can also make out the word "community" (Hebrew: *yahad*) on the ostracon. If this reading is correct, we would have a direct link between the Qumran ruins and the DSS, for the scrolls speak of new members handing over their property to the community (e.g., 1QS 1:11–12: "All who volunteer for His truth are to bring the full measure of their . . . wealth into the Community [*Yahad*] of God").

Other archaeological evidences supporting the link between Qumran, the Essenes, and the DSS include jars, pottery, inkwells, and what could be remnants of writing desks discovered in the nearby caves. The caves also yielded documents that appear to be nothing more than writing exercises, a fitting habit for a community of religious scribes.[8] Finally, among the

Possible writing desks from Qumran.

DSS were also found many calendrical texts, indicating that the community was intent on marking special days throughout the year. Consistent with this interest was a sundial recovered from the ruins.

All of these evidences show a correspondence between the subjects mentioned in the DSS and the lifestyle and values of the Qumran community, suggesting that the community produced and collected the scrolls found in the nearby caves.

Why Live in the Wilderness?

What was the purpose of the wilderness compound? After all, Josephus said most Essenes lived among their fellow Jews around Israel. Why did a few of them choose to live in a remote, harsh environment surrounded by hundreds of books, separated from mainstream Jews? The answer is hinted at in their constitution document, which is called the Rule of the Community:

> When such men as these come to be in Israel, conforming to these doctrines, they shall separate from the session of perverse men to go to the wilderness, there to prepare the way of truth, as it is written, "In the wilderness prepare the way of the Lord, make straight in the desert a highway for our God" (Isa 40:3). This means the expounding of the Law, decree by God through Moses for obedience, that being defined by what has

been revealed for each age, and by what the prophets have revealed by His holy spirit. (1QS 8:12–16)

Expounding on the Law of Moses appears to have been the primary purpose of the community's immense library, for we find many scrolls concerned with its meaning.

It seems the founder(s) of the Essenes took Isaiah's wilderness summons quite literally—and allegorically too. "Preparing the way of the Lord" was understood to mean "expounding of the Law." That appears to have been the primary purpose of the community's immense library, for we find many scrolls concerned with the meaning of the Law. The Rule also includes phrases saying "what has been revealed for each age . . . by what the prophets have revealed by His holy spirit," which suggests that the community had a futuristic outlook. This in turn explains the community's great interest in interpreting the prophets, as seen in their commentaries.

Meeting Physical Needs in the Wilderness

Several tools have been recovered at Qumran, including a pickax, a sickle, a hoe, and shears. Fragments of clothing and sandals were also recovered, plus shoe nails (thanks to highly sensitive metal detectors). Below we examine a few of these findings and suggest how they bear on the question of Qumran identity.

Shoe Nails: The discovery of shoe nails is quite interesting. Some of them were found along paths connecting the ruins of the Qumran compound to the nearby caves, thus establishing a solid link between Qumran and the caves in which DSS were found. However, some point out that only Roman sandals were held together with nails, so the "nail trails" might not have been made by members of the Qumran compound. This is possible. Nevertheless, the trails indicate regular traffic between Qumran and the caves. Additionally, it is doubtful that sandal-shod soldiers, whose visit to Qumran was surely brief, could have dropped so many nails. Maybe the nails came from Essene sandals after all.

Simple Clothing: Ancient writers say the Essenes wore simple, unadorned clothing (Josephus, *War* 2.123, "always clothed in white garments"). Judging by the undyed cloth found at Qumran, it seems that the men of this community dressed in the Essene fashion.[9]

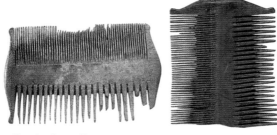

Combs from Qumran.

Modesty: Another interesting observation has to do with what has not been found at Qumran: jewelry, mirrors, art, and other items usually linked to comfort and the presence of women. The absence of these things is consistent with the ancient writers who say Essenes lived without women. It also fits with the conclusion that the Qumran ruins do *not* represent an ancient villa. The overall modesty hinted at by archaeological findings supports identifying the men of Qumran with the Essenes.

Dietary Laws: The Essenes were greatly concerned with pure food as well as who could eat it and who could not. These facts are clearly seen in the following excerpts from the Rule of the Community (1QS):

> *The Essenes were greatly concerned with pure food as well as who could eat it and who could not.*

If he does proceed in joining the Council of the Yahad, he must not touch the pure food of the general membership before they have examined him as to his spiritual fitness and works, and not before a full year has passed. (6:16–17)

If there be found among them a man who has lied about money and done so knowingly, they shall bar him from the pure meals of the general membership for one year. (6:24–25)

If anyone speaks angrily against one of the priests who are inscribed in the book, he is to be punished by reduced rations for one year and separated from the pure meals of the general membership, eating by himself. (7:2–3)

No man belonging to the Covenant of the Community who flagrantly deviates from any commandment is to touch the pure food belonging to the holy men. (8:16–17)

The archaeological finds at Qumran are consistent with these statements. About 200 fragments of stone vessels have been found in and around the ruins of Qumran. This is significant, because in Jewish thinking stone is resistant to contamination. One thinks of the wedding feast at Cana of Galilee, where "six stone water jars had been set there for Jewish purification" (John 2:6). Water for

Water for purification was kept in stone jars because stone was not susceptible to impurity.

purification was kept in stone jars because stone was not susceptible to impurity. The presence of the stone vessels at the

Qumran compound suggests that members of this community were greatly concerned with purity and pure food, an emphasis found throughout the DSS.[10]

So far as pottery is concerned, hundreds of dishes, bowls, cups, and various cooking utensils have been found.[11] Even fragments of baskets, dates, date pits, and faunal remains have been uncovered. The kiln in which the pottery was baked has been found in the compound's ruins. Scientists have determined that the clay used in the making of the jars and other pottery found in the caves where scrolls were found is the same clay from which the bowls, cups, and dishes found in the ruins were made. This significant finding strongly supports a link between the ruins and the caves.

Over 400 bones from goats and sheep have been recovered from a burial pit. Some 69 bones from four cows have also been recovered. Many of the scrolls were made from the skins of a species of cow that is now extinct. Very few of the bones showed signs of scorching, suggesting that the meat was normally boiled.

Meeting Spiritual Needs in the Wilderness

Since archaeology deals in artifacts and ruins, you might be surprised to learn that this science also sheds light on spiritual life at Qumran.

The DSS speak of liturgy, prayer, and study of Scripture, giving us a glimpse of the ways in which the men of Qumran maintained spiritual vitality. Since archaeology deals in artifacts and ruins, you might be surprised to learn that this science also sheds light on spiritual life at Qumran. Here's how:

Josephus tells us that the Essenes regularly bathed in cold water and that they did so before their meals (*War* 2.129). The DSS say that their members were to purify themselves in proper water (CD 10:10–13).[12] The ruins at Qumran suggest members of this community did exactly this. Excavations have exposed 16 water installations and 10 *miqva'ot* (ritual immersion pools).[13] One of the large, plastered immersion pools was damaged by an earthquake. Running down its steps is a divider, the purpose of which was to separate descending impure persons from ascending pure persons who had already been cleansed in the pool. Curiously enough, this practice is attested in an early second-century nonbiblical Christian writing, where a priest in the temple precincts is portrayed as saying to Jesus: "I am clean, for I washed in the pool of David, and having descended by one set of steps I ascended by another" (Papyrus Oxyrhynchus no. 840).

We are told that the Essenes dug holes, squatted over them, and then buried their excrement. According to Josephus, each man who joined the Essenes was given a hatchet with which to dig a hole for his waste (*War* 2.137 "he is given a hatchet"; 2.148 "they dig a hole one foot deep"). One or two of the tools found in the ruins may have been for this purpose.

Burial of the Dead at Qumran

About 100 feet east of the ruins at Qumran is a necropolis, or cemetery. A low wall separated the community proper and the cemetery. This was in keeping with the command to bury the dead "outside the camp" (Num 5:2–3). The grave sites are for the most part obvious, with the result that the number of burials can be counted. Some 1,200 graves have been identified, but only 50 or so have been excavated. No inscriptions have been found with the graves, which fits with the Essene emphasis on equality. One grave, however, seems a bit more pronounced than the others, leading to speculation that perhaps it is the grave of the Teacher of Righteousness.

The graves sit in neat rows that are oriented north to south. The head is situated at the south end with small stones piled in a heap beside it. The bodies lie on their backs, with arms at sides or crossed on the pelvis.[14] All the skeletons examined in the main cemetery are male, while a few of the remains found in the extended area are female. A string of beads and earrings were found with two of the female skeletons. The segregation of the female skeletons from the main cemetery is consistent with the male orientation of the Essenes, as especially emphasized in Josephus and Pliny.[15]

All the skeletons examined in the main cemetery at Qumran are male, while a few of the remains found in the extended area are female.

The body count and analysis of remains have been complicated by what appear to be a number of Bedouin burials that intrude into the Qumran site. However, the archaeologists and anthropologists have for the most part sorted out these problems, separating burials of Qumran community members from those of the wandering Bedouin people.

Summary

The literary evidence and the evidence gleaned from archaeological discoveries point in the same direction: The men who collected and wrote many of the DSS lived within the Qumran compound and its immediate vicinity. In all probability these men were none other than the Essenes mentioned by Philo, Pliny, Dio, and Josephus.

Notes

1. For a general discussion of the evidence of the archaeology of Qumran, see J. Patrich, "Archaeology," and M. Broshi, "Qumran: Archaeology," in L. H. Schiffman and J. C. VanderKam (eds.), *Encyclopedia of the Dead Sea Scrolls* (2 vols., Oxford: Oxford University Press, 2000), 1:57–63 and 2:733–39, respectively; J. Magness, *The Archaeology of Qumran and the Dead Sea Scrolls* (Grand Rapids: Eerdmans, 2002).

2. A. D. Crown and L. Cansdale, "Qumran: Was It an Essene Settlement?" *Biblical Archaeology Review* 20/5 (1994): 24–36, 73–78.

3. R. Donceel and P. Donceel-Voute, "The Archaeology of Khirbet Qumran," in M. O. Wise et al. (eds.), *Methods of Investigation of the Dead Sea Scrolls and the Khirbet Qumran Site* (New York: The New York Academy of Sciences, 1994), 1–38.

4. N. Golb, *Who Wrote the Dead Sea Scrolls?* (New York: Simon & Schuster, 1996).

5. See I. Rabin et al., "On the Origin of the Ink of the Thanksgiving Scroll (1QHodayota)," *Dead Sea Discoveries* 16 (2009): 97–106.

6. Y. Hirschfeld, *Qumran in Context: Reassessing the Archaeological Evidence* (Peabody, MA: Hendrickson, 2004).

7. J.-B. Humbert, "Some Remarks on the Archaeology of Qumran," in K. Galor (ed.), *Qumran, the Site of the Dead Sea Scrolls: Archaeological Interpretations and Debates* (Leiden: Brill, 2006), 19–39.

8. For more on this topic, see M. Bar-Ilan, "Writing Materials," in Schiffman and VanderKam (eds.), *Encyclopedia of the Dead Sea Scrolls*, 2:996–97.

9. For more on this topic, see Magness, *The Archaeology of Qumran and the Dead Sea Scrolls*, 193–202; A. Sheffer, "Textiles," in Schiffman and VanderKam (eds.), *Encyclopedia of the Dead Sea Scrolls*, 2:938–43.

10. For more on this topic, see R. Rosenthan-Heginbottom, "Stoneware," in Schiffman and VanderKam (eds.), *Encyclopedia of the Dead Sea Scrolls*, 2:892–95; Magness, *The Archaeology of Qumran and the Dead Sea Scrolls*, 212–13.

11. For more on this topic, see J. Magness, "Pottery," in Schiffman and VanderKam (eds.), *Encyclopedia of the Dead Sea Scrolls*, 2:681–86; J. Magness, "The Community at Qumran in Light of Its Pottery," in Wise et al. (eds.), *Methods of Investigation of the Dead Sea Scrolls and the Khirbet Qumran Site*, 39–50.

12. For more on this topic, see H. Lichtenberger, "Baths and Baptism," and H. K. Harrington, "Purity," in Schiffman and VanderKam (eds.), *Encyclopedia of the Dead Sea Scrolls*, 1:85–89 and 2:724–28, respectively.

13. For more on this topic, see B. G. Wood, "Cisterns and Reservoirs," and B. G. Wood, "Water Systems," in Schiffman and VanderKam (eds.), *Encyclopedia of the Dead Sea Scrolls*, 1:131–33 and 2:968–70, respectively.

14. For more on this topic, see R. Hachlili, "Cemeteries, " in Schiffman and VanderKam (eds.), *Encyclopedia of the Dead Sea Scrolls*, 1:125–29; Magness, *The Archaeology of Qumran and the Dead Sea Scrolls*, 163–87.

15. For more on this topic, see P. Smith, "Skeletal Remains," in Schiffman and VanderKam (eds.), *Encyclopedia of the Dead Sea Scrolls*, 2:880–82.

Photo: Berthold Werner.

Part VI

Faith and Practice
According to the Scrolls

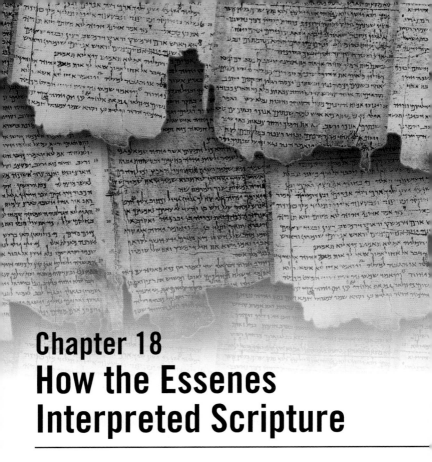

Chapter 18
How the Essenes Interpreted Scripture

Careful study of Scripture was of central importance to the men of the Qumran community because they saw this task as a fulfillment of Isaiah 40:3, which says: "Prepare the way of the LORD in the wilderness." Thus by interpreting Scripture correctly and living in accordance with its teaching, they believed they were preparing the way for Messiah. How they handled Scripture is the focus of this chapter.

Literal and Semi-allegorical Interpretations

The Dead Sea Scrolls (DSS) manifest two basic approaches to biblical interpretation: A mostly literal approach and a semi-allegorical approach called *pesher* (from the Hebrew, meaning "interpretation" or "meaning").[1] Understanding these approaches helps us appreciate the distinctive teachings of the DSS.

Literal: The Essenes typically used the literal approach when interpreting the Law of Moses. This more conservative approach did not mean that the men of Qumran could not expand the legal elements of Scripture. In fact they believed the laws could be rewritten, paraphrased, applied to new situations, and even "corrected" in light of new customs. Paraphrasing and rewriting Scripture were regarded as forms of commentary, not forms of corruption or deviation from the sacred text. Among the more fascinating examples are the three Temple Scrolls (11Q19–21), in which the laws of Deuteronomy are restat-

Moses by Rembrandt. The Essenes typically used the literal approach when interpreting the Law of Moses.

ed. A similar set of scrolls is called the Reworked Pentateuch (4Q158, 4Q364–367).

The Law of Moses could also be "interpreted" by expanding certain laws, retelling parts of the Pentateuch, or focusing on particular characters such as Moses or Abraham in a made-up vision or revelation. In these ways the Essenes updated the Law of Moses so that it would speak more clearly to their time and the specific concerns of the Qumran community.

Pesher: Another important area of biblical interpretation in the DSS is what we find in the pesharim. These are commentaries on some of the Prophets and a few of the Psalms. These scrolls are called pesharim (which is the plural form of the singular *pesher*) because they quote passages line by line, stating the meaning of each.[2] As we shall see in the case studies below, this approach to interpretation stresses allegorical over literal and contemporary over original.

Commentary on Habakkuk 2:1-2

The pesharim drew immediate attention among scholars largely because of 1QpHab, the commentary on the prophecy of Habakkuk. This spelled out the community's understanding of prophetic Scripture and how it related to them. Below I quote some of the commentary and then comment on a few key phrases:

> "So I will stand on watch and station myself on my watchtower and wait for what He will say to me, and what he will reply to my rebuke. Then the Lord answered me and said, Write down the vision plainly on tablets, so that with ease someone can read it" (Hab 2:1–2). This refers to . . . then God told Habakkuk to write down what is going to happen to the generation to come; but when that period would be complete He did not make known to him. When it says, "so that with ease someone can read it," this refers to the Teacher of Righteousness to whom God made known all the mysterious revelations of his servants the prophets. "For still the prophecy is for a specific period; it testifies of that time and does not deceive" (Hab 2:3a). This means that the Last Days will be long, much longer than the prophets had said; for God's revelations are truly mysterious. "If it tarries, be patient, it will surely come true and not be delayed" (Hab 2:3b). This refers to those loyal ones, obedient to the Law, whose hands will not cease from loyal service even when the Last Days seems long to them, for all the times fixed by God will come about at their proper time as He ordained that they should by his inscrutable insight. (1QpHab 6:12–7:14)

The commentary on Habakkuk spelled out the community's understanding of prophetic Scripture and how it related to them.

We learn many things from this interesting "interpretation" of Habakkuk. The commentator begins this section by quot-

...ng from Habakkuk 2:1–2, which says in part, "Write down the vision plainly on tablets." The commentator took this as a command to write this specific commentary! This provides an important clue as to what motivated the men of Qumran to collect and write so many commentaries on prophecies, visions, and revelations (apocalypses). They believed their doing so was a direct fulfillment of prophecy.

The men of Qumran believed they were fulfilling prophecy by writing biblical commentaries.

Let's examine a few more phrases from this pesher on Habakkuk. In the phrase, "What is going to happen to the generation to come" (7:1–2), we see that the commentator understands Habakkuk's words to be fulfilled in the future. There was a basic futuristic outlook among the Essenes.

The phrase, "When that period would be complete He did not make known to him" (7:2), shows that the commentator believed God kept Habakkuk himself unaware of the time of fulfillment. As we shall see, however, the time of fulfillment was revealed to the Teacher of Righteousness, indicating his importance as God's messenger.

By the statement, "With ease someone can read it" (6:15–16 and 7:3, citing Hab 2:2), the commentator means that the "someone" who can read the vision "with ease" is none other than the Teacher of Righteousness (7:4).

The statement, "To whom God made known all the mysterious revelations of his servants the prophets" (7:4–5), indicates that the Teacher of Righteousness can understand the true meaning of Habakkuk's vision because God made it known to him. In effect, the commentator is claiming divinely inspired interpretation. The Teacher not only understands the meaning of Habakkuk's vision; he understands "all the mysterious revelations" of the prophets. Not surprisingly, the DSS also included pesharim on Isaiah, Hosea, Nahum, and other prophets.

By saying, "The Last Days will be long, much longer than the prophet said" (7:7), the commentator explained that the words of Habakkuk 2:3 imply that the last days are further in the future than Habakkuk himself had believed. This means the prophecy was not fulfilled hundreds of years ago in

Habakkuk's time but will instead be fulfilled in the time of the Teacher of Righteousness.

The Habakkuk commentary helps us understand the prophetic perspective and worldview of the men of Qumran. They believed the prophetic Scriptures spoke of their time, not some time in the past or some very distant future time. The men of the Renewed Covenant saw themselves as men of the last days, the days in which the prophecies would be fulfilled.

The Essenes believed the prophetic Scriptures spoke of their time, not some time in the past or some very distant future time.

Commentary on Habakkuk 2:7–8

"Yes, you yourself have plundered many nations, now the rest of the peoples will plunder you" (Hab 2:7–8a), refers to the later priests of Jerusalem, who will gather ill-gotten riches from the plunder of the peoples, but in the Last Days their riches and plunder alike will be handed over to the army of the Kittim, for they are "the rest of the peoples." "For the murder of a man and injustice in the land, the city and all who live in it" (Hab 2:8b). This refers to the Wicked Priest. Because of the crime he committed against the Teacher of Righteousness and the members of his party, God handed him over to his enemies, humiliating him with a consuming affliction with despair, because he had condemned his chosen. (1QpHab 9:3–12)

The author of the commentary on Habakkuk anticipated a future Roman attack in which Israel's corrupt priesthood would suffer judgment. Model of the Jerusalem temple. Photo of Second Temple Model: Daniel Ventura.

The commentator applies the prophecy to specific events and opponents of the Teacher of Righteousness. The "later priests of Jerusalem" have plundered the peoples, but "in the Last Days" their wealth will be seized by "the army of the Kittim," that is, the Roman legions. The commentator anticipated a future Roman attack in which Israel's corrupt priesthood would suffer judgment. The commentator then cited the first part of Habakkuk 2:8 and predicted that it would be fulfilled when the Wicked Priest, who had committed crimes against the Teacher of Righteousness, would be handed over to his enemies.

Summary

The commentary on Habakkuk makes crystal clear that the Qumran community believed themselves to be at the center of end-time fulfillments. Of special importance was their righteous Teacher, who was wronged by the Wicked Priest and would someday suffer at the hands of the Romans as well. Thus he is the continuation and culmination of Israel's ancient prophets.

> *The commentary on Habakkuk makes crystal clear that the Qumran community believed themselves to be at the center of end-time fulfillments.*

Notes

1. For a general survey of this topic, see M. Bernstein, "Interpretation of Scriptures," in L. H. Schiffman and J. C. VanderKam (eds.), *Encyclopedia of the Dead Sea Scrolls* (2 vols., Oxford: Oxford University Press, 2000), 1:376–83.

2. For more on this approach to Scripture in the Scrolls, see S. L. Berrin, "Pesharim," in Schiffman and VanderKam (eds.), *Encyclopedia of the Dead Sea Scrolls*, 2:644–47.

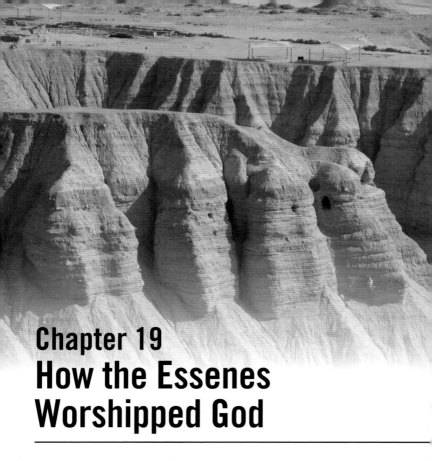

Chapter 19
How the Essenes Worshipped God

When Jerusalem's magnificent temple was destroyed by the Romans in AD 70, the sacrificial system came to an end. What were the faithful to do? Devotions must go on, and so righteous deeds took the place of sacrifice, and prayer replaced the smoke of incense. The rabbis began prescribing this soon after the temple's destruction. They had little or no choice since the centerpiece of their religion was gone. What is interesting to discover, however, is that the idea of temple-free worship was expressed by the Essenes in the Dead Sea Scrolls (DSS) two or three generations *before* the temple was destroyed.

> *The idea of temple-free worship was expressed by the Essenes in the Dead Sea Scrolls two or three generations before the temple was destroyed.*

The concept of worship without the temple helped prepare the way for expression of a key Christian belief developed in the book of Hebrews—that the temple was not necessary be-

...ause Jesus provided the final sacrifice, a sacrifice that does not ...eed to be repeated. Thus we have evidence for three basic po-...itions on the role of the temple in worship of God: (1) some ...ews saw no need for a temple since it had been destroyed; ...2) the Essenes saw no need for the temple even before it was ...destroyed because the priesthood of the temple had been cor-...upted; and (3) Christians said the temple was unnecessary be-...ause it had been superseded by the sacrificial death of Jesus. ...As you can see, these three rationales for temple-free worship ...re vastly different.

If the Essenes were es-...ranged from the temple ...n Jerusalem in the years ...before its destruction, and ...f they did not participate ...so far as we know) in the ...village synagogues, how ...did they worship? The ...DSS provide the answers. ...The Essenes emphasized ...worship of God through ...prayer, singing of praises, ...and even visiting God and ...he angels in heaven (or

The Essenes believed they could worship God wherever they found themselves, even in a wilderness far from the temple.

...he angels visiting the Essenes on earth).[1] In short, they be-...ieved they could worship God wherever they found them-...elves, even in a wilderness far from the temple.

Praise and War

...From Qumran we have scrolls called *Berakhot* ("Blessings") ...which extol God and other scrolls called *Barkhi Nafshi* ..."Bless, O my soul"), which bless God. In fact praise of God is ...ound almost everywhere in the DSS in one form or another.

Praise of God is found almost everywhere in the DSS in one form or another.

According to the Rule of the Community, a member of Qumran was to declare: "I praise God for His righteousness, the Most High for His glory. Blessed are you, O my God, who has opened to knowledge the mind of your servant" (1QS 11:15–16).

Throughout the *Hodayot*, or Hymn Scrolls, God is praised:

> "You bring forth . . . the utterances of breath in re-
> spect to their reckoning in order to make known Your
> glory and recount Your wonders in all Your works of
> truth and Your righteous judgments and to praise Your
> name." (1QH^a 9:31–32)

> "And for humanity, You have allotted an eternal des-
> tiny with the spirits of knowledge, to praise Your name
> together with shouts of joy, and to recount Your won-
> ders before all Your creatures." (1QH^a 11:23–24)

From statements such as these, we understand that the men
of Qumran believed the very purpose of humanity is to praise
God. Injunctions to praise God appear in some odd places too.
In the War Scroll we read:

> "When they return from battle they shall write on
> their banners, 'The Exaltation of God,' 'The Greatness
> of God,' 'The Praise of God,' 'The Glory of God,' with
> their names in full." (1QM 4:8)

> "When they return from battle they shall write on
> their banners, 'The Deliverance of God,' 'The Victory
> of God,' 'The Help of God,' 'The Support of God,' 'The
> Joy of God,' 'The Thanksgivings of God,' 'The Praise of
> God,' and 'The Peace of God.'" (1QM 4:13–14)

For the men of Qumran, the battle for the cause of truth, light, and righteousness was nothing less than holy war.

Imagine slogans such as these on the uniforms and standards of modern soldiers! For the men of Qumran, the battle for the cause of truth, light, and righteousness was nothing less than holy war. Thus in some sense the future battle would be an act of worship, and the men of Qumran planned to shout praises to God in the midst of the tumult.

Phylactery cases, small containers that held Scripture and were worn on the forehead, found at Qumran.

Life of Prayer

Prayer was also an important activity in the lives of the Essenes. Numerous DSS are devoted to the subject of prayer (e.g., 4Q291–293, 443–444, 449–457). Many prayers are for specific occasions. Let's review a few examples of these.

Festival Prayers: A few prayers are composed with festivals in mind (e.g., 4Q507–509). Here are brief excerpts from two of them, one concerned with the Day of Atonement (observed in September) and the other concerned with Day of First Fruits (observed the day after the Sabbath during Passover Week):

> Prayer for the Day of Atonement: Remember, Lord, the festival of Your mercies and the time of return . . . for You established it for us as a festival of fasting, an everlasting statute. (4Q508 frag. 2, lines 2–3)

> Prayer for the Day of First Fruits: Remember, O Lord, the festival of . . . and the freewill offerings of Your will which You commanded . . . we shall present before You the first fruits of our labors . . . upon the earth to be. (4Q509 frags. 131–32, column ii, lines 5–8)

The first prayer mentions the practice of fasting and refers to the Day of Atonement as a "festival of [God's] mercies and the time of return," where "return" probably refers to the return to the promised land after the exile. Because the traditional Jewish calendar does not match exactly with the modern Western calendar, the date of the Day of Atonement occurs on various dates in September and October. In 2008 the observance was held on October 8 beginning at sundown and extending to October 9 at sundown. In 2009 the date was September 27 to September 28. The Jewish people traditionally observe the day with fasting and prayer, usually spending much of the day in synagogue services.

The second prayer celebrates the offerings of the first fruits where the first of the crops to ripen are presented at the temple (the festival usually falling in late April). These crops traditionally were wheat, barley, figs, pomegranates, and dates.

Mealtime Prayer: One fragmentary scroll (sometimes called Grace after Meals) may contain a supper-time prayer. Here is some of it:

> [God] will renew the activity of heaven and earth and they will rejoice and His glory fills all the earth. . . . their . . . He will forgive and console them with abundant goodness . . . to eat its fruit and its goodness. Like one whose mother comforts him, so He will comfort them in Jerusalem as a bridegroom does his bride. His presence will rest upon it forever, for His throne will last forever and ever, and His glory. (4Q434a frag. 2, lines 2–7, with some restoration)

The Statute for Prayer: Here is a prayer the members of the Qumran community were to utter on various occasions. Notice the role music played:

> On the first of each month in its season, and on holy days laid down for a memorial, in their seasons by a prayer shall I bless Him—a statute forever engraved. When each new year begins and when its seasons turn, fulfilling the law of their decree, each day as set forth, day after day: harvest giving way to summer, planting to the shoots of spring, Seasons, years and weeks of years. When weeks of years begin, Jubilee by Jubilee, while I live, on my tongue shall the statute be en-

graved—with praise its fruit, even the gift of my lips. With knowledge shall I sing out my music, only for the glory of God, my harp, my lyre for His holiness established; the flute of my lips will I lift, His law its tuning fork. (1QS 10:5–9)

> *"With knowledge shall I sing out my music, only for the glory of God," says the supplicant in one of the prayer scrolls at Qumran.*

Prayer to Begin a New Day: This prayer was to be said at the beginning of every day:

> When the sun rises out of the firmament of heaven, they shall offer praise. They shall respond, "Blessed is the God of Israel, who has . . . This day You have renewed . . . in fourteen gates of light . . . for us the dominion of light . . . ten flags of . . . the heat of the sun . . . when the sun passes over . . . by the might of Your powerful hand . . . Peace be upon you, O Israel." On the fifteenth of the month, in the evening, they shall offer praise. They shall say, "Blessed is the Go[d of Israel], who conceals . . . before Him in every division of His glory." (4Q503 frags. 1–6, column iii, lines 1–7, with some restoration)

Psalms, Hymns, and Songs

The men of Qumran also believed praises should be sung to God. Some of these are dedicated to special days and festivals. One interesting collection represents songs for the Sabbath sacrifice (4Q400–407, 11Q17, Mas1k). Here are excerpts from two of them:

> A text belonging to the Instructor. The song accompanying the sacrifice on the fourth Sabbath, sung on the twenty-fifth of the first month. Praise the God of . . . who stand before . . . the kingdom of . . . with all the chiefs of . . . the King of the gods . . . . (4Q401 frags. 1–2, lines 1–5)

A song of musical praise will be spoken in the language of the seventh chief prince, a powerful musical praise to the God of holiness incorporating his language's seven wonderful praise elements. Then he will sing praise to the King of holiness seven times with seven wondrous words of musical praise, together with seven psalms of blessing to Him, seven psalms of exaltation of His righteousness, seven psalms of glorification of His kingdom, seven psalms of praise of His glory, seven psalms of thanksgiving for His wondrous doings. (4Q404 frag. 1, lines 1–3, with restorations)

One of the intriguing features of the Songs of the Sabbath Sacrifice is the frequent reference to God's kingdom and to God as King, for these are themes which Jesus would later emphasize in his ministry.

One of the intriguing features of the Songs of the Sabbath Sacrifice is the frequent reference to God's kingdom and to God as King.

The scrolls also include several noncanonical psalms. Although these psalms introduce new elements, some reflecting specific concerns of the Qumran community, they are heavily indebted to the psalms of the OT.[2] One sounds forth this way:

I have declared, and of his marvels I will speak. And Wisdom will teach me what is right . . . my mouth, and to the simple, so that they will understand, and to the ignorant, that they may gain knowledge. O Lord, how great . . . miracles are, in the day He made heaven and earth, and by the word of His mouth. . . . He perfected the watercourses, its lakes and pools, and every body of water . . . night, and the stars, and constellations . . . trees, and every fruit of the vineyard, and all the produce of the field, and by the utterance of His words. (4Q381 frag. 1, lines 1–6)

Heavenly Worship

Perhaps the most intriguing feature of worship in the Qumran community is the belief that worshippers could enter heaven and that heaven or its representatives were present on earth during worship. The emphasis on heaven's presence motivated rules excluding people with defects and impurities from participating in liturgical activities. The law of

The Essene emphasis on heaven's presence motivated rules excluding people with defects and impurities from participating in liturgical activities.

the Essenes states that "none of these shall enter the congregation, for the holy angels are in your midst" (CD 15:17). Indeed, only the pure "may enter to take a place in the congregation of the men of reputation. For the holy angels are a part of their congregation" (1QSa 2:8–9).

This rule even applied to the anticipated holy war, when the Sons of Light would engage the Sons of Darkness in battle. A person who is impure or has a defect "on the day of battle shall not go down with them into battle, for holy angels are present with their army" (1QM 7:6).

Not only were angels thought to be present during worship and other sacred functions; pure worshippers could seemingly be caught up into heaven.

Not only were angels thought to be present during worship and other sacred functions; pure worshippers could seemingly be caught up into heaven. For instance, the author of one hymn, from the *Hodayot* (a.k.a. Thanksgiving Hymns), thanks God by saying:

> I give thanks to You, O Lord, for You have redeemed my soul from the pit. From Sheol and Abaddon You have raised me up to an eternal height, so that I might walk about on a limitless plain, and know that there is hope for him whom You created from the dust for the eternal council. (1QH^a 11:20–21)

We find similar expressions in the Rule of the Community, the document that lays down the rules and regulations for life in the community of the Essenes:

> To them He has chosen all these has He given—an eternal possession. He has made them heirs in the legacy of the Holy Ones; with the angels has He united their assembly, a Community Council. They are an assembly built up for holiness, an eternal Planting for all ages to come. (1QS 11:7–9)

Are these statements to be taken literally? Were the pure and the righteous actually "raised up to an eternal height," to "walk about on a limitless plain"? Has the earthbound assembly of the righteous Essenes been united "with the angels"? The next passage apparently does envision such a thing:

> . . . a mighty throne in the congregation of the angels. None of the ancient kings shall sit on it, and their nobles shall not. . . . There are none comparable to me in my glory, no one shall be exalted besides me; none shall come against me. For I have dwelt on high . . . in the heavens, and there is no one. . . . I am reckoned with the angels and my abode is in the holy congregation. My desire is not according to the flesh . . . everything precious to me is in the glory of the holy habitation. Who has been considered contemptible like me? Who is comparable to me in my glory? Who of those who sail the seas shall return telling of my equal? Who has borne troubles like me? And who like me has refrained from evil? I have never been taught, but no teaching compares with my teaching. Who then shall

assault me when I open my mouth? Who can endure the utterance of my lips? Who shall challenge me and compare with my judgment? . . . For I am reckoned with the angels, and my glory with that of the sons of the King. Neither pure gold, nor the renowned gold of Ophir. (4Q491 frag. 11, column i, lines 12–18, with some restoration)

When first published, some scholars believed that this text portrayed an angel speaking. After all, what man could make his abode in heaven, "reckoned with angels"? But other scholars objected. Why would an angel, whose home is heaven, boast of being in heaven, serving "in the holy congregation"? Isn't this what all angels do by right of who they are? These scholars suggested that the speaker is indeed a human, a member of the Qumran community who in a mystical state had experienced "soul ascent." He entered heaven, participated with the angels in their wor-

Some Essenes appear to have had mystical experiences where they claimed to have entered heaven and participated with the angels in their worship of God.

ship of God, and saw and heard things that mortals on earth are never permitted. His worship took him into heaven itself. This is why he can exult and say, "I am reckoned with the angels" and "my glory [is reckoned] with that of the sons of the King." ("Sons of the King" is another way of referring to the angels.) Thus the rhetorical question, "Who is comparable to me in my glory?" and "Who shall challenge me and compare with my judgment?" Because of what he has seen and heard in heaven, no one on earth (not even the priests in Jerusalem, who are corrupt) can challenge him.[3] When others speak of heaven, they rely on conjecture. Not this worshipper! He claims to speak from experience.

Notes

1. For learned discussion of the topic of worship at Qumran, see G. A. Anderson, "Worship, Qumran Sect," in L. H. Schiffman and J. C. VanderKam (eds.), *Encyclopedia of the Dead Sea Scrolls* (2 vols., Oxford: Oxford University Press, 2000), 2:991–96; E. Schuller, "Worship, Temple, and Prayer in the Dead Sea Scrolls," in A. J. Avery-Peck, J. Neusner, and B. D. Chilton (eds.), *Judaism in Late Antiquity. Part Five: The Judaism of Qumran: A Systemic Reading of the Dead Sea Scrolls. Volume One: Theory of Israel* (Leiden: Brill, 2001), 125–43.

2. For more on the psalms and hymns of Qumran, see E. Chazon, "Psalms, Hymns, and Prayers," in Schiffman and VanderKam (eds.), *Encyclopedia of the Dead Sea Scrolls*, 2:710–15; M. Weinfeld, "Prayer and Liturgical Practice in the Qumran Sect," in D. Dimant and U. Rappaport (eds.), *The Dead Sea Scrolls: Forty Years of Research* (Leiden: Brill, 1992), 241–58.

3. C. A. Newsom, "Mysticism," in Schiffman and VanderKam (eds.), *Encyclopedia of the Dead Sea Scrolls*, 1:591–94.

Model of the Second Temple
Photo: Ariely.

Chapter 20
How the Essenes Related to the Priests of Jerusalem

How did the Essenes relate to the priests of Jerusalem? In short, *not well*. The disparaging epithet "Wicked Priest" has already been mentioned. Originally it referred to one of the Hasmonean high priests in the second century BC, shortly after the Jews successfully repelled the Greek Syrians and gained freedom for Israel. In time the nasty nickname probably came to refer to other high priests.

There is evidence in the Dead Sea Scrolls (DSS) of general disapproval of the worship and the sacrificial system in Jerusalem. Disputes over the calendar (when festivals and days of sacrifice should take place),[1] purity laws, ethics, and behavior drove a deep wedge between the priests of Jerusalem and the priests of the Qumran community. The Essenes

> *There is evidence in the Dead Sea Scrolls of general disapproval of the worship and the sacrificial system in Jerusalem.*

lost out in the struggle with the Jerusalem priesthood, and so they withdrew from Jerusalem and the temple establishment in order to create a purist community in the desert.

Corrupt Jerusalem Priesthood

Three of the commentaries (pesharim) on the Prophets found among the DSS disparage the Jerusalem priesthood. For instance, the commentary on Habakkuk says:

> "Yes, you yourself have plundered many nations, now the rest of the peoples will plunder you" (Hab 2:7–8a), refers to the later priests of Jerusalem, who will gather ill-gotten riches from the plunder of the peoples. (1QpHab 9:3–5)

One relevant line, with some restoration, can just be made out in the Micah commentary:

> . . . the priests of Jerusalem which went astray. (1Qp-Mic frag. 11, line 1)

The Essenes lost out in the struggle with the Jerusalem priesthood, and so they withdrew into the wilderness to form a purist community.
Photo: Ariely.

This brief snatch of text summarizes the Essene assessment of the authorized priesthood in Jerusalem. Two scathing references to the Jerusalem priests are also found in the commentary on Nahum:

> I will burn with smoke your horde, the sword will con-

sume your lions, and I will annihilate its prey from the land. Your messengers' voice shall no longer be heard" (Nah 2:13b). The meaning of the passage: "your horde" are the troops of his army which are in Jerusalem; "its lions" are his nobles . . . "its prey" is the wealth that the priests of Jerusalem gathered. (4QpNah frag. 3–4, column i, lines 9–11)

"All because of the harlot's many fornications. Beautiful is she, a witch indeed, who acquires peoples through fornication, whole clans through sorcery" (Nah 3:4). This refers to the deceivers from Ephraim, who through their deceptive teaching, lying talk, and dishonest speech deceive many: kings, princes, priests, native and foreigner alike. (4QpNah frag. 3–4, column ii, lines 7–9)

Qumran's criticism of the Jerusalem priesthood is severe and uncompromising. Those who were called to be spiritual guides instead led Israel astray. Thus the day of judgment was coming for the false priesthood.[2]

Qumran's criticism of the Jerusalem priesthood is severe and uncompromising.

Since they were estranged from the sacrificial system of the Jerusalem temple, it is not surprising to hear the Essenes say that a wicked man's hope for purification cannot be fulfilled outside their righteous community:

He lacks the strength to repent. He is not to be reckoned among the upright. His knowledge, strength and wealth are not to enter the society of the Community. Surely, he plows in the muck of wickedness, so defiling stains would mar his repentance. Yet he cannot be justified by what his willful heart declares lawful, preferring to gaze on darkness rather than the ways of light. With such an eye he cannot be reckoned faultless. Ceremonies of atonement cannot restore his innocence, neither cultic waters his purity. He cannot be sanctified by baptism in oceans and rivers, nor purified

> by mere ritual bathing. Unclean, unclean shall he be
> all the days that he rejects the laws of God, refusing to
> be disciplined in the Community of His society. (1QS
> 3:1–6a)

The wicked man, unwilling to repent and embrace the teaching of the Qumran community, cannot be restored through any priestly ritual, most certainly not one performed in Jerusalem. Indeed, even if an ocean of "cultic waters" were poured over him, he would remain impure since purity cannot be obtained outside of the faithful community of Essenes.

Priestly Service Apart from the Temple

Since they had separated from the "corrupt" priesthood of Jerusalem and thus forfeited access to the temple, the men of Qumran had to offer *symbolic* sacrifices and incense. These acts required true, heartfelt repentance, prayer, sincere praise, and songs of thanksgiving. Though they could not offer the traditional temple-based sacrifices, these are the men who are at peace, truly reconciled with the God of Israel.

Since they had separated from the "corrupt" priesthood of Jerusalem and thus forfeited access to the temple, the men of Qumran had to offer symbolic sacrifices and incense.

Seeing themselves as the lone practitioners of true religion, the Essenes spelled out the practice of acceptable religion in the Rule of the Community, the constitution of the Qumran establishment:

> For only through the spirit pervading God's true society can there be atonement for a person's ways, all of his iniquities; thus only can he gaze upon the light of life and so be joined to His truth by His holy spirit, purified from all iniquity. Through an upright and humble attitude his sin may be covered, and by humbling himself before all God's laws his flesh can be made clean. Only thus can he really receive the purifying

waters and be purged by the cleansing flow. Let him order his steps to walk faultless in all the ways of God, just as He commanded for the times appointed to him. Let him turn aside neither to the right nor the left, nor yet deviate in the smallest detail from all of His words. Then indeed will he be accepted by God, offering the sweet savor of atoning sacrifice, and then only shall he be a party to the Covenant of the eternal Community. (1QS 3:6b–11)

The Community Rule Scroll was the constitution for the Qumran community.

They will be "the tested wall, the precious cornerstone" (Isa 28:16) whose foundations shall neither be shaken nor swayed, a fortress, a Holy of Holies for Aaron, all of them knowing the Covenant of Justice and thereby offering a sweet savor. They shall be a blameless and true house in Israel, upholding the covenant of eternal statutes. They shall be an acceptable sacrifice, atoning for the land and ringing in the verdict against evil, so that perversity ceases to exist. (1QS 8:7b–10)

When, united by all these precepts, such men as these come to be a community in Israel, they shall establish eternal truth guided by the instruction of His holy spirit. They shall atone for the guilt of transgression and the rebellion of sin, becoming an acceptable sacrifice for the land through the flesh of burnt offerings, the fat of sacrificial portions and prayer, becoming—as it were—justice itself, a sweet savor of righteousness and blameless behavior, a pleasing free-will offering. At that time the men of the Community shall withdraw, the holy house of Aaron uniting as a Holy of Holies, and the synagogue of Israel as those who walk blamelessly. (1QS 9:3–6)

Recognizing that the mere "mechanics" of religion and ritual cannot make atonement, the men of Qumran saw themselves as forming a society centered on true righteousness and faithfulness. Through purification by God's Holy Spirit and by obedience to God's law, a member of their community would "be accepted by God, offering the sweet savor of atoning sacrifice" (3:11). This atoning sacrifice came through obedience rather than the offering of an animal in Jerusalem. The men of the Qumran community "shall atone for the guilt of transgression and the rebellion of sin, becoming an acceptable sacrifice for the land" (9:4), whose prayer becomes "justice itself, a sweet savor of righteousness" and whose "blameless behavior" becomes "a pleasing free-will offering" (9:5).[3]

The Qumran community, "uniting as a Holy of Holies, and the synagogue of Israel as those who walk blamelessly," believed they had lost nothing by withdrawing from Jerusalem (9:6).

> *The Qumran community believed they had lost nothing by withdrawing from Jerusalem.*

Sure, some traditional rituals were no longer possible since they no longer accessed the temple, but the Essenes were confident they could offer up spiritual sacrifices and the sweet aroma of incense by being obedient. As mentioned in the previous chapter, they also believed they could ascend into the heavenly sanctuary itself and worship God in the presence of the angels. With these privileges in hand, who needed Jerusalem and its corrupted temple priests?

Notes

1. On this controversial matter, see S. Talmon, "Calendars and Mishmarot," in L. H. Schiffman and J. C. VanderKam (eds.), *Encyclopedia of the Dead Sea Scrolls* (2 vols., Oxford: Oxford University Press, 2000), 1:108–17.

2. For more on Qumran's view of the priests, see R. A. Kugler, "Priests," in Schiffman and VanderKam (eds.), *Encyclopedia of the Dead Sea Scrolls*, 2:688–93; T. H. Lim, "Wicked Priest," in Schiffman and VanderKam (eds.), *Encyclopedia of the Dead Sea Scrolls*, 2:973–76.

3. J. Milgrom, "Sacrifice," in Schiffman and VanderKam (eds.), *Encyclopedia of the Dead Sea Scrolls*, 2:807–12; J. Maier, "Temple," in Schiffman and VanderKam (eds.), *Encyclopedia of the Dead Sea Scrolls*, 2:921–27.

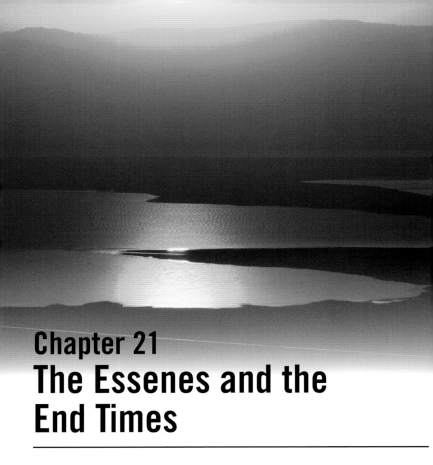

Chapter 21
The Essenes and the End Times

The Dead Sea Scrolls (DSS) provide a broad outline of eschatological (end times) expectations among the Essenes. They expected their beliefs and practices to be vindicated in the not too distant future even as false priests would fall under judgment. They expected the Messiah of Israel, by which they meant the Branch of David, the messianic king, to appear. Messiah and the anointed high priest would take the reins of power, purging the wicked of Israel and annihilating the Romans. It is less clear whether the Qumran community anticipated that its members would be raised from the dead.

We will not be able to tie up all the loose ends in this chapter, but we shall see that while some of the eschatological expectations outlined in the DSS were unique to the

While some of the eschatological expectations outlined in the DSS were unique to the Qumran community, many of them were in line with what average Jews anticipated in that era.

Qumran community, many of them were in line with what average Jews anticipated in that era.[1]

The Coming of the Messiahs of Aaron and Israel

What did the men of Qumran believe about Messiah? Surprising from the Christian vantage point is the mention of the rise of "Messiah of Aaron and of Israel." Usually "Messiah" is in the singular. However, when modified by two nouns, such as we have here, it is understood as plural. Elsewhere in the DSS it is even clearer that Messiah is plural (e.g., "Messiahs of Aaron and of Israel," in 1QS 9:11).

The Messiah of Aaron is the high priest. Many times in the OT the high priest is said to be "anointed," which is what "Messiah" means. For instance, Moses' brother Aaron was Israel's first high priest and was anointed (Exod 28:41). Aaron's successor, to be selected among Aaron's sons, was to be anointed (Lev 6:22).

According to the Damascus Document the era of wickedness would continue "until arise the Messiah of Aaron and of Israel" (CD 12:23–24; 14:19). The righteous "will escape in the time of punishment, but all the rest will be handed over to the sword when the Messiah of Aaron and of Israel come" (CD 19:10–11).

The Damascus Document said the era of wickedness would end "when the Messiah of Aaron and of Israel come."

The Rule of the Community espouses a similar view, declaring that the faithful men of their community would continue in study and obedience "until there come the Prophet and the Messiahs of Aaron and Israel" (1QS 9:10–11). According to the Rule of the Congregation, the Messiah would sit at the banquet table with the great ones of the community (1QSa 2:11–21).

According to a commentary on selected passages from Genesis the Messiah would come in fulfillment of Jacob's blessing on his son Judah (Gen 49:8–12):

A ruler shall not depart from the tribe of Judah while Israel has dominion. And the one who sits on the throne of David shall never be cut off, because the "ruler's staff" is the covenant of the kingdom, and the thousands of Israel are "the standards," until the Righteous Messiah, the Branch of David, has come (Gen 49:10). For to him and to his seed the covenant of the kingdom of His people has been given for the eternal generations, because he has kept . . . Interpreter of the Law with the men of the Community. (4Q252 5:1–5, with some restoration)

One of the commentaries on Isaiah explains how the coming Messiah would fulfill the prophecy of Isaiah 11:

"A rod will grow from Jesse's stock, a sprout will bloom from his roots; upon him will rest the spirit of the Lord: a spirit of wisdom and insight, a spirit of good counsel and strength, a spirit of true knowledge and reverence for the Lord, he will delight in reverence for the Lord. He will not judge only by what his eyes see, he will not decide only by what his ears hear; but he will rule the weak by justice, and give decisions in integrity to the humble of the land. He will punish the land with the mace of his words, by his lips' breath alone he will slay the wicked. 'Justice' will be the sash around his waist, 'Truth' the sash around his hips" (Isa 11:1–5). This saying refers to the Branch of David, who will appear in the last days . . . his enemies; and God will support him with a spirit of strength . . . and God will give him a glorious throne, a sacred crown, and elegant garments. . . . He will put a scepter in his hand, and he will rule over all the Gentiles, even Magog and his army . . . all the peoples his sword will control. (4Q161 frags. 8–10, lines 11–21, with restorations)

Messiah is called "Branch of David" because he was to spring from David's line. His coming would be in fulfillment of Isaiah 11. God would give him the royal scepter, a glorious throne, a sacred crown, and elegant garments. He would rule over all the Gentiles, even the much feared Magog (Ezek 38:2; Rev 20:8).[2]

> *Messiah is called "Branch of David" because he was to spring from David's line.*

The Final War

The Messiah would lead Israel in her final eschatological war, which in the War Scroll (1QM) is described as the War of the Sons of Light against the Sons of the Darkness. The action taken by the Messiah is not described in the War Scroll, thanks in all probability to the poor condition of the end of the scroll. However, a legible portion does say that the Messiah's name will appear on battle implements (e.g., 1QM 3:16; 5:1). And we know from a related document, called the Rule of War (4Q285), that the Essenes did indeed expect Messiah to be involved in the final battle.

The War Scroll prescribes a remarkably elaborate set of requirements and preparations for the great eschatological battle. Participants are to be properly dressed, ritually pure, and free of defects:

> No one crippled, blind or lame, nor a man who has a permanent blemish on his skin, or a man affected with ritual uncleanness of his flesh; none of these shall go with them to battle. All of them shall be volunteers for battle, pure of spirit and flesh, and prepared for the day of vengeance. (1QM 7:4–5)

This is holy war in the extreme. The warriors are to be prepared for battle as though they were priests preparing to conduct a temple sacrifice. The slaughter of the Romans (the Kittim) was seen as sacred duty:

The blowing of rams' horns signaled the attack on the Kittim, according to the War Scroll.

When the infantry has approached the battle line of the Kittim, within throwing range, each man shall raise his hand with his weapon. Then the priests shall blow on the trumpets of the slain and the Levites and the all the people with rams' horns shall sound a signal for battle. The infantry shall attack the army of the Kittim, and as the sound of the signal goes forth, they shall begin to bring down their slain. Then all the people shall still the sound of the signal, while the priests continuously blow on the trumpets of the slain, and the battle prevails against the Kittim, and the troops of Belial are defeated before them. (1QM 17:11–15)

At that time the priests shall sound a signal on the six trumpets of remembrance, and all the battle formations shall be gathered to them and divide against all the camps of the Kittim to completely destroy them. (1QM 18:3–5)

The Romans are equated with the "troops of Belial," that is, the troops of Satan. They will be defeated and their camps plundered.[3]

The Slaying of the Roman Emperor

When the unpublished scroll fragments from Cave 4 began to pour forth in the early 1990s, one that caught everyone's attention was 4Q285. A couple of scholars pounced on the text, claiming that it spoke of a "wounded" or "pierced Messiah." This interpretation, as it turned out, was quite mistaken. It failed to handle the Hebrew properly or take full account of the context. Although this misguided interpretation is now a thing of the past,[4] scholars still remain keenly interested in this fragmentary scroll. Here is a fragment that has especially received attention:

> Just as it is written in the book of Isaiah the prophet, "And the thickets of the forest shall be cut down with an ax, and Lebanon with its majestic trees will fall. A shoot shall come out from the stump of Jesse and a branch shall grow out of his roots" (Isa 10:34–11:1). This is the Branch of David. Then all forces of Belial shall be judged, and the king of the Kittim shall stand for judgment and the Prince of the congregation—the Branch of David—will have him put to death. Then all Israel shall come out with timbrels and dancers, and the high priest shall order them to cleanse their bodies from the guilty blood of the corpses of the Kittim. (4Q285 frag. 7, lines 1–6, with restoration)

Here again we have an interpretation of Isaiah 11, though beginning with the last verse of Isaiah 10, which speaks of the cutting down of the trees of Lebanon. For the Rule of War Scroll, this cutting down refers to the defeat of the Roman army. The "shoot" that grows up from the "stump of Jesse" refers to the Davidic Messiah, the "Branch of David." The Branch of David will kill the "king of the Kittim," that is, the Roman emperor.

The Branch of David will kill the "king of the Kittim," that is, the Roman emperor.

The scroll presents Israel's Messiah as none other than the "Prince of the congregation," that is, the leader of the Qumran community. When God raises up the Messiah of Israel, he would naturally ally himself to the Essenes, who are the faithful of Israel.[5] Also important to note is that the priests are concerned to cleanse the land of Israel from the defilement of the corpses of the slain Romans.

Christian Scripture teaches that the dead will be resurrected at the end of time. Do the Dead Sea Scrolls teach the same thing?

Did the Qumran Community Anticipate the Resurrection of the Dead?

Do the DSS speak of the resurrection of the dead? The fact that I raise the question suggests that the answer is not obvious. There is only one scroll that clearly mentions the resurrection, and not all scholars think it was produced by the Essenes themselves. Here is the key passage:

> For the heavens and the earth shall listen to His Messiah and all which is in them shall not turn away from the commandments of the holy ones. Strengthen yourselves, O you who seek the Lord, in His service. Will you not find the Lord in this, all those who hope in their heart? For the Lord attends to the pious and calls the righteous by name. Over the humble His spirit hovers, and He renews the faithful in His strength. For He will honor the pious upon the throne of His eternal kingdom, setting prisoners free (Ps 146:7; Isa

61:1), opening the eyes of the blind, raising up those who are bowed down (Ps 146:8; Isa 35:5). And forever I shall hold fast to those who hope and in His faithfulness shall . . . and the fruit of good deeds shall not be delayed for anyone and the Lord shall do glorious things which have not been done, just as He said. For He shall heal the critically wounded, He shall revive the dead (Isa 26:19), He shall send good news to the afflicted (Isa 61:1), He shall satisfy the poor, He shall guide the uprooted, He shall make the hungry rich. (4Q521 frag. 2, column ii, lines 1–13)

This remarkable passage will receive attention in a later chapter. For now it is sufficient to call attention to line 12, where the Messiah (or God—the subject of the verbs in these lines is not clear) will "heal the critically wounded" and "revive" (lit. "make alive") the "dead." Is this text speaking of the general resurrection that takes place on the day of judgment? It is not clear. In my opinion, what we have in 4Q521 is the healing and raising up (as Elijah and Elisha of old did) of those wounded and killed in battle against the Romans. Such acts reverse the horrors of the Roman era. The prisoners are set free, the blind regain their sight, and those wounded and killed in the great battle are restored to health and life.

If 4Q521 does not speak of a general eschatological resurrection, do other scrolls? Two copies of a text scholars call "Pseudo-Ezekiel" (4Q385 and 4Q386) might. They allude to Ezekiel's vision of the dry bones, but the scrolls are fragmentary, and it is difficult to be sure what is really being described. Also, these scrolls may not actually reflect Essene thought.

Others point out that the collectors of the scrolls at Qumran seemed very fond of the book of Daniel, which explicitly teaches the resurrection (Dan 12:2). From this some infer that the Essenes must have believed in the resurrection.[6]

Essene collectors of the scrolls at Qumran seemed very fond of the book of Daniel, which explicitly teaches the resurrection (Dan 12:2).

Notes

1. For more on the eschatology of Qumran and the Jewish people in the first century, see L. H. Schiffman, *The Eschatological Community of the Dead Sea Scrolls* (Society of Biblical Literature Monograph Series 38; Atlanta: Scholars Press, 1989); J. J. Collins, "Eschatology," in L. H. Schiffman and J. C. VanderKam (eds.), *Encyclopedia of the Dead Sea Scrolls* (2 vols., Oxford: Oxford University Press, 2000), 1:256–61.

2. For more on this topic, see J. J. Collins, *The Scepter and the Star: The Messiahs of the Dead Sea Scrolls and Other Ancient Literature* (Anchor Bible Reference Library 10; New York: Doubleday, 1995); C. A. Evans, "Messiahs," in Schiffman and VanderKam (eds.), *Encyclopedia of the Dead Sea Scrolls*, 1:537–42.

3. For further discussion, see P. R. Davies, "War of the Sons of Light Against the Sons of Darkness," in Schiffman and VanderKam (eds.), *Encyclopedia of the Dead Sea Scrolls*, 2:965–68.

4. For a learned study of this aspect of 4Q285, see M. G. Abegg, "Messianic Hope and 4Q285: A Reassessment," *Journal of Biblical Literature* 113 (1994), 81–91.

5. See C. A. Evans, "Prince of the Congregation," in Schiffman and VanderKam (eds.), *Encyclopedia of the Dead Sea Scrolls*, 2:693–94.

6. For more on resurrection ideas at Qumran and in Judaism and early Christianity, see G. W. E. Nickelsburg, "Resurrection," in Schiffman and VanderKam (eds.), *Encyclopedia of the Dead Sea Scrolls*, 2:764–67.

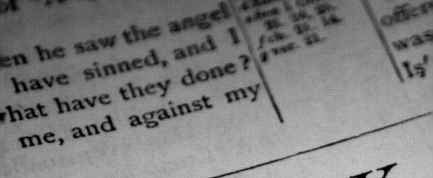

en he saw the angel
have sinned, and I
what have they done?
me, and against my

FIRST BOOK

COMMONLY

BOOK

Part VII

The Scrolls and the Old Testament

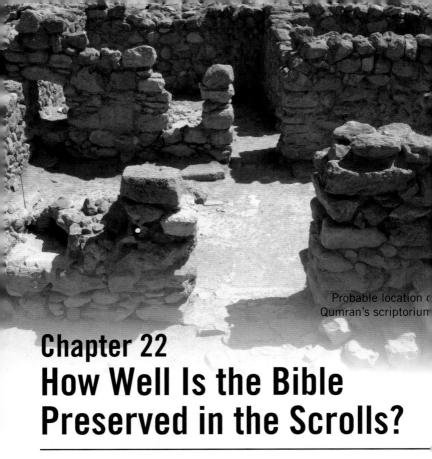
Probable location of Qumran's scriptorium

Chapter 22
How Well Is the Bible Preserved in the Scrolls?

One of the questions that held the public's attention as the first Dead Sea Scrolls (DSS) were published was whether the OT books represented among them would match the OT as we have it in our modern Bibles. Would the Bible scrolls among the DSS show evidence that the Hebrew manuscripts that have come down to us, and which serve as the basis for our translations, had been significantly altered over the centuries?

Prior to the discovery of the DSS, the oldest complete Hebrew Bible (called the OT by Christians) was the Leningrad Codex, which dates to AD 1008. Another old manuscript contains large portions of the OT. Called the Aleppo Codex, it dates to about AD 900. Ancient Greek translations of the OT have also survived. Almost all of the OT is found in the great Greek codices called Vaticanus and Sinaiticus, which date to the fourth century AD. Smaller portions of the

Prior to the discovery of the DSS the oldest complete Hebrew Bible was the Leningrad Codex, which dates to AD 1008.

Greek version of the OT survive in even older forms among Egyptian papyri dating to the first, second, and third centuries AD, with a few examples dating to the first or second century BC. It seems odd, but our oldest copies of the OT were Greek translations, not the original Hebrew. This left us uncertain of how well the original had been preserved.

Until the discovery of the DSS, the oldest portion of the OT in Hebrew was the Nash Papyrus, acquired in Egypt in 1898 by W. L. Nash and given to Cambridge University Library. The papyrus dates to between 150 and 100 BC. It contains the Ten Commandments and the beginning of the famous Shema ("Listen, Israel") of Deuteronomy 6:4–5. This is not much text, so it is easy to see why scholars were excited about the Scripture scrolls from the Dead Sea, for they date back to the first and second centuries BC and represent a large amount of the Hebrew OT.

Until the discovery of the DSS, the oldest portion of the OT in Hebrew was the Nash Papyrus, acquired in Egypt in 1898 by W. L. Nash and given to the Cambridge University Library.

When photographs of the Great Isaiah Scroll were published, Hebrew scholars compared the text of this ancient scroll to the Masoretic Text (MT). The Masoretes (seventh to eleventh centuries AD) were scribes who copied the Hebrew manuscripts and supplied marks indicating how the words should be pronounced. As a result of their work a standard version of the Hebrew Bible was produced. Since then the MT has been used in Jewish synagogues around the world; it has also served as the basis for most translations of the OT since the time of the King James Version. It was always said that the Masoretes had taken great care to preserve their manuscripts

The Great Isaiah Scroll is evidence of the care with which ancient and medieval scribes copied and transmitted Scripture.

from error, but here finally was proof. Examination revealed that the Hebrew text of Isaiah represented in the Great Isaiah Scroll was essentially the same as Isaiah of the MT. There were some spelling differences, a few scribal errors, and variant readings; but on the whole it was the same Hebrew text! The Great Isaiah Scroll is evidence of the care with which ancient and medieval scribes copied and transmitted Scripture.

Interestingly, Scripture scrolls discovered at Qumran represented not only a pre- or proto-Masoretic form of the Hebrew text but also a slightly different form that agreed with the Greek translation called the Septuagint (abbreviated LXX). Scholars also discovered a version of the Pentateuch that agreed with the Samaritan version, plus another that apparently does not agree with the other three versions. Thus, the Scripture scrolls at Qumran attest four versions of the Hebrew text of the OT:

1. the proto-Masoretic Text
2. a version that underlies the LXX
3. a version that agrees with the Samaritan Pentateuch (SP)
4. a fourth, independent version.[1]

This diversity surprised scholars. It seems that several versions of the Hebrew Bible were available at the beginning of the first century, plus different versions of the Greek translation as well. The men of Qumran clearly placed high value on Scripture. Among the 900 or so scrolls discovered there were more than 200 copies of Scripture. Judging by the number of scrolls representing them, the favorites were the books of Moses (especially Deuteronomy), the prophets (especially Isaiah), and the writings (especially Psalms).

Several versions of the Hebrew Bible were available at the beginning of the first century.

Number of Scripture Scrolls: The Law

Genesis	20
Exodus	18
Leviticus	16
Numbers	11
Deuteronomy	30

Number of Scripture Scrolls: The Former Prophets

Joshua	2
Judges	3
Samuel	4
Kings	3

Number of Scripture Scrolls: The Latter Prophets

Isaiah	21
Jeremiah	6
Ezekiel	10

Number of Scripture Scrolls: The Writings

Psalms	40
Proverbs	2
Job	4
Song of Songs	4
Ruth	4
Lamentations	4
Ecclesiastes	2
Esther	no scroll
Daniel	8
Ezra-Nehemiah	1
Chronicles	1

These Scripture scrolls have been collated and made into *The Dead Sea Scrolls Bible*,[2] which makes it convenient to find out how much of the Bible has survived among the many scrolls found in the Dead Sea region and to find out where the Scripture scrolls read differently from the MT. Let's look at a few examples of the differences.

Studies on the Variant Readings

The Scripture scrolls have helped clear up a few mysteries. In three cases they supply us with missing verses (as will be explained below); in other places they help settle controversial readings. Let's take a look.

Missing Verses in Samuel 11: Anyone who reads 1 Samuel 11 is struck by the ruthlessness of Nahash, king of the Ammonites. When he besieged Jabesh-Gilead, the besieged citizens called for a truce, offering to make a treaty. Nahash agreed but stipulated that each person had to allow his right eye to be gouged out.

When Jewish historian Josephus told the story, he provided extra details that help the reader understand that Nahash regularly required eye-gouging of subjugated peoples. Was Josephus just trying to make sense of the story by creating a context, or did his Bible have a few verses that our Bible doesn't have? When the Samuel Scroll from Cave 4 at Qumran was read, we discovered that indeed the version of the Bible available to Josephus had a couple verses which ours lack. It seems that the equivalent of two or three verses from the beginning of chapter 11 somehow went missing in the text tradition we've inherited. As it turns out, Nahash was regularly ruthless. His eye-gouging policy was his customary way of oppressing his foreign subjects. By gouging out the right eye, he made it difficult for his potential enemies to make war against him. When men fled and took refuge in Jabesh-gilead, Nahash agreed to a treaty, but his original policy was still in force. Compare the two columns below from the RSV and the NRSV translation of the Samuel Scroll. What Qumran's Samuel Scroll adds is in bold.

1 Sam 10:27–11:1

RSV	4QSamuel^a NRSV
10:27 But some worthless fellows said, "How can this man save us?" And they despised him, and brought him no present. But he held his peace.	10:27 But some worthless fellows said, "How can this man save us?" And they despised him and brought him no present. But he held his peace.
	Now Nahash, king of the Ammonites, had been grievously oppressing the Gadites and the Reubenites. He would gouge out the right eye of each of them and would not grant Israel a deliverer. No one was left of the Israelites across the Jordan whose right eye Nahash, king of the Ammonites, had not gouged out. But there were seven thousand men who had escaped from the Ammonites and had entered Jabesh-gilead.
11:1 Then Nahash the Ammonite went up and besieged Jabesh-gilead; and all the men of Jabesh said to Nahash, "Make a treaty with us, and we will serve you."	About a month later, 11:1 Nahash the Ammonite went up and besieged Jabesh-gilead; and all the men of Jabesh said to Nahash, "Make a treaty with us, and we will serve you."

Height of Goliath: One of the all-time favorite OT stories is the contest between the mighty Philistine giant Goliath and David, the youthful shepherd who was destined to become Israel's most famous king. David dropped the giant with a slingshot-fired stone and then beheaded him with a sword (1 Sam 17:1–54). As remarkable as that seems, the most notable feature of the story was Goliath's great stature. The biblical narrator tells us:

> Then a champion named Goliath, from Gath, came out from the Philistine camp. He was nine feet, nine inches tall and wore a bronze helmet and bronze scale armor that weighed 125 pounds. There was

bronze armor on his shins, and a bronze sword was slung between his shoulders. His spear shaft was like a weaver's beam, and the iron point of his spear weighed 15 pounds. In addition, a shield-bearer was walking in front of him. (1 Sam 17:4–7)

Everything about Goliath and his gear was huge, but most remarkable of all is the claim that he was nearly 10 feet tall. This is an astounding height in any era but especially in antiquity when most men were no taller than five feet six inches. Interestingly, the Greek translation of 1 Samuel says something different about Goliath's height. It says he was "four cubits and a span," or about six feet six inches tall. That is still very tall for antiquity, but it is at least within the conceivable anatomical range of humans.

Faced with the difference between the Greek and Hebrew versions, one must ask which figure was original. Did the Greek translator modify Goliath's great size in an attempt to make it sound more realistic? It turns out that the Samuel Scroll from Qumran, which is in Hebrew, reads the same as the Greek version (6' 6"). This implies that the Greek translator of 1 Samuel did not modify the details about Goliath. Rather, the Hebrew text he used said Goliath was six feet six inches rather than nearly ten feet tall. Thus the findings at Qumran suggest

David and Goliath by Doré.

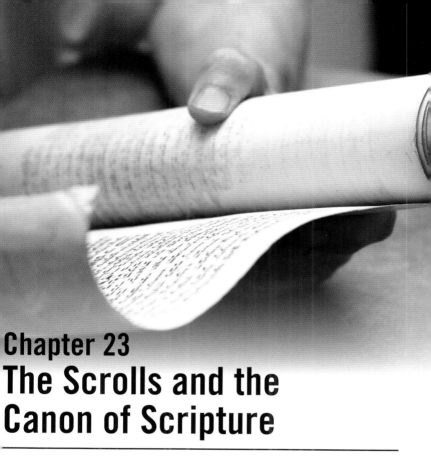

Chapter 23
The Scrolls and the Canon of Scripture

In the preceding chapter we saw that the Dead Sea Scrolls (DSS) help demonstrate the accuracy of the OT manuscripts that lie behind our English translations. They also prove that somewhat different versions of the Hebrew text were circulating in antiquity. Our Bible translations have been based on the Masoretic Text (MT), not the alternative versions witnessed among the DSS. Finally, the Scripture scrolls assist us in clearing up a few textual questions about portions of the OT. Do the DSS also cast light on the question of what books were or were not regarded as Holy Scripture at the turn of the era? Yes, the scrolls cast light on this complicated question, but they raise new questions as well.

The Protestant canon of OT Scripture includes 39 books. The Roman Catholic, Eastern, Greek Orthodox, and Coptic Churches have more than this in their OT canon. Who is correct? Is one or the other canon supported by evidence from the DSS? We examine these questions in this chapter. But first, let's compare the Protestant OT canon to the Jewish canon.

The Protestant OT Canon

Genesis	2 Chronicles	Daniel
Exodus	Ezra	Hosea
Leviticus	Nehemiah	Joel
Numbers	Esther	Amos
Deuteronomy	Job	Obadiah
Joshua	Psalms	Jonah
Judges	Proverbs	Micah
Ruth	Ecclesiastes	Nahum
1 Samuel	Song of Solomon	Habakkuk
2 Samuel	Isaiah	Zephaniah
1 Kings	Jeremiah	Haggai
2 Kings	Lamentations	Zechariah
1 Chronicles	Ezekiel	Malachi

The Jewish Bible, often called the Hebrew Bible or Tanak (an acronym where **T** = Torah; **N** = Nebi'im [the Prophets]; and **K** = Ketuvim [the Writings]) is made up of the same books as the Protestant OT canon, though arranged in a different order. The books of the Hebrew Bible, as the Jewish people have traditionally arranged them, fall into three basic groupings: The first book is Genesis, but the last is Chronicles rather than Malachi.

The Jewish Canon

Law (or Torah)	Prophets	Writings
Genesis	Joshua	Psalms
Exodus	Judges	Proverbs
Leviticus	Samuel	Job
Numbers	Kings	Song of Solomon
Deuteronomy	Isaiah	Ruth
	Jeremiah	Lamentations
	Ezekiel	Ecclesiastes
	The Twelve (i.e.,	Esther
	the twelve Minor	Daniel
	Prophets)	Ezra-Nehemiah
		Chronicles

How many books are in this list? Protestants count them as 39, but Jewish rabbis traditionally refer to the Hebrew Bible as comprising 24 books. They arrive at this number by combining several of the books that Protestants separate. Jews enumerate *five* books of Law, *eight* books of prophecy (with Samuel and Kings counted as two books, not four, and the 12 Minor Prophets counted as one, not 12); and *11* books classified as writings (with Ezra and Nehemiah combined, as was done in antiquity).

A few writers in antiquity either state or seem to imply that there are 24 books in the Bible (e.g., 4 Ezra 14:45). Others say there were 22 books (e.g., *Jubilees* 2:23–24; Josephus, *Against Apion* 1.39). Whether these statements truly correspond to the 39 books of our OT is debated, though a correspondence is genuinely possible.

Thirty-seven of the 39 books of the Protestant OT have been found, in whole or in part, among the Bible scrolls in the Dead Sea Caves. Missing are 1 Chronicles and Esther. However, because we have a small fragment of 2 Chronicles, we assume that 1 Chronicles was also among the Bible scrolls.[1] Thus only Esther seems truly to have been missing. Scholars have suggested several reasons to account for Esther's absence among the DSS.

> *Thirty-seven of the 39 books of the Protestant OT have been found, in whole or in part, among the Bible scrolls in the Dead Sea Caves.*

First, the Feast of Purim, which originates from the story of Esther, is not one of the festivals prescribed in the Law of Moses. Perhaps the men of Qumran, being in all ways conservative, had no interest in the festival or the book that established it since it did not originate with Moses.

Second, the book of Esther contains very little theology and does not even once mention the divine name. The men of Qumran may have regarded Esther as unimportant or even secular given this lack of theological subject matter.

Third, the story of Esther revolves around a Jewish woman who marries a Gentile king. Perhaps the men of Qumran found the story distasteful and unedifying since it went against their ideals of purity.

Fourth, the book of Esther approves of violent retaliation, which flies in the face of teaching in the Rule of Community scroll (see 1QS 10:17–18: "Against no man do I return evil for evil").

Esther by Benouville.

Apocrypha and Pseudepigrapha

We have seen that the books of the Protestant OT canon are well represented among the DSS. What about popular books that failed to make it into the canon? These are part of the Apocrypha and the Pseudepigrapha. The word *apocrypha* is the plural form of the Greek word *apocryphon*, meaning something "hidden away." In biblical studies, Apocrypha thus refers to "hidden" writings related to but not included in the OT canon. Basically, hidden books were for scholars, not general readers. We see this in a passage in one of the books of the Apocrypha. Writing as if he were the great scribe and priest Ezra, the late-first-century author of 4 Ezra says:

> And you alone were worthy to learn this secret of the Most High. Therefore write all these things that you have seen in a book, and put it in a hidden place; and you shall teach them to the wise among your people. (4 Ezra 12:36–38)

> So during the forty days ninety-four books were written. And when the forty days were ended, the Most High spoke to me, saying, "Make public the twenty-four books that you wrote first and let the worthy and the unworthy read them; but retain the seventy that were written last, in order to give them to the wise among your people. (4 Ezra 14:44–46)

As for the Pseudepigrapha, this set of works is named after the Greek word meaning "falsely signed (books)," that is, books that are published under a pen name. Usually these pen names are the names of famous OT figures such as Adam, Enoch, Abraham, Moses, Solomon, Elijah, Baruch, and others. In biblical studies, *Pseudepigrapha* refers to a specific collection of writings that are related to the OT books.

Books of the Old Testament Apocrypha

1 Esdras	Prayer of Azariah and the Song of the Three Young Men
2 Esdras	
Tobit	Susanna
Judith	Bel and the Dragon
Additions to Esther	Prayer of Manasseh
Wisdom of Solomon	1 Maccabees
Wisdom of Jesus ben Sirach (or Ecclesiasticus)	2 Maccabees
Baruch	3 Maccabees
Letter of Jeremiah	4 Maccabees
	Psalm 151

Some of the Books of the Old Testament Pseudepigrapha

1 Enoch	Testament of Moses
2 Enoch	Testament of Solomon
4 Ezra	Letter of Aristeas
Apocalypse of Ezra	Jubilees
Vision of Ezra	Joseph and Aseneth
2 Baruch	Life of Adam and Eve
3 Baruch	Ps.-Philo, Biblical Antiquities
Testament of the Twelve Patriarchs	Lives of the Prophets
Testament of Job	Jannes and Jambres
	Eldad and Modad

In the quotation of 4 Ezra above, the "twenty-four books" that Ezra wrote first and was commanded by God to make public are the canonical books of the OT, which number 24 in the Jewish system and 39 in the Protestant. The "seventy" books that Ezra was commanded to retain are the books of the Apocrypha and Pseudepigrapha. They are to be "put in a hidden place," recalling the meaning of the Greek word *apocrypha.*

As it so happens, some of the books of the Apocrypha and Pseudepigrapha are found among the DSS. Were any or all of these books regarded as authoritative Scripture at Qumran or elsewhere in the Jewish world at the beginning of the first century AD? This is a good question. Notice in the diagram below that 20 scrolls of the book of Enoch were found. That compares to the number of Genesis scrolls. Indeed, only Isaiah (21 scrolls) and the book of Psalms (40 scrolls) are better represented than the book of Enoch. In short, there are more Enoch scrolls than

A fragment of Enoch found at Qumran.

scrolls of most of the other books that came to be recognized as part of the OT canon of Scripture. Apparently the book of Enoch, a pseudepigraphal work, was highly prized among the Essenes.

Another book that stands out is Jubilees, which is a retelling of OT history revolving around the number seven and the jubilee (cycles of 49 years). There are 15 Jubilees scrolls, which again outnumbers most of the canonical Scripture scrolls found in the Dead Sea region. Even the five Tobit scrolls place Tobit ahead of about one-third of the books of the OT, so far as representation among the DSS is concerned.

Based on the number of scrolls alone, some scholars suspect the books of Enoch, Jubilees, and Tobit were regarded as authoritative Scripture by the men of Qumran and perhaps other Jews in late antiquity.[2] The evidence of the DSS suggests that the OT canon was not firmly closed among all Jews in the time of Jesus and his disciples.

Apocrypha Among the Scrolls

Wisdom of Ben Sira	3
Tobit	5
Letter of Jeremiah	1
Psalm 151	1
Psalm 154	1
Psalm 155	1
Jubilees	15
Enoch	20

Finally, the DSS have yielded up a great number of new apocryphal and pseudepigraphal texts. I group them together as Visions and Apocalypses, Testaments, Prayers, and Apocrypha (in the sense of hidden or secret books, not the traditional Apocrypha).

Visions and Apocalypses

Vision of Samuel (4Q160)

Messianic Apocalypse (4Q521)

Son of God Apocalypse (4Q246)

Visions of Amram (4Q543–548)

Testaments

Testament of Levi (4Q213–214)

Testament of Naphtali (4Q215)

Testament of Judah (4Q484)

Testament of Qahat (4Q542)

Prayers

Prayer of Nabonidus (4Q242)

Prayer of Enosh (4Q369)

Prayer of Michael (4Q471b)

Apocrypha

Apocryphon of Jacob (4Q537)

Apocryphon of Judah (4Q538)

Apocryphon of Joseph (4Q371–373, 539)

Apocryphon of Moses (4Q375–377)

Apocryphon of Joshua (4Q378–379)

Apocryphon of Jeremiah (4Q383–384, 387b, 389a)

Apocryphon of Malachi (5Q10)

Apocryphal Psalms (11Q11)

Notes

1. Technically 1 Chronicles also has not been found among the scroll fragments. But the survival of fragments of 2 Chronicles (4QChron, which preserves portions of 2 Chron 28:17 and 29:1–3) suggests that there was at least one copy of 1 Chronicles at Qumran, for 1–2 Chronicles, like 1–2 Samuel and 1–2 Kings, were united as a single scroll in antiquity.

2. On the question of what books were authoritative, see J. C. VanderKam, "Authoritative Literature in the Dead Sea Scrolls," *Dead Sea Discoveries* 5 (1998), 382–402; and M. Bernstein, "Scriptures: Quotation and Use," in L. H. Schiffman and J. C. VanderKam (eds.), *Encyclopedia of the Dead Sea Scrolls* (2 vols., Oxford: Oxford University Press, 2000), 2:839–42. For a convenient assemblage of the books of the Apocrypha and Pseudepigrapha that at Qumran and elsewhere might have been regarded as authoritative Scripture, see M. G. Abegg, P. W. Flint, and E. Ulrich, *The Dead Sea Scrolls Bible: The Oldest Known Bible Translated for the First Time into English* (San Francisco: HarperCollins, 1999).

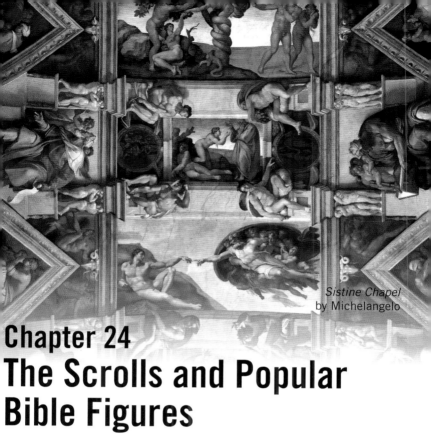

Sistine Chapel
by Michelangelo

Chapter 24
The Scrolls and Popular Bible Figures

The Dead Sea Scrolls (DSS) make frequent mention of Israel's great heroes. They serve as models of piety and faithfulness and are rarely criticized, even when their failings are quite serious. The heroes were also co-opted to serve as authors of additional biblical-like books, that is, the books of the Apocrypha and Pseudepigrapha. There was no better way to win a readership than to present your book as if someone like Moses or Enoch had endorsed or even written it.

Adam

Adam is famous by virtue of being the first human (see Genesis 1–4). Since he sinned and broke God's law, the writers of the scrolls understandably give Adam mixed reviews. He is a hero of sorts but also an example of failure.[1] For example, the Damascus Document reminds and admonishes readers that "when Adam broke faith, his life was shortened" (CD 10:8–9). The commentary on Hosea quotes Hosea 6:7: "They, like Adam, broke the covenant." Unfortunately the comment that follows is lost, so we are unsure what application was made. The commentary on Psalm 37 also mentions Adam:

> "They will not be put to shame in an evil time" (Ps 37:19a). This refers to the ones who return from the wilderness, who will live a thousand generations in virtue. To them and their descendants belongs all the heritage of Adam forever. (4Q171 frags1–4, column ii, line 26–column iii, line 2)

The reference to Adam in this case appears to be positive. Those who have lived in the wilderness (perhaps signifying the men of Qumran?) have lived in virtue. To them and their descendants "belongs all the heritage of Adam forever." The "heritage of Adam" may refer to the opportunity to live in paradise forever.

Elsewhere we find an interesting interpretation of Adam and Eve in a scroll comprising various laws. The author explains the role the garden of Eden played in making Adam and Eve holy:

> In the first week Adam was created but he had no holiness until he was brought to the Garden of Eden. And a bone from his bones was taken for the woman, but she had no holiness until she was

Adam by Dürer. The Dead Sea Scrolls give Adam mixed reviews.

brought to him in the Garden of Eden after eighty days because the Garden of Eden is holy, and every growing thing in its midst is holy. (4Q265 frag. 7, lines 11–14, with restorations)

Another scroll prayerfully recalls Adam's creation and fall:

You fashioned Adam, our father, in the image of Your glory; You breathed the breath of life into his nostrils, and filled him with understanding and knowledge. You set him to rule over the garden of Eden that You had planted. . . . and to walk about in a glorious land . . . he guarded it. You enjoined him not to turn aside from Your commands. . . . Flesh is he, and to dust he shall return. (4Q504 frag. 8, lines 4–9, with restoration)

Noah by Meister. Noah receives a lot of attention in the Dead Sea Scrolls.

Noah

Given his rather ambiguous moral portrait in Scripture (see Genesis 6–9; recall his drunkenness), it is surprising that Noah is the subject of so much attention among the DSS, and yet there are books among the scrolls that bear the name Noah or are about him. 1Q19–20 may have been originally titled "Book of the Words of Noah" (see 1Q20 5:29). According to Jubilees 10:1–14, Noah wrote a book. Possibly that was a reference to this book, making it a pseudepigraphal book. The Genesis Apocryphon devotes four large columns of text to the birth of Noah (columns ii–v) written from the perspective of his father, Lamech. Another 12 columns are devoted to his life (columns vi–xvii).

Several scrolls mention Noah's flood (e.g., 4Q176 frags. 8–11, lines 10–11; 4Q252 1:1–2:7; 4Q422 2:3–4). The author of the Damascus Document appeals to the event in order to teach that hearts that refuse to obey God are the cause of judgment and annihilation:

Everything mortal on dry land expired and became as if they had never existed, because they did their own will, and did not keep the commandments of their Maker, until finally His anger was aroused against them. By it the sons of Noah and their families went astray, and by it they were exterminated. (CD 2:20–3:1)[2]

Abraham

Abraham is the Jewish hero par excellence, for he is the ethnic fountainhead of the Hebrew race and exemplar of faith for all to follow. He answered God's summons, showed remarkable faith and patience, and received from God covenant promises that became foundational for the people of Israel (see Genesis 12–25). Not surprisingly the DSS take great interest in him. His name (either as Abraham or the older form Abram) occurs some 100 times in the DSS.

Abraham by Dolabella. Abraham (or Abram) is mentioned some 100 times in the Dead Sea Scrolls.

In sharp contrast to the mention of the sons of Noah, who were led astray by a willful heart, the Damascus Document says, "Abraham did not live by it (the willful heart) and was considered God's friend, because he observed the commandments of God and he did not choose to follow the will of his own spirit" (CD 3:2–3).

Abstracting the famous man's life in a column and a half of text (4Q252 2:8–3:14), the author of a work usually called Patriarchal Narratives begins the story of Abraham with the words "[God] gave the land to Abraham His beloved" (4Q252 2:8). The aforementioned Genesis Apocryphon, after its lengthy treatment of Noah, focuses on Abraham. This scroll makes clear that Pharaoh would have killed Abraham had he suspected that Sarah was his wife rather than his sister. Relating the event himself, Abraham says:

> He sought to kill me, but Sarah said to the king, "He is my brother," so that I might be benefited by her. And I, Abram, was spared because of her. I was not killed. But I wept bitterly—I, Abram, and Lot, my nephew, with me—on the night when Sarah was taken away from me by force. That night I prayed . . . "Mete out justice to him for me and show forth your great hand against him and against all his house." (1QapGen 20:9–15)

Abraham knew of the danger because of a dream in which he had been warned of Pharaoh's evil intentions.

> And I, Abram, had a dream in the night of my entering into the land of Egypt and I saw in my dream that there was a cedar, and a date-palm (which was) very beautiful; and some men came intending to cut down and uproot the cedar, but leave the date-palm by itself. Now the date-palm remonstrated and said, "Do not cut down the cedar, for we are both from one family." So the cedar was spared with the help of the date-palm, and it was not cut down. (1QapGen 19:14-16)

Such dreams were interpreted as warnings from God. In mortal danger Abraham had no choice but to deceive Pharaoh. Thus his deceptive actions are recast in a better light in the Genesis Apocryphon.

Abraham's deceptive actions are recast in a better light in the Genesis Apocryphon.

The comparison of Abraham and Sarah to a cedar and date-palm was likely drawn from Psalm 92:12: "The righteous flourish like the palm tree, and grow like a cedar in Lebanon" (see also the Aramaic paraphrase of Num 21:34: "Abraham and Sarah are like beautiful trees planted firmly next to springs of water" [*Fragment Targum*]).

Perhaps the most interesting paraphrase of events in Abraham's life is found in 4Q225. Most of what survives is concerned with the "the covenant which was made with Abraham" (frag. 1, line 4). According to this scroll God tested

Abraham in Genesis 22 because of "Prince Mastemah" (frag. 2, column i, lines 9–11). Mention of Mastemah, who is Satan ("Belial" in 4Q225 frag. 2, column ii, line 14), coheres with Jewish interpretive lore (see Jubilees 17:15–16) and probably owes its origin to Job 1:6–12.[3]

Moses

In fame and respect Moses ranks alongside Abraham. Moses is known as the great lawgiver through whom God gave his law to Israel at Mount Sinai. The name of Moses occurs in the DSS some 200 times. Many times his name is virtually synonymous with the Law, as in "as Moses said," "the Law of Moses," or, "as it is written in the book of Moses."

Josephus remarks that "after God, [the Essenes] hold most in awe the name of their lawgiver; any blasphemer of which is punished with death" (*War* 2.145).

Moses by Michelangelo. Moses is mentioned some 200 times in the Dead Sea Scrolls.

The Essenes held Moses in such high esteem they multiplied his works through rewriting and expansion and named a number of pseudepigraphal works after him (such as 4Q376, an Apocryphon of Moses, or 4Q385a, 387a, 385–390, all copies of a work scholars call Pseudo-Moses).

A distinctive element in the scrolls is the portrayal of Moses as a prophet foretelling the ups and downs of Israel's future. One scroll declares: "That is why You have caused the scourge of Your plagues to cleave to us, that of which Moses and Your servants the prophets wrote: You would send evil against us in the Last Days." (4Q504 frags. 1–2, column iii, lines 11–14). The point here is not simply that Moses foretold the future but that he spoke of the last days, which the men of Qumran believed were at hand.

One of the longest prophecies attributed to Moses is found in a work called *The Words of Moses* (1Q22). God tells the lawgiver:

> I declare to you that they will abandon Me and choose to follow the idols of the Gentiles and their abominations and their filthy deeds, and they will worship the false gods, which will become a trap and snare, and they will violate every sacred assembly and covenant Sabbath and the festivals, the very ones I am commanding them today to observe. They will suffer a great defeat within the very land that they are about to cross the Jordan to possess. And so it will be, that all the curses will come upon them and catch them until they perish and until they are destroyed and they will know that a just judgment has been passed on them. (1Q22 frag. 1, column i, lines 7–11, with restorations)

The scrolls not only study Moses but also expand on his teachings. These interpretive expansions are similar to the oral "traditions" that developed among the scribes and Pharisees, against which Jesus complained.

The reference to the "Law of Moses" was understood by the men of the scrolls to refer to their legal interpretations that go beyond the explicit teaching of the books of the Law. Thus, we find that the scrolls not only study Moses but also expand on his teachings.[4] These interpretive expansions are similar to the oral "traditions" that developed among the scribes and Pharisees, against which Jesus complained (see Mark 7).

Aaron

Aaron, the brother of Moses, is cited by name more than 100 times in the DSS. The anointed high priest who will someday rule over Israel, alongside the anointed king (i.e., the Messiah), is several times in the scrolls called the "anointed (or

Adoration of the Golden Calf by Poussin. The Dead Sea Scrolls downplay Aaron's role in crafting the calf idol.

messiah) of Aaron" (e.g., CD 12:23; 14:19; 19:11; 20:1; 1QS 9:11). Israel's priests are several times called "sons of Aaron" (1QS 5:21; 9:7; 1QSa 1:23; 1QM 7:10). We also hear of "holy house of Aaron" (1QS 9:6). The name of Aaron will be printed on the banners of the holy army that will engage the Sons of Darkness in the great and final war (1QM 3:14; 5:1).

Most of the references to Aaron are honorary and are used to identify other people. However, a few times the historical Aaron plays a role in a narrative. One of the most interesting instances of this is an allusion to his contest with Pharaoh's magicians, who in later Jewish lore are identified as Jannes and Jambres. Here is what is said in the Damascus Document:

> For in times past Moses and Aaron stood in the power of the Prince of Lights and Belial raised up Yannes and his brother in his cunning when seeking to do evil to Israel the first time. (CD 5:17b–19)

Here we have one of Qumran's favorite themes, the contest between light and darkness, God and Satan. Moses and his brother Aaron "stood in the power of the Prince of Lights" (to be identified as God himself or one of archangels) and were opposed by Belial (Satan) who "raised up Yannes and his brother" Yambres. The story of the infamous brothers who served Pharaoh is also alluded to in one of the NT letters:

> Just as Jannes and Jambres resisted Moses, so these also resist the truth, men who are corrupt in mind, worthless in regard to the faith. But they will not make further progress, for their lack of understanding will be clear to all, as theirs was also. (2 Tim 3:8–9)

One of the fragmentary scrolls from Cave 4 relates some of the highlights of the life of Aaron, especially when he met his brother Moses in the wilderness and learned of God's plan to rescue his people from Egyptian bondage:

> The Lord said to Aaron, "Go into the wilderness to meet Moses." So he went, meeting him at the mountain of God, and kissed him. Moses told Aaron all the Lord's words with which He had sent him, and all the signs with which He had charged him . . . (Exod 4:27–28). Moses told Aaron, "The Lord has spoken to me, saying, 'When you have brought the people out of Egypt.'" (4Q158 frags. 1–2, lines 13b–16)

In the Bible Aaron's greatest failing was overseeing the making of the golden calf (Exod 32:1–6). The making of the idol is recounted in the scrolls, but Aaron's role goes unmentioned

The foibles of biblical heroes are often overlooked in the Dead Sea Scrolls.

(see 4Q364 frag. 26, column ii, lines 5–9). It merely says, "Behold, I saw you had sinned against the Lord your God. You had made for yourself a molten calf"). By omitting the role played by Aaron, the author cleansed Aaron's reputation, thus heightening his status as a hero of the faith.[5] The foibles of other heroes are overlooked in similar fashion in the DSS.

Joshua

One of the Bible's most beloved characters is Joshua, Moses' successor. Joshua led Israel into the promised land. His capture of Jericho was his signature military stroke and even became the subject of the famous black spiritual, "Joshua Fought the Battle of Jericho."

The men of Qumran also took interest in Joshua. In Cave 4 alone two Joshua scrolls were found (4Q47–48), along with two apocryphal books of Joshua (4Q378–79). Joshua and Eleazar son of Aaron are given the responsibility of repeating the law to the people of Israel. "So Moses called Eleazar son of [Aaron] and Joshua [son of Nun and said to] them, Repeat [all the words of the Law up to] the very end" (1Q22 frag. 1, column i, lines 11–12).

According to a work called the Psalms of Joshua, Joshua prophesies the coming of two or three wicked men, the first regarded as a son of Belial (Satan), who will lead Israel astray:

> Behold, one cursed man, one belonging to Belial, is about to arise to be a fowler's net to his people and a source of ruin for all his neighbors. Then shall arise sons after him, the two of them to be instruments of wrongdoing. They shall rebuild this city and set up for it a wall and towers, creating a stronghold of evil and a great wickedness in Israel, a thing of horror in Ephraim and Judah. . . . They shall work blasphemy in the land, a great uncleanness among the children of Jacob. They shall pour out blood like water upon the bulwark of the daughter of Zion and within the city limits of Jerusalem. (4Q175 1:23b–30, quoting Psalms of Joshua [4Q379 frag. 22, column ii, lines 9–14])

We happen to have two fragmentary copies of the Psalms of Joshua, though the part that refers to Joshua is best preserved in the lengthy quotation found in 4Q175.[6]

David

David is another favorite of the DSS, both as a youthful shepherd and warrior king. In what was probably supposed to be a prophecy of the birth and reign of David as well as his plans to build the temple, we read:

> For, behold, a son is born to Jesse, son of Perez, son of Judah. . . . He will choose the rock of Zion and drive out from there all the Amorites from Jerusalem . . . to build the house for the Lord, God of Israel. (4Q522 frag. 1, column ii, lines 2–5)

The reference to David's birth is reminiscent of the oracle of Isaiah 9:6a: "For a child will be born for us, a son will be

given to us, and the government will be on His shoulders."

The War Scroll alludes to David's greatest personal military triumph, his defeat of Goliath:

King David by Leighton. The Dead Sea Scrolls mention David as both a shepherd boy and a warrior king.

Truly the battle is yours, and by the strength of your hand their corpses have been broken to pieces, without anyone to bury them. Indeed, Goliath the Gittite, a mighty man of valor, you delivered into the hand of David, your servant, because he trusted in your great name and not in sword and spear. For the battle is yours. (1QM 11:1–2).

The Great Psalm Scroll of Cave 11 catalogues David's literary and musical compositions:

Now David the son of Jesse was wise and shone like the light of the sun, a scribe and man of discernment, blameless in all his ways before God and men. The Lord gave him a brilliant and discerning spirit, so that he wrote: psalms, 3,600; songs to sing before the altar accompanying the daily perpetual burnt-offering, for all the days of the year, 364; for the Sabbath offerings, 52 songs; and for the New Moon offerings, all the festival days and the Day of Atonement, 30 songs. The total of all the songs that he composed was 446, not including four songs for charming the demon-possessed with music. The sum total of everything, psalms and songs, was 4,050. All these he composed through prophecy given him by the Most High. (11QPsa 27:2–11)

Jewish lore held that both David and his son Solomon were skilled exorcists.

Note line 10, where the author says David composed "four songs for charming the demon-possessed with music." The idea that Israel's king was also an exorcist is seen in the legends that grew up around Solomon, David's son. Solomon was so well known for his medicinal and exorcistic skills that professional exorcists claimed to possess charms and incantations that had been composed by him, and a work called the Testament of Solomon was composed sometime in the first century AD.

Later in the Cave 11 Psalms Scroll, we find statements attributed to David. God "anointed me with the holy oil" and "set me as a prince to his people, a ruler over the children of his covenant" (11QPsa 28:11). This language again echoes Psalm 89, in which God says: "I have found David My servant, I have anointed him with My sacred oil" (Ps 89:20).

The men of Qumran were forgiving toward David's sins. For instance, observe the understanding tone in this passage from the Damascus Document:

> Concerning the Leader it is written "he shall not multiply wives to himself" (Deut 17:17); but David had not read the sealed book of the Law in the Ark; for it was not opened in Israel from the day of the death of Eleazar and Joshua. . . . It lay buried and was not revealed until the appearance of Zadok. Nevertheless the deeds of David were all excellent, except the murder of Uriah and God forgave him for that. (CD 5:1b–6a)

Whoever wrote this passage recognized that David disobeyed Deuteronomy 17:17 by taking multiple wives. However, he is excused because the book of Deuteronomy was hidden and not revealed until *after* David's time. The author goes on to praise David, claiming that his deeds "were all excellent, except the murder of Uriah." The author is referring to David's adultery with Bathsheba and the murder of her husband. If adultery and murder don't disqualify a man for the biblical hall of fame, what does? The author of the Damascus Document assures his readers that "God forgave [David] for that" sin.

In a work called the Words of the Heavenly Lights (4Q504–506), God's election of Jerusalem, the people of Israel, especially the tribe of Judah, and the Davidic monarchy are recalled. The author reminds God: "You have established your covenant with David, so that he would be like a shepherd, a prince over your people, and would sit upon the throne of Israel before you forever" (4Q504 frag. 1, column ii, lines 6–8). This language again recalls Psalm 89, where God is reminded of having promised David: "I have made a covenant with My chosen one; I have sworn an oath to David My servant" (Ps 89:3).[7]

Elijah and Elisha

Elijah and his disciple-successor Elisha were the great prophets of the "nonwriting prophets" era. They were famous for confronting the stray leaders of Israel and Syria and for working wonders. Thanks to the prophecy of Malachi, Elijah came to be associated with the Day of the Lord and, eventually, with the appearing of the Messiah.

It is not surprising that the men of Qumran took interest in Elijah and Elisha since they were famous for confronting sin and, in Elijah's case, being

Elijah with the Chariot of Fire by Cifrondi. The men of Qumran identified strongly with prophets such as Elijah who confronted sin boldly.

connected to end times. The two prophets figure prominently in a fragmentary scroll (4Q382) that appears to be an alternate version of 1–2 Kings. The following fragment parallels 2 Kings 2:2–8, though with a few differences:

And the sons of the prophets said to Elisha, "Do you know that today the Lord will take your master away from you?" He replied, "I know." Elijah said to Elisha, "Stay here, my son; for the Lord has sent me as far as Bethel." But Elisha said, "As the Lord lives, and as you yourself live, I will not leave you." So they went down to Bethel. . . . The sons of the prophets who were in Jericho said to Elisha . . . "Hold your tongue. . . . Everyone who descends alive to Sheol . . ." (4Q382 frag. 9, lines 5–10, with restorations)

The last part of this version of 2 Kings 2 is very interesting. It is unfortunate that more of the scroll is not preserved. It would have been fascinating to hear more about "everyone who descends alive to Sheol."

There is a second fragmentary scroll at Qumran that appears to contain another version of 2 Kings 2, this time verses 15–16:

And Elisha arose and saw the sons of the prophets which were in Jericho opposite him; and they said, "The spirit of Elijah is resting on Elisha," and they came toward Elisha and bowed down to him on the ground. And they said to him, "Look, please, your servants have fifty men, valiant men; please, let them come and seek my lord lest the spirit of the Lord be removed." And they threw him upon one of the mountains. (4Q481a frag. 2, lines 3–6)

In this version of the story, the strong men threw Elisha upon one of the mountains. Compare this to what is said in 2 Kings 2:16–17, where fear is expressed that the Spirit of the Lord might cast Elisha upon a mountain or into a valley.[8]

Daniel

Daniel apparently held special fascination for the men of Qumran. Not only were eight Daniel scrolls found, several other writings were found that relate to the Daniel tradition. Among these are a scroll called the Prayer of Nabonidus (4Q242), which parallels the confession and prayer of Nebuchadnezzar (Dan 4:34–37)

Daniel in the Lions' Den by Rubens. Not only were eight Daniel scrolls found, among the Dead Sea Scrolls several other writings were found that relate to the Daniel tradition. Among these is a scroll called the Prayer of Nabonidus (4Q242), which parallels the confession and prayer of Nebuchadnezzar (Dan 4:34–37).

There are fragmentary copies of three scrolls that scholars have dubbed Pseudo-Daniel (4Q243–245), another scroll that is an apocalypse involving the interpretation of a dream (4Q246), something for which Daniel was well known (Dan 2:28–45; 4:19–27). All of these scrolls are in Aramaic. Half of the biblical book of Daniel is in Aramaic (unlike almost all other books of the OT, which are in Hebrew).

There are also two Hebrew scrolls, another apocalypse revolving around weeks (4Q247), and a narrative of the acts of a great king (4Q248). Finally, there are three more Aramaic scrolls, one a possible version of Susanna (4Q551) and two fragmentary copies of scrolls concerned with the four kingdoms (4Q552–553), which roughly parallel the visions of the four kingdoms in the book of Daniel (Dan 2:31–45; 7:3–17 "Four huge beasts"; 8:22 "four kingdoms").

Daniel was nothing if not a prophet. One of his prophecies is key to the eschatological expectation of one of the scrolls:

> That will be the time of persecution that is to come upon the House of Judah, to the end of sealing up the wicked in consuming fire and destroying all the children of Belial. Then shall be left behind a remnant of chosen ones, the predestined. They shall perform the whole of the Law, as God commanded through

Moses. This is the time of which it is written in the book of Daniel the prophet, "The wicked will act ever more wickedly and shall not understand. But the righteous will be purified, cleansed and refined" (Dan 12:10). (4Q174 frags. 1–3, column ii, lines 1–4a, with restoration)

A prophecy of Daniel also plays an important role in the Melchizedek Scroll:

This visitation is the Day of Salvation that He has decreed through Isaiah the prophet concerning all the captives, inasmuch as scripture says, "How beautiful upon the mountains are the feet of the messenger who announces peace, who brings good news, who announces salvation, who says to Zion, 'Your God reigns'" (Isa 52:7). This scripture's interpretation: "the mountains" are the prophets, they who were sent to proclaim God's truth and to prophesy to all Israel. "The messenger" is the Anointed of the Spirit, of whom Daniel spoke, "After the sixty-two weeks, an Anointed one shall be cut off" (Dan 9:26). The "messenger who brings good news, who announces salvation" is the one of whom it is written, "to proclaim the year of the Lord's favor, the day of vengeance of our God; to comfort all who mourn" (Isa 61:1–2). (11Q13 2:14b–20a)

This is a fascinating vision in which the prophecies of Isaiah and Daniel are invoked. The two passages from Isaiah (52:7 and 61:1–2) are important in the NT.[9] What is especially interesting is that the messenger of Isaiah 52 is also the "Anointed of the Spirit" mentioned in Daniel and Isaiah 61. This interpretation agrees with what Jesus says of himself (Luke 4, where he quotes Isa 61:1–2 and applies it to himself) and what his apostles say of him and his ministry. The appeal to Daniel 9:26, which says that the "Anointed" (remember, "Anointed" can be translated "Messiah") will be "cut off" (i.e., killed), is important in the light of the death of Jesus the Messiah.

Notes

1. See G. A. Anderson, "Adam," in L. H. Schiffman and J. C. VanderKam (eds.), *Encyclopedia of the Dead Sea Scrolls* (2 vols., Oxford: Oxford University Press, 2000), 1:7–9.

2. See J. C. Reeves, "Noah," and M. E. Stone, "Noah, Texts of," in Schiffman and VanderKam (eds.), *Encyclopedia of the Dead Sea Scrolls*, 2:612–13 and 2:613–15, respectively.

3. See C. A. Evans, "Abraham," in Schiffman and VanderKam (eds.), *Encyclopedia of the Dead Sea Scrolls*, 1:2–4.

4. For more on Moses in the Scrolls, see D. K. Falk, "Moses" and "Moses, Texts of," in Schiffman and VanderKam (eds.), *Encyclopedia of the Dead Sea Scrolls*, 1:576–77 and 1:577–81, respectively.

5. For more discussion, see G. A. Anderson, "Aaron," in Schiffman and VanderKam (eds.), *Encyclopedia of the Dead Sea Scrolls*, 1:1–2.

6. For more discussion, see E. Tov, "Joshua, Book of," in Schiffman and VanderKam (eds.), *Encyclopedia of the Dead Sea Scrolls*, 1:431–34.

7. For more discussion, see C. A. Evans, "David in the Dead Sea Scrolls," in S. E. Porter and C. A. Evans (eds.), *The Scrolls and the Scriptures: Qumran Fifty Years After* (Sheffield: Sheffield Academic Press, 1997), 183–97; P. W. Flint, "David," in Schiffman and VanderKam (eds.), *Encyclopedia of the Dead Sea Scrolls*, 1:178–80.

8. For more discussion, see J. Trebolle Barrera, "Elijah," and J. Trebolle Barrera, "Elisha," in Schiffman and VanderKam (eds.), *Encyclopedia of the Dead Sea Scrolls*, 1:246 and 1:246–47, respectively.

9. For more discussion, see E. Ulrich, "Daniel, Book of: Hebrew and Aramaic Text," G. W. E. Nickelsburg, "Daniel, Book of: Greek Additions," and J. J. Collins, "Daniel, Book of: Pseudo-Daniel," in Schiffman and VanderKam (eds.), *Encyclopedia of the Dead Sea Scrolls*, 1:170–74, 1:174–76, and 1:176–78, respectively.

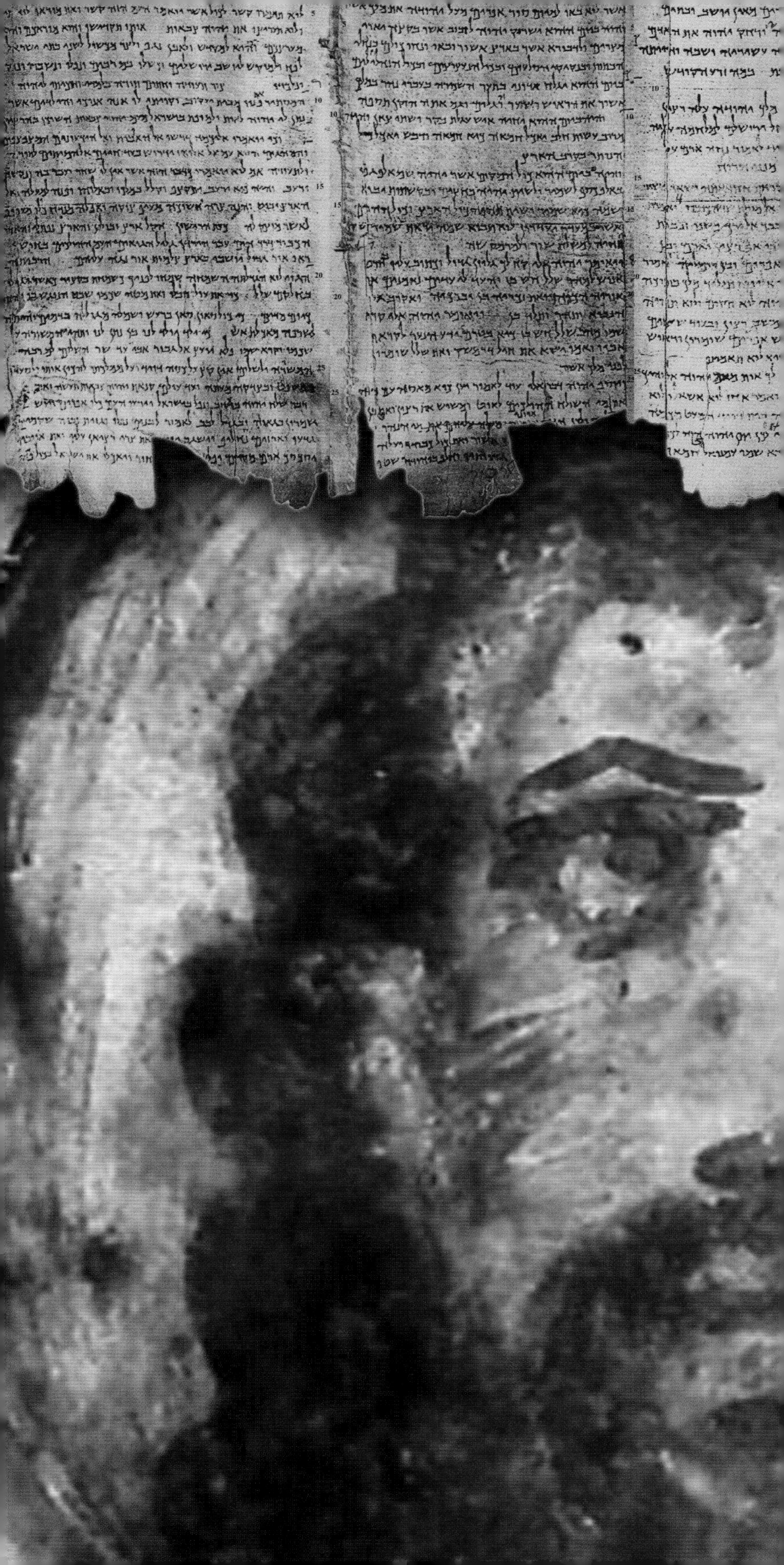

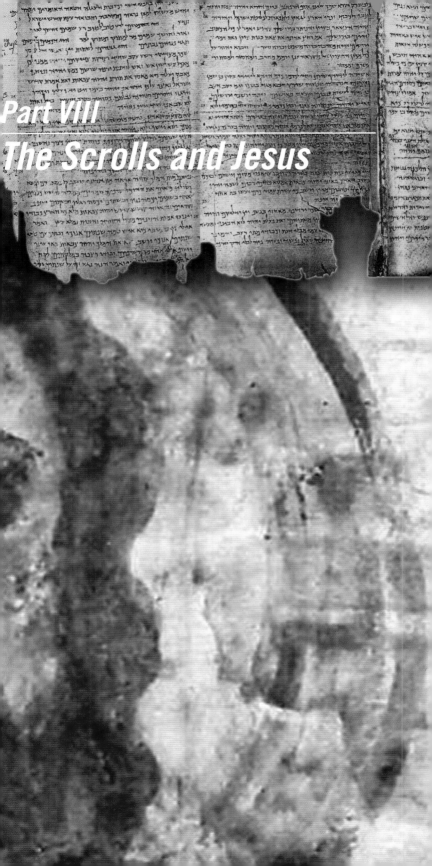

Part VIII
The Scrolls and Jesus

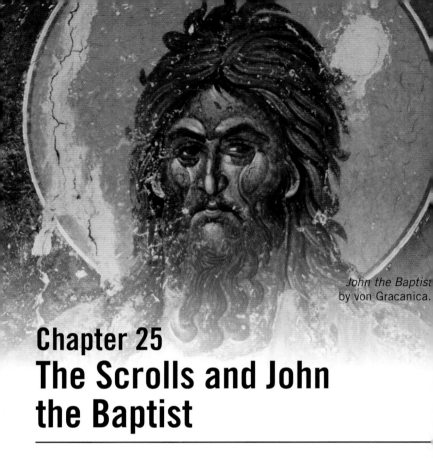

John the Baptist
by von Gracanica.

Chapter 25
The Scrolls and John the Baptist

Before considering in what ways the Dead Sea Scrolls (DSS) are helpful in understanding the teaching and actions of Jesus, we should briefly look at John the Baptist, the colleague and forerunner of Messiah.

The discovery of the Qumran scrolls raised the question of John's possible relationship with the Essenes. Some openly suggested that John might have been a member of the Essene community. This was not surprising, for there are at least six important parallels between the Baptist, the content of the DSS, and descriptions of the Essenes found in ancient sources.

Parallels between John the Baptist and the Scrolls

First, both John and the men of Qumran (presumed to be Essenes) appealed to Isaiah 40:3 ("A voice of one crying out: 'Prepare the way of the LORD in the wilderness'") as their rationale for retreating to the wilderness and engaging in ministries focused on the redemption and restoration of Israel (cf. 1QS

3:12–16; 9:19–20; Matt 3:1–3; Mark 1:2–4; Luke 3:2–6; John 1:23). John's upbringing in the wilderness (cf. Luke 1:80) allows for the possibility of his association with the wilderness community, especially in light of the fact that Josephus said, "The Essenes . . . adopt the children of others at a tender age in order to instruct them" (Josephus, *War* 2.120). It is very easy to imagine John as one of these children, raised to shun wealth and mainstream Jewish life in favor of strict devotion to God and the Scriptures. Furthermore, both Essenes and Christians called their respective movements "the Way" because of Isaiah 40:3 (see 1QS 9:17–18; Luke 20:21; Acts 9:2; 16:17; 18:26; compare also John 14:6). John's emphasis on Isaiah 40:3 likely paved the way for Christian adoption of this description.

> *Both Essenes and Christians called their respective movements "the Way" because of Isaiah 40:3.*

Excavation of the ruins at Qumran has uncovered the presence of baptismal reservoirs, confirming the importance of ritual immersion for the Essene community.

Second, both John and the men of Qumran called for repentance and practiced baptism (see 1QS 5:7–15; Pliny the Elder, *Natural History* 5.17.4; Matt 3:5; Mark 1:4–5; Luke 3:7; John 1:25). Excavation of the ruins at Qumran has uncovered the presence of baptismal reservoirs, confirming the importance of ritual immersion for the Essene community.

Third, both John and the men of Qumran anticipated the soon-coming appearance of the kingdom of God, including an anointed figure or Messiah (1QS 8:13–14; Matt 3:2; Mark 1:7).

Fourth, John and the men of Qumran employed similarly the words "water, spirit, and fire" (cf. 1QS 4:11–21; Isa 5:24; Matt 3:11–12; Mark 1:8; Luke 3:16; John 1:26).

Fifth, John's strange diet may have reflected the strict food laws (*kashruth*) that were observed by the Essenes. Josephus says Essenes who were evicted from the community often starved to death because they are unwilling "to share the food of others," preferring to eat grass rather than violate their food laws (cf. Josephus, *War* 2.143). John's strict diet included eating locusts and wild honey, and he "came neither eating nor drinking" the common foodstuffs (see Matt 3:4; 11:18; Mark 1:6; Luke 1:15).

Sixth, John harshly criticized Israel's religious leaders, calling them such things as a "brood of vipers (Matt 3:7–9). This confrontational approach coheres with the harsh epithets frequently found in the writings of Qumran. For example, the Essenes labeled their enemies as:

- Man of Lies (1QpHab 2:1–2)
- Wicked Priest (1QpHab 8:8)
- Preacher of Lies (1QpHab 10:9)
- Men of the Pit (1QS 9:16)
- Men of Perversity (1QS 9:17)
- Sons of Darkness (1QM 1:1)
- Host of Belial (1QM 15:2-3)

Conclusion

These parallels may or may not suggest that John at one time had been an Essene, but for certain it demonstrates that he embraced a worldview quite similar to that of the Essenes. The

John the Baptist embraced a worldview quite similar to that of the Essenes.

possible connection between John and the Essenes is important since Jesus in all likelihood was associated with John even before inaugurating his own public ministry. Remember Jesus and John were related to one another through their mothers (Luke 1:36). They could have had ties many years before Jesus went public. Therefore the writings of Qumran may supply vital background for understanding the ministries of both John and Jesus.[1]

Note

1. For more on this topic, see O. Betz, "Was John the Baptist an Essene?" *Bible Review* 6/6 (1990), 18–25.

Chapter 26
The Scrolls and the Coming Messiah

The Dead Sea Scrolls (DSS) have shed light on many aspects of Jesus' life, activities, and teaching, sometimes in very significant ways. In this chapter we explore how the scrolls clarify (1) why the followers of Jesus came to believe that he was God's Son and (2) what Jesus proclaimed.

The Divinity of Jesus the Messiah

Many Jews in Jesus' time expected Messiah just to be human despite the fact that the OT contains important hints about his divinity. Judging from the literature produced in the time between the Testaments, however, we know that some Jews expected Messiah to be much more than merely a human descendant of King David.

Many Jews in Jesus' time expected Messiah just to be human despite the fact that the OT contains important hints about his divinity.

One of the oldest suggestions that there would be something special about a future male descendant of David is found in a prophecy given by Nathan. The passage is sometimes called the Davidic Covenant (2 Sam 7:8–16). The key element is seen in the promises: "I will establish the throne of his kingdom for ever. I will be a father to him, and he will be a son to Me" (7:13b–14a). The promise of a filial relationship with God is also given in two psalms:

> The kings of the earth take their stand and the rulers conspire together against the LORD and His Anointed One. . . . I will declare the LORD's decree: He said to Me, "You are My Son; today I have become Your Father." (Ps 2:2,7)

> I have found David My servant; I have anointed him with My sacred oil. . . . He will call to Me, "You are my Father, my God, the rock of my salvation." (Ps 89:20, 26)

The prophet Isaiah uttered a very unusual oracle that adds significantly to these passages:

> For a child will be born for us, a son will be given to us, and the government will be on His shoulders. He will be named Wonderful Counselor, Mighty God, Eternal Father, Prince of Peace. The dominion will be vast, and its prosperity will never end. He will reign on the throne of David and over his kingdom, to establish and sustain it with justice and righteousness form now on and forever. The zeal of the LORD of Hosts will accomplish this (Isa 9:6–7).

In light of passages such as these, it is not surprising that some who longed for the coming of the Messiah expected him to be divine. Nor is it surprising that when Jesus was recognized as the Messiah, his followers also regarded him as God's Son.

In light of passages such as Isaiah 9:6–7, it is not surprising that some who longed for the coming of the Messiah expected him to be divine.

Nevertheless, some scholars have believed that the OT teachings could not adequately explain why the early Church proclaimed Jesus as the divine Son of God. Some of them have argued that the early Church's proclamation of a divine Messiah was due to the influence of the Roman imperial cult, in which the emperor was believed to be a "son of God." This Roman belief is expressed in many surviving ancient documents (papyri) and stone monuments (inscriptions). Here are a few examples:[1]

- Of Julius Caesar (ruled 48–44 BC) one public inscription proclaims: "The manifest god from Mars and Aphrodite, and universal savior of human life" (SIG 760).

- Another announces: "The Carthaean people honor the god and emperor and savior of the inhabited world Gaius Julius Caesar son of Gaius Caesar" (IG 12.5).

Julius Caesar. Photo: Andrew Bossi.

- Julius Caesar's famous nephew and eventual successor, Caesar Augustus (ruled 31 BC to AD 14), is proclaimed "Emperor Caesar Augustus, son of god" (BGU 628) and "Emperor Caesar, god from god" (SB 8895).

- Even the madman Nero (ruled AD 54–68) said of himself: "Nero Claudius Caesar . . . the savior and benefactor of the inhabited world" (OGIS 668); and "The good god of the inhabited world, the beginning of all good things" (P.Oxy. 1021).

Such proclamations strike us moderns as extraordinary, but

2,000 years ago they were rather conventional among many non-Hebrew peoples. Rulers were often divinized and worshipped as a matter of course. Are skeptical scholars right to suggest that these widespread beliefs gave early Christians the idea that Jesus was God, or is it instead the case that Christians proclaimed Jesus as God because his teachings and the teachings of the OT led to this conclusion?

The DSS suggests that Jews who longed for the appearance of the Messiah thought of him as God's Son. The evidence of the DSS suggests that Jews who longed for the appearance of the Messiah thought of him as God's Son apart from an influence from pagan belief systems. This implies that the OT itself was a major source of the belief that Messiah is divine. Let's look at the most important evidence in the scrolls.

Messiah as Divine in the Scrolls

The Rule of the Congregation Scroll (1QSa) envisions a day when the Messiah will sit with Israel's elders at the banquet table. This is what the scroll says:

> This is the procedure for the meeting of the men of repute when they are called to the banquet held by the Council of the Community, when God has begotten the Messiah among them. (1QSa 2:11–12)

Some scholars have disputed the reading "begotten." In truth it is hard to tell for certain what the word is since the scroll has a hole in that spot. In any event, the first scholar to look at it concluded the reading was indeed "begotten," and the language of these verses reminds us of Psalm 2:2,7, which says that the Messiah would be "begotten." Thus the rendering that includes "begotten" is probably correct.

A major theme in 1QSa is that the Essenes longed for the great eschatological banquet that was foretold by Isaiah the prophet:

> The L<small>ORD</small> of Hosts will prepare a feast for all the peoples on this mountain—a feast of aged wine, choice meat, finely aged wine. . . . He will destroy death forever. The Lord G<small>OD</small> will wipe away the tears from every face and removed His people's disgrace from the whole earth, for the L<small>ORD</small> has spoken. On that day it will be said, "Look, this is our God; we have waited for Him, and He has saved us. This is the L<small>ORD</small>; we have waited for Him. Let us rejoice and be glad in His salvation." (Isa 25:6,8–9)

This biblical passage inspired the hope that someday God would spread a table and feast with "all peoples." It lies behind Jesus' parable of the Great Banquet (Luke 14:15–24), which was told in response to the man who cried out, "The one who will eat bread in the kingdom of God is blessed!" The day will come when God will prepare a banquet for the faithful. At this time his Anointed, the Messiah, will sit at the head of the table.

Another important scroll offers compelling evidence that the expected one will be acclaimed God's Son. But first, we need to recall what the angel Gabriel told Mary, the mother of Jesus:

> Then the angel told her: Do not be afraid, Mary, for you have found favor with God. Now listen: You will conceive and give birth to a son, and you will call his name JESUS. *He will be great and will be called the Son of the Most High*, and the Lord God will give Him the throne of His father David. *He will reign* over the house of Jacob *forever*, and *His kingdom will have no end.* Mary asked the angel, "How can this be,

The Annunciation by Barocci.

since I have not been intimate with a man?" The angel replied to her: "The Holy Spirit will come upon you, and the power of the Most High will overshadow you. Therefore the holy One to be born *will be called the Son of God.*" (Luke 1:30–35)

Key elements in this passage have been placed in italics. One of the surprising Qumran texts to come to light was a small rectangular-shaped piece of leather, comprising two columns of Aramaic text. This is all we have of the document, but what we have is very important. The document (4Q246) is sometimes called the Son of God Apocalypse. Here it is, with elements that parallel themes in the Lukan passage placed in italics:

[O ki]ng, wrath is coming to the world, and your years shall be shortened . . . such is your vision, and all of it is about to come unto the world. . . . Amid great signs, tribulation is coming upon the land. . . . After much killing and slaughter, a prince of nations will arise . . . the king of Assyria and Egypt . . . he will be ruler over the land . . . will be subject to him and all will obey him. Also his son *will be* called *Great*, and be designated by his name. He *will be called the Son of God*, they will call him the *son of the Most High*. But like the meteors that you saw in your vision, so will be their kingdom. They will reign only a few years over the land, while people tramples people and nation tramples nation, until the people of God arise; then all will have rest from warfare. Their kingdom *will be an eternal kingdom*, and all their paths will be righteous. They will judge the land justly, and all nations will make peace. Warfare will cease from the land, and all the nations shall do homage to them. The great God will be their help, He Himself will fight for them, putting peoples into their power, overthrowing them all before them. God's rule will be an eternal rule and all the depths of [the earth are His.] (4Q246 1:2–2:9, with restorations, including the probable beginning of column iii)

When this remarkable text was published, scholars immediately noticed amazing parallels with the Gospel of Luke. These include:

Luke	4Q246
He will be great (1:32).	"Great" he shall be called (1:9).
and will be called the Son of the Most High (1:32).	"Son of the Most High" he shall be called (2:1).
will be called the Son of God (1:35).	"Son of God" he shall be addressed (2:1).
He will reign . . . forever, and His kingdom will have no end (1:33).	His kingdom shall be an eternal kingdom (2:5).

The Son of God Apocalypse (4Q246) dates to the first century BC. The text is Aramaic, the language of Jesus and his disciples, and it was found in Israel, obviously where Jesus lived and ministered. These facts alone make it relevant for NT studies, but its importance is greatly heightened by its clear parallels with NT material. The figure foretold in this scroll fragment, very probably understood to be the Messiah, will be called "Great," "Son of God," and "Son of the Most High," and his kingdom shall be an eternal one. These things are said of Jesus also. Thus the proclamations made about Jesus showed continuity with already-established Jewish thought and would not have depended on borrowing ideas from the Roman world. Long before the apostles and missionaries of the Christian faith took the good news about Jesus to places where the Roman emperor was worshipped as god, Jewish people thought of Messiah as the Son of God.

The proclamations made about Jesus showed continuity with already-established Jewish thought and would not have depended on borrowing ideas from the Roman world.

Thus the Christian understanding of Jesus as the Son of God was not the result of contact with the Greco-Roman world but grew out of OT Scripture itself and the messianic expectations current in Israel at the turn of the era, as demonstrated in at least two scrolls from Qumran that speak of a divine Messiah.

The Temptation of Jesus the Messiah

After Jesus was baptized, he went into the wilderness and was tempted by the devil. Matthew and Luke tell us that there were three specific temptations. In one of them the devil cites Scripture, saying: "If You are the Son of God, throw Yourself down. For it is written: He will give His angels orders concerning you, and they will support you with their hands so that

Temptation of Christ by Kramskoi

you will not strike your foot against a stone" (Matt 4:6; quoting Ps 91:11–12).

Satan cited this passage because it was understood to offer assurance of divine protection against evil spirits. This is not so obvious from reading the psalm in its original context. In order to see the psalm's relevance to protection from evil spirits, we need to compare the Hebrew version of Psalm 91 with the Aramaic paraphrase that came to be used in Aramaic-speaking synagogues:

RSV	Aramaic
5 You will not fear the terror of the night, nor the arrow that flies by day,	5 Be not afraid of the terror of demons who walk at night, of the arrow of the angel of death that he looses during the day;
6 nor the pestilence that stalks in darkness, nor the destruction that wastes at noonday.	6 Of the death that walks in darkness, of the band of demons that attacks at noon.
9 Because you have made the Lord your refuge, the Most High your habitation,	9 Solomon answered and said: "For you are my confidence, O Lord; in the highest dwelling place you have placed the house of your presence."
10 no evil shall befall you, no scourge come near your tent.	10 The lord of the world responded and thus he said: "No harm shall happen to you; and no plague or demon shall come near to your tents."

Notice that whereas the Hebrew original speaks of the "terror of the night" and the "arrow that flies," the Aramaic paraphrase speaks of the "terror of demons" and the "arrow of the angel of death" (Ps 91:5). In verse 6 the Hebrew speaks of "destruction that wastes," but the Aramaic reads, "The band of demons that attacks." Verse 9 of the Aramaic introduces Solomon, a king who in noncanonical Jewish traditions was famed for his reputed power over demons. In verse 10 the Hebrew assures readers that "no scourge (shall) come near," but the Aramaic paraphrase turns the subject toward spiritual warfare by saying, "No plague or demon shall come near."

Clearly the Aramaic paraphrase of Psalm 91 emphasizes demonic activity and spiritual warfare, but how early did this paraphrase circulate among the Jews? Does it go all the way back to the first century, thus establishing that in the time of Christ Psalm 91 was popularly understood as touching on the topic of demons? In the form *The Aramaic paraphrase of Psalm 91 emphasizes demonic activity and spiritual warfare.* we cited above, it does not stretch back that far. However, a copy of Psalm 91 was found among the DSS. It was grouped in a scroll along with three noncanonical psalms that speak of protection against evil spirits. This Psalms Scroll (11Q11) is in very poor condition. I offer excerpts of the noncanonical exorcism psalms below, using square brackets to show what is missing and where we can plausibly restore it. Key words are placed in bold type:

First Exorcism Psalm

[. . .] and the one who weeps for him [. . .] the curse [. . .] by the Lord [. . .] **dragon** [. . .] the ear[th . . .] **exor[ci]sing** [. . .] to [. . .] this [. . .] to the **demon** [. . .] he will dwe[ll . . .]. (11Q11 1:1–11)

Second Exorcism Psalm

[. . . A Psalm of] Solomon. He took [. . .] the **demons** [. . .] these are [the de]mons [. . . I]sr[ael . . .] with me [. . .] **healing** [. . . the righteous] leans on Your name and calls [. . . He says to Is]rael, "Be strong [. . .] the heavens [. . .]" who has separated [light from darkness . . . .] and the earth [. . .] the earth, who m[ade the host of heaven for seasons] and for sig[ns . . .] He is the Lord [. . .] He made the [. . . I] **adjure** all [. . .] and all [. . .] which [. . .] before [. . .]

[. . .] the curses of des[truction . . .] the fierce wrath of [. . .] darkness [. . .] affliction [. . .] your portion [. . .] which [. . .] and those **possessed by [demon**s . . .] those crushed [by **Belial** . . . on Isra]el, peace [eternal . . . .]. (11Q11 2:2–5:3)

Third Exorcism Psalm

A Psalm of David, against [. . .] in the name of the Lor[d . . .] against **Resheph** [. . .] he will come to you at ni[ght, and] you will say to him, "Who are you? [Withdraw from] humanity and from the ho[ly] race! For your appearance is [nothing], and your **horns** are horns of sand. You are darkness, not light, [wicked]ness, not righteousness [. . .] the Lord. (11Q11 5:4–13)

These psalms were employed as charms or prayers against evil spirits.

Although they are in terrible condition, we learn several interesting things from these psalms. First, it is clear that psalms were employed as charms or prayers against evil spirits, including an interesting character named Resheph. Resheph was an ancient deity or demon understood to be punitive and dangerous. He was also thought to have horns! I suspect that in the third exorcism psalm above he was probably regarded as none other than Satan himself.

Second, one of the psalms is attributed to Solomon and another is attributed to his father David. Both David and Solomon were popularly believed to have had power over evil spirits and to have written psalms that offered protection against them.

Third, following these three noncanonical psalms is the canonical Psalm 91. Unlike the standard Hebrew text that underlies our English translations, the version found in this Qumran scroll begins with the words, "Of David," and then continues with the whole of Psalm 91 (see 11Q11 6:3–14). I suspect if we had the entire text of the first exorcistic psalm found in this scroll, we would find that it, too, was attributed either to David or to Solomon since both these men were reputed in popular Jewish culture to exercise power over demons.

All of this shows that Psalm 91 *in and before the time of Jesus* was understood as a psalm that promised divine protection from evil spirits. Even Jesus apparently appealed to this psalm with the same understanding. According to Luke 10:17–19 the disciples returned from a preaching mission, saying, "Lord, even the demons submit to us in Your name." Jesus replied to this by saying, "I watched Satan fall from heaven like a lightning flash. Look, I have given you the authority to trample on snakes and scorpions and over all the power of the enemy; nothing will ever harm you." Jesus' statement about "the authority to trample [*patein*] on snakes and scorpions" almost certainly alludes to Psalm 91:13, which says, "You will tread on [Greek: *katapatein*] the lion and the cobra." This verse probably underlies a prophecy found in an intertestamental writing called the *Testament*

Psalm 91 in and before the time of Jesus was understood as a psalm that promised divine protection from evil spirits.

of Levi, forms of which were also found among the DSS (such as 4Q213–14 and 540–41). This fictional work portrays the aged patriarch Levi as prophesying the coming of a Redeemer, a time when "Beliar shall be bound by him. And he shall grant to his children au-

Temptation of Christ by Duccio.

thority to trample [Greek: *patein*] on wicked spirits" (*Testament of Levi* 18:12).

Far from being an isolated incident, the temptation of Jesus foreshadowed the coming struggle between the rule of God and the rule of Satan, and Psalm 91 was popularly understood as foreshadowing several elements in the battle between good and evil. The DSS helped us understand this by supplying vital context (the exorcism psalms) for Jewish use of Psalm 91.

The Proclamation of Jesus the Messiah

If one wished to sum up Jesus' message, a good way of doing it would be to quote his statement in Mark 1:15, which says: "The time is fulfilled, and the kingdom of God has come near." Scholars recognize that by "kingdom" Jesus did not mean territory or boundaries, as in the modern political sense, but sphere of power or rule. Scholars also recognize that Jesus' proclamation was the fulfillment of the prophecy of Isaiah, as in these passages:

> Zion, herald of good news, go up on a high mountain. Jerusalem, herald of good news, raise your voice loudly. Raise it, do not be afraid! Say to the cities of Judah, "Here is your God!" (Isa 40:9)

> How beautiful on the mountains are the feet of the herald, who proclaims peace, who brings news of good things, who proclaims salvation, who says to Zion, "Your God reigns!" (Isa 52:7)

> The Spirit of the Lord God is on Me, because the Lord has anointed Me to bring good news to the poor. He has sent Me to heal the brokenhearted, to proclaim liberty to the captives, and freedom to the prisoners; to proclaim the year of the Lord's favor. (Isa 61:1–2)

What is especially interesting is that in the Aramaic version of Isaiah, the words "Here is your God" and "Your God reigns"

become "The king-
dom of your God
is revealed." This is
what Jesus was pro-
claiming: The king-
dom (or rule) of God
prophesied by Isaiah
is now fulfilled in
my ministry.

The War Scroll.

The hope for the
kingdom of God is
also expressed in the DSS. A fragment of the War Scroll from
Cave 4 prophesies that "the kingdom shall be for God and the
salvation for His people . . . as a few to Belial. But God's covenant is peace for Israel in all the times of eternity . . . (4Q491
frag. 11, column ii, lines 17–18).

In the Rule of Blessings Scroll, the blessing for the future
high priests petitions: "May you serve in the temple of the
kingdom of God, ordering destiny with the Angels of the Presence, a council of the Community with the Holy Ones forever,
for all the ages of eternity!" (1QSb 4:25b–26, with restoration).
The scroll goes on to pronounce a blessing on the coming
Messiah, who will live up to the expectations expressed in the
prophecy of Isaiah 11: "And He shall renew for him the Covenant of the Community, so as to establish the kingdom of
His people forever, that 'with righteousness he may judge the
poor, and decide with equity for the meek of the earth' (v. 4)
and walk before Him blameless in all the ways of His heart'"
(1QSb 5:21–22, with restoration).

We find many references to "His kingdom" and "Your kingdom" in the Songs of the Sabbath Sacrifice scrolls and elsewhere (esp. 4Q400–5; 1QHa 3:27; 4Q286 frag. 7, column i,
line 5). The hope of God's rule was an important theme for the
men of Qumran.

For Jesus, of course, the
rule of God cannot coex-
ist peacefully with the
rule of Satan. This is why
he declares, "If I drive
out demons by the finger

Jesus not only proclaimed God's rule (after all, anyone can do that); he actually demonstrated its reality by attacking the rule of Satan.

of God, then the kingdom of God has come to you" (Luke 11:20). Jesus not only *proclaimed* God's rule (after all, anyone can do that); he actually *demonstrated* its reality by attacking the rule of Satan. Jesus' remarkable success in healing the sick and casting out evil spirits was evidence of the divine power at work in him.

Jesus also proclaimed the jubilee, the time when all debts were traditionally cancelled. Of course, the debts of which Jesus spoke were the debts of sin. This is what lies behind Jesus' sermon in the synagogue at Nazareth (Luke 4:16–30), where he quotes Isaiah 61:1–2 ("The Spirit of the Lord GOD is on Me, because the LORD has anointed Me to bring good news . . .") and declares that it has been fulfilled in the very ears of those who heard it.

Initially the response of the synagogue congregation was very positive: "They were all speaking well of Him and were amazed by the gracious words that came from His mouth" (Luke 4:22). But things soured quickly when Jesus cited the examples of Elijah and Elisha, implying that the good news foretold by Isaiah and proclaimed by Jesus was in fact as much for Gentiles as it was for Israelites. The synagogue congregation became enraged and threw Jesus out of town.

Why such a negative reaction? The Melchizedek Scroll (11Q13) provides the answer. The scroll agrees with Jesus that Isaiah 61 promises a jubilee in which all sin debt is forgiven. The scroll agrees with Jesus that it is indeed good news. But it *disagrees* with Jesus that this good news will be extended to those outside the righteous circle as the insiders defined it. Here is part of the text, where the work of the Redeemer is described:

> He will proclaim to them the jubilee, thereby releasing th[em from the debt of a]ll their sins . . . by his might he will judge God's holy ones and so establish a righteous kingdom. . . . Therefore Melchizedek will thoroughly prosecute the vengeance (Isa 61:2) required by God's statutes. Also, he will deliver all the captives from the power of Belial, and from the power

of all the spirits predestined to him. Allied with him will be all the "righteous divine beings." The . . . is that which . . . all the divine beings. This visitation is the day of salvation that He has decreed through Isaiah the prophet concerning all the captives, inasmuch as scripture says, "How beautiful upon the mountains are the feet of the messenger who announces peace, who brings good news, who announces salvation, who says to Zion, 'Your God reigns'" [Isa 52:7]. . . . (11Q13 2:6–16, with restoration)

Because of this fascinating scroll, we now are better able to understand why the Nazareth congregation was initially delighted to hear that the prophecy of Isaiah 61 was fulfilled in Jesus' ministry. This was a popular prophecy, one associated with the coming era of forgiveness and blessing. But the congregation was outraged when Jesus said nothing about vengeance against Israel's enemies (note that Jesus did not quote all of Isa 61:2, which goes on to *The congregation at Qumran was outraged when Jesus said nothing about vengeance against Israel's enemies.* speak of God's vengeance), but instead implied by citing the examples of Elijah and Elisha (Luke 4:25–27) that God's mercy would also extend to Gentiles such as the widow of 1 Kings 17:8–16 and the Syrian commander of 2 Kings 5:8–14. What Jesus said seemed like treason against Israel to his listeners!

Jesus taught us to forgive people of their sins (e.g., Luke 17:3–4). We find it very difficult to obey this command, and the men of Qumran were no exception. Copies of two scrolls angrily petition: "May God have no mercy upon you when you cry out, nor forgive, so as to atone for your sins" (4Q256 3:2 = 4Q257 2:5). These angry sentiments, perhaps uttered by a prophet in a moment of anger (see Isa 2:9 "Forgive them not!"), stand in stark contrast to the words of the dying Jesus: "Father, forgive them, because they do not know what they are doing" (Luke 23:34).

The Sermon on the Mount by Bloch.

The Blessings of Jesus the Messiah

The Beatitudes (Matt 5:3–12 and Luke 6:20–23) are among the most well-known words that Jesus spoke. They reflect his understanding of the good news of God's rule, offering hope and blessing to those who are humble, pure, meek, and hungry for righteousness. Bible interpreters hear echoes of Isaiah 61 in these teachings.

Until the discovery of the DSS, we had no other examples of beatitudes strung together in the way Jesus presented them. There are a few examples of two but never four, as we have in Luke 6, or nine (or 10), as we have in Matthew 5. The scroll known as 4Q525 changed all of that, for though its beatitudes are not exactly like those of Jesus, the similarities are striking. In demonstration of this fact, notice the parallels between 4Q525 and select beatitudes of Jesus in the following diagram:

> *Until the discovery of the DSS, we had no other examples of beatitudes strung together in the way Jesus presented them.*

Jesus (Matthew 5:3–12 RSV)

3 Blessed are the poor in spirit, for theirs is the kingdom of heaven.

4 Blessed are those who mourn, for they shall be comforted.

5 Blessed are the meek, for they shall inherit the earth.

6 Blessed are those who hunger and thirst for righteousness, for they shall be satisfied.

7 Blessed are the merciful, for they shall obtain mercy.

8 Blessed are the pure in heart, for they shall see God.

9 Blessed are the peacemakers, for they shall be called sons of God.

10 Blessed are those who are persecuted for righteousness' sake, for theirs is the kingdom of heaven.

11 Blessed are you when men revile you and persecute you and utter all kinds of evil against you falsely on my account.

12 Rejoice and be glad, for your reward is great in heaven, for so men persecuted the prophets who were before you.

4Q525 frags. 2–3 ii 1–10

. . . with a pure heart and does not slander with his tongue (Ps 15:3).

Blessed are those who hold fast to its statutes and do not hold fast to the ways of injustice.

Blessed are those who rejoice in it, and do not exult in paths of folly.

Blessed are those who seek it with pure hands, and do not search for it with a deceitful heart.

Blessed is the man who attains wisdom, and walks in the law of the Most High: establishes his heart in its ways, restrains himself by its corrections, is continually satisfied with its punishments, does not forsake it in the face of his trials, at the time of distress he does not abandon it, does not forget it in the day of terror, and in the humility of his soul he does not abhor it. But he meditates on it continually, and in his trial he reflects on it, and with all his being he gains understanding in it, and he establishes it before his eyes so as not to walk in the ways of wickedness . . . and . . . together, and kept his heart fixed on it, and . . . You place a crown of gold upon his head, and with kings You shall seat him, and . . . by His scepter up with equity and among brothers He shall scatter. . . .

Scrolls scholars debate how many beatitudes were originally listed in 4Q525. The beginning of the first one is missing, and four more or less complete beatitudes follow thereafter. It is speculated that originally there were seven or perhaps even 10 beatitudes in this document. In any case, reading through the above comparison reveals several significant parallels, including:

- Jesus spoke of the "pure in heart" while 4Q525 reads "pure heart" and "pure hands."
- Jesus spoke of righteousness while 4Q525 refers to avoiding injustice (which could be rendered "unrighteousness").
- The concluding beatitude of 4Q525 speaks of being seated "with kings" while Jesus spoke of righteous persons who are persecuted being in the company of the prophets.

The parallels are impressive, but important differences exist as well. The greatest difference is in the perspectives of Jesus and the Essene author. Whereas the beatitudes of 4Q525 have a wisdom orientation and focus on doing the Law, Jesus' beatitudes promise that righteous persons will be vindicated when God judges the earth.

Whereas the Essene beatitudes have a wisdom orientation and focus on doing the Law, Jesus' beatitudes promise that righteous persons will be vindicated when God judges the earth.

We have seen striking similarities between the DSS and things said by and of Jesus. In some cases it seems clear that the DSS content came first; in other cases the DSS content may have arisen after Jesus, for some of the scrolls likely date to the latter part of the first century AD. In the chapter that follows, we examine examples where Jesus' teachings differ noticeably from those in the DSS.

Note

1. The following is a key for abbreviations of collections of inscriptions and papyri cited in this chapter. BGU stands for *Ägyptische Urkunde aus den Staatlichen Museen zu Berlin, Griechische Urkunden* (18 vols., Berlin: Staatliche Museen zu Berlin, 1895–2000). IG stands for *Inscriptiones graecae* (Deutsche Akadamie der Wissenschaften zu Berlin; Berlin: G. Reimer, 1873–). OGIS stands for W. Dittenberger (ed.), *Orientis graeci inscriptions selectae* (2 vols., Leipzig: S. Hirzel, 1903–1905; repr. Hildesheim: Olms, 1960). P.Oxy. stands for Oxyrhynchus Papyri. SB stands for F. Preisigke (ed.), *Sammelbuch griechischer Urkunde aus Ägypten* (5 vols., Strassburg: K. J. Trübner, 1915–1955). SIG stands for W. Dittenberger (ed.), *Sylloge inscriptionum graecarum* (4 vols., 3rd ed., Leipzig: Hirzelm 1915–1924).

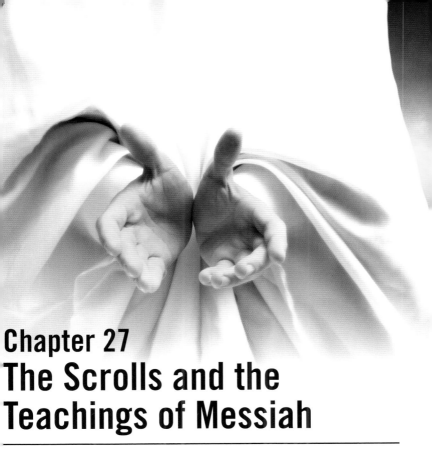

Chapter 27
The Scrolls and the Teachings of Messiah

Some of Jesus' most interesting and controversial teachings concerned the sensitive issue of who was chosen (or elect), who was not, and on what basis this distinction is made. At the center of this discussion was the Law of Moses. How should the God-ordained Law be understood and applied? Everyone agreed that the Law was good, but what did it say about divorce and taxes? And what did Jesus think of the ruling priests who interpreted and applied the Law? Did he agree with their interpretations or oppose them? Once again the Dead Sea Scrolls (DSS) help us understand the issues more clearly.

Parable of the Great Banquet and the Recognized in God's Kingdom

In the parable of the Great Banquet (Luke 14:15–24), Jesus teaches that the healthy and wealthy may not be present at the eschatological banquet hosted by God himself (see Isa 25:6: "The LORD of Hosts will prepare a feast for all the peoples on this mountain"). That Jesus was referring to the great banquet at the end of days is clear from the context, for he told the parable in response to a devout man at a table who said: "The one who will eat bread in the kingdom of God is blessed!" (Luke 14:15).

In this familiar parable Jesus tells those reclining about him that the wealthy, who initially accepted the invitation to the banquet, declined to attend when the announcement was made that all was ready. One said, "I have bought a field, and I must go out and see it. I ask you to excuse me" (Luke 14:18) Another said, "I have bought five yoke of oxen, and I'm going to try them out. I ask you to excuse me" (v. 19). The third man claimed his right of exemption due to his having just married (v. 20). Jesus' audience would have recognized these as affluent persons, signaled by their having enough resources to buy land before seeing it and oxen before testing them. In this light, the audience would assume that such men were enjoying the blessings of God. Of all people, surely *they* number among the elect and would be present for God's banquet. Jesus overturns this expectation by portraying the banquet host as saying, "I tell you, not one of those men who were invited will enjoy my banquet!" (v. 24).

Jesus' audience would have assumed that the wealthy were favored by God.

Instead, "the poor, **maimed**, **blind**, and **lame**" (v. 21, bold font mine) will recline at the banquet table. In Jewish late antiquity the healthy and wealthy were viewed as blessed of God, whose election was assured. The election of the poor and sick, on the other hand, was very much in doubt, a sentiment perhaps inspired by Leviticus 21:17ff.

> None of your descendants throughout your generations who has a physical defect is to come near to present the food of his God. No man who has any defect is to come near: no man who is blind, lame, facially disfigured, or deformed.

These strict rules applied to the priests and the animals offered for sacrifice. The idea was to treat God as holy, offering him sacrifices free of blemishes. Offering a lame lamb, for in-

The Blind Leading the Blind by Bruegel.

stance, would entail offering God an animal that was worth less than a healthy one. It would be giving God the leftovers rather than the first fruits. The men of Qumran took these requirements very seriously. They also applied them to the anticipated final war between the Sons of Light and the Sons of Darkness. This conflict was seen as a spiritual battle more than a physical battle. Indeed, fighting in this battle amounted to an act of worship. Therefore, all participants were to be dressed in white and to be free of physical defects and impurities, as stated in the War Scroll:

> No one **maimed**, **blind** or **lame**, nor a man who has a permanent blemish on his skin, or a man affected with ritual uncleanness of his flesh; none of these shall go with them to battle. All of them shall be volunteers for battle, pure of spirit and flesh, and prepared for the day of vengeance. Any man who is not ritually clean . . . on the day of battle shall not go down with them into battle, for holy angels are present with their army. (1QM 7:4–6)

Notice that the "**maimed**, **blind** or **lame**" at the beginning of this passage parallel the words of Jesus' parable. But what has the great holy war at the end of time to do with the banquet of Jesus' parable? The War Scroll tells us that after the eschatological war, the banquet of celebration takes place. It will be then that the Messiah reclines at table with the righteous of Israel. According to the men of Qumran, however, those with defects and impurities cannot recline at this table. According to the Rule of the Congregation Scroll:

> No man with a physical handicap—**maimed** in both legs or hands, **lame**, **blind**, deaf, dumb or possessed of a visible blemish in his flesh—or a doddering old man unable to do his share in the congregation—may enter to take a place in the congregation of the m[e]n of reputation. For the holy angels are a part of their congregation. (1QSa 2:5–9)

Here again we find the familiar list of excluded persons, such as the "**maimed** in both legs or hands, **lame**, **blind**," the very people who Jesus says will be included in God's great end-times banquet. Whereas the Essenes believed that reclining at table with the Messiah would be forbidden to anyone with defects because the banquet itself was an act of worship, Jesus said the way was open for all to worship him and join in the celebration.

Whereas the Essenes believed that reclining at table with the Messiah would be forbidden to anyone with defects, Jesus said the way was open for all to worship him and join in the celebration.

Jesus' parable of the Great Banquet would have surprised his dinner companions and anyone else who heard of it. He effectively overturned popular conceptions and expectations with this teaching, just as he had done by actions such as his tendency to eat and drink with despised persons such as "sinners and tax collectors" (Mark 2:16). This should give all of us occasion to reflect on our outlooks and practices. Do we exclude those whom Jesus is prepared to accept?

Law and Life: What Shall I Do to Inherit Eternal Life?

On one occasion an expert in the Law put Jesus to the test by asking him a question. Luke tells the story this way:

> Just then an expert in the law stood up to test Him, saying, "Teacher, what must I do to inherit eternal life?"
>
> "What is written in the law?" He asked him. "How do you read it?"
>
> He answered: "Love the Lord your God with all your heart, with all your soul, with all your strength, and with all your mind; and your neighbor as yourself."
>
> "You've answered correctly," He told him. "Do this and you will live." (Luke 10:25–28)

The man answered Jesus by appealing to Deuteronomy 6:4–5 ("Listen, Israel: The LORD our God, the LORD is One. Love the LORD your God with all your heart, with all your soul, and with all your strength") and Leviticus 19:18 ("Love your neighbor as yourself").

Jesus agreed with the man's answer. In fact, when asked the same question on another occasion, Jesus gave the same reply (see Mark 12:29–31). But it is not enough simply to say, "I love God; I believe he is one" and "I love my neighbor as myself." One actually has to *do* these things. This is the point Jesus' brother James makes in his NT letter. He says it is not enough to believe God is one (Jas 2:19),

It is not enough simply to say, "I love God; I believe he is one" and "I love my neighbor as myself." One actually has to *do* these things.

or tell your needy neighbor, "Go in peace, keep warm, and eat well" (v. 16), as though that proves your love for your neighbor (v. 8). One has actually to meet the neighbor's needs, putting faith into action.

This is why after agreeing with the legal expert's answer, Jesus added, "Do this and you will live." This alludes to Leviticus 18:5, where God commanded his people: "Keep My statutes and ordinances; a person will live if he does them. I am the LORD."

Keep in mind that the legal expert asked Jesus specifically about inheriting "eternal life." He was not just asking about long life in the land of Israel, which was the primary point being made in Leviticus 18:5. Given the context of His answer, Jesus' words, "Do this, and you will live," imply that if the man truly loves God and his neighbor as himself he will inherit eternal life. Interestingly, this is exactly how Leviticus 18:5 was understood by the men of Qumran, as we see in the Damascus Document:

> But when those of them who were left held firm to the commandments of God he instituted His covenant with Israel for ever, revealing to them things hidden, in which all Israel had gone wrong: His holy Sabbaths, His glorious festivals, His righteous laws, His reliable ways. The desires of His will, which Man should carry out and so have life in them (Lev 18:5), He opened up to them. So they "dug a well," yielding much water. . . . Those who hold firm to it shall receive eternal life, and all human honor is rightly theirs. (CD 3:12b–16, 20)

The men of Qumran interpreted "neighbor" too narrowly. For them the only neighbors worthy of love were Israelites who joined their group and followed their rules.

If one does what God commands, then he "shall receive eternal life." The only problem for the men of Qumran is that they interpreted "neighbor" too narrowly. For them the only neighbors worthy of love were Israelites who joined their group and followed their rules. Jesus had a much broader definition of neighbor. The legal expert suspected this, and so asked Jesus: "And who is my neighbor?" (Luke 10:29). Jesus answered with the famous parable of the Good Samaritan (Luke 10:30–35).

Who fulfilled the law to love one's neighbor as one's self? The Samaritan did! Not the priest. Not the Levite. Only the Samaritan fulfilled the law and did so by helping a person who in all likelihood held strong personal bias against him. Jesus' command to the legal expert as well as to you and me is, "Go and do the same" (Luke 10:37).

The Works of the Messiah

When the Messiah comes, what will he do? A variety of ideas were entertained among the people of Israel, but faithful Israelites turned to the Prophets for answers. John the Baptist had his ideas, too, and while in prison he grew discouraged and sent messengers to Jesus. Here is how Matthew tells it:

> When John heard in prison what the Messiah was doing, he sent a message by his disciples and asked Him, "Are You the One who is to come, or should we expect someone else?"
>
> Jesus replied to them, "Go and report to John what you hear and see: the blind see, the lame walk, those with skin diseases are healed, the deaf hear, the dead are raised, and the poor are told the good news. And if anyone is not offended because of Me, he is blessed." (Matt 11:2–6)

John the Baptist by El Greco. While in prison, John grew discouraged and sent messengers to Jesus to ask if he was really Messiah.

Jesus' reply echoes selections from Isaiah and Psalm 146. For instance, "the blind see" comes from Isaiah 35:5 and Psalm 146:8; "the lame walk" comes from Isaiah 35:6; "the deaf hear" comes from Isaiah 35:5; "the dead are raised" comes from Isaiah 26:19; and "the poor are told the good news" comes from Isaiah 61:1. In a DSS called a Messianic Apocalypse (4Q521), we find impressive parallels to all of these texts. One column reads as follows:

For the heavens and the earth (Ps 146:6) shall listen to His Messiah and all which is in them (Ps 146:6) shall not turn away from the commandments of the holy ones. Strengthen yourselves, O you who seek the Lord, in His service. Will you not find the Lord in this, all those who hope in their heart? For the Lord attends to the pious and calls the righteous by name. Over the humble His spirit hovers, and He renews the faithful in His strength. For He will honor the pious upon the throne of His eternal kingdom, setting prisoners free (Ps 146:7; Isa 61:1), opening the eyes of the blind, raising up those who are bowed down (Ps 146:8; Isa 35:5). And forever I shall hold fast to those who hope and in His faithfulness shall . . . and the fruit of good deeds shall not be delayed for anyone and the Lord shall do glorious things which have not been done (before), just as He said. For He shall heal the critically wounded, He shall revive the dead (Isa 26:19), He shall send good news to the afflicted (Isa 61:1), He shall satisfy the poor, He shall guide the uprooted, He shall make the hungry rich (Ps 46:7). (4Q521 frag. 2, column ii, lines 1–13, with restorations)

What is especially interesting in this apocalypse (revelation) is that the remarkable things it describes are to take place when the Lord's Messiah appears, one to whom "the heavens and the earth will listen." From this we may infer that doing things like opening the eyes of the blind, enabling the lame to walk and the deaf to hear, raising the dead, and proclaiming good news to the poor are things the Messiah was expected to do. Accordingly, the evangelist Matthew rightly says that John sent word to Jesus when he "heard in prison what the Messiah was doing" (Matt 11:2).

Doing things like opening the eyes of the blind, enabling the lame to walk and the deaf to hear, raising the dead, and proclaiming good news to the poor are things the Messiah was expected to do.

But what caused John to doubt? The answer is found in the very passages of Scripture to which Jesus and the author of 4Q521 alluded. According to Isaiah 61:1 and Psalm 146:7, prisoners were to be set free when Messiah came. But John had not been set free! He was still bound in prison, beginning to wonder whether Jesus was really the Messiah.

Jesus understood the cause of John's doubt and so answered with the words of Scripture to signify that he was in fact performing the works of the Messiah even if John happened to remain in prison. Suffering was necessary for Jesus. This was the path the Father called him to walk. He did not come immediately to take his position at the right hand of power. One implication of this is that even his followers must suffer a little while before their ultimate and permanent vindication. This is why Jesus concluded his reply to John by saying, "And if anyone is not offended because of Me, he is blessed" (Matt 11:6).

The Parable on the Vineyard

In the climactic drama of his life, Jesus entered Jerusalem about a week before Passover, taught in the temple precincts, offended the ruling priests, was seized at night by thugs employed by the ruling priests, and then was handed over to the Roman governor, who crucified him. One of the most threatening things Jesus uttered in the days leading up to his trial

Parable of the Vineyard by de Wet. Jesus' parable of the vineyard depicts the rejection of God's messengers and ultimately his own son.

and crucifixion was his parable of the Wicked Vineyard Tenants (Mark 12:1–12). Jesus' parable begins with an allusion to the much-loved song of the vineyard of Isaiah 5:1–7. Here is the opening verse of the parable:

> Then He began to speak to them in parables: "A man planted a vineyard, put a fence around it, dug out a pit for a winepress, and built a watchtower. Then he leased it to tenant farmers and went away." (Mark 12:1)

Jesus drew about a dozen words in this verse from the vineyard song in Isaiah 5:

> I will sing about the one I love, a song about my loved one's vineyard: The one I love had a vineyard on a very fertile hill. He broke up the soil, cleared it of stones, and planted it with the finest vines. He built a tower in the middle of it and even hewed out a winepress there. (Isa 5:1–2a)

Jesus transformed Isaiah's song of the vineyard by introducing tenant farmers who refuse to comply with the terms of the lease. When it came time to collect payment, the owner sent his servants. But the tenants attacked them and sent them away empty-handed. Finally the owner sent his beloved son, but the tenants killed him. In response, said Jesus, the owner "will come and destroy the farmers and give the vineyard to others" (Mark 12:9).

The evangelist Mark concludes the scene by remarking that the ruling priests "knew He had said this parable against them" (Mark 12:12). But why should the priests think a parable based on Isaiah 5 was directed specifically against them and not against all Israel? After all, Isaiah's song of the vineyard identifies the guilty this way: "For the vineyard of the LORD of Hosts is the house of Israel, and the men of Judah, the plant He delighted in. He looked for justice but saw injustice, for righteousness, but heard cries of wretchedness" (Isa 5:7). The prophet Isaiah said nothing about the ruling priests in specific.

Rather than strictly depending on the original context of Isaiah's words, Jesus' parable reflects the way the song of the vineyard had come to be popularly understood in his time. According to the Aramaic paraphrase of Isaiah 5, the wine press is the altar of sacrifice, and the tower is the temple. Thus the song of the vineyard in the Aramaic version is focused on the temple establishment, which includes the ruling priests.

Rather than strictly depending on the original context of Isaiah's words, Jesus' parable reflects the way the song of the vineyard had come to be popularly understood in his time.

Some scholars doubt the Aramaic Targum can help us understand Jesus' parable because the Targum arose late in Jewish history and thus may not reflect the way Isaiah 5 was understood in Jesus' time. While it is true that the Aramaic version is late, it does sometimes contain readings and interpretations that predated its composition. I think this is so in the case of the song of the vineyard, and evidence from Qumran backs this conclusion. A scroll fragment (4Q500 frag. 1, lines 1–7) found among the DSS preserves six incomplete lines that help us understand how Isaiah 5 was interpreted among the Essenes and by inference possibly among many other Jews. Here is how it reads:

1 [. . .]
2 [. . .] your [tereb]inths flower [. . .]
3 [. . .] the press for your wine is built among stones [. . .]
4 [. . .] to the gate of holy height [. . .]
5 [. . .] your planting and the your glorious channels [. . .]
6 [. . .] your delightful palm leaves [. . .]
7 [. . .] your vine[yard. . . .]

The words in line 3, "The press for your wine is built among stones," confirm that the author had in mind Isaiah 5:1–7. The words in line 4, "the gate of holy height," allude to the sanctuary on the temple mount. The partially restored word "your vineyard" confirms that the scroll had something to say about the vineyard of Isaiah's old song.

In summary, this scroll fragment confirms the antiquity of understanding Isaiah's song as specifically having to do with the temple. Jesus presupposed this understanding in his adapted form of the parable, and the ruling priests who heard his parable understood it and resented it deeply. Who was Jesus to teach publicly that God was unhappy with his ruling priests? And so they strengthened their resolve to be rid of Jesus.

John and Jesus on Divorce

The Gospels tell us that John criticized Herod Antipas for abandoning his wife in order to take up with Herodias, the wife of his brother Philip. John was imprisoned and eventually beheaded because of this rebuke (Mark 6:14–29). Biblically speaking, was John right to criticize Herod? After all, according to many experts in the Law of Moses, the OT permits divorce (see Deut 24:1–4).

For John Herod's offense was not so much that he divorced his wife (the daughter of Aretas IV, the king of Nabatea). Rather, it was that Herod took up with his sister-in-law. John said to Herod, "It is not lawful for you to have your brother's wife!" (Mark 6:18). Herod's action was a clear violation of Mosaic Law, which says, "If a man marries his brother's wife, it is impurity" (Lev 20:21; see also Lev 18:16). This same law is mentioned in the DSS: "No man is to marry his brother's ex-wife, for that would violate his brother's rights, even if the brother shares only the same father or only the same mother. Surely that would be unclean" (4Q524 frags. 15–22, lines 2b–3a; and 11Q19 66:12–13).

Besides the prohibitions, Qumran documents also admonish married men in a positive way: "But you, live together with the wife of your bosom" (4Q416 frag. 2, column iv, line 5). That is, live with your wife, don't divorce her, and by all means do not take up with your sister-in-law!

What were Jesus' views on divorce? They were consistent with John's. In fact, his critics knew this, which is why some Pharisees approached Jesus, to put him to the test. They asked:

Herodias by Levy. John the Baptist criticized Herod Antipas for abandoning his wife in order to take up with Herodias, the wife of his brother Philip.

"Is it lawful for a man to divorce his wife?"

He replied to them, "What did Moses command you?"

They said, "Moses permitted us to write divorce papers and send her away." But Jesus told them, "He wrote this commandment for you because of the hardness of your hearts. But from the beginning of creation God made them male and female. For this reason a man will leave his father and mother and be joined to his wife, and the two will become one flesh. So they are no longer two, but one flesh. Therefore what God has joined together, man must not separate." (Mark 10:2–9)

Jesus here appealed to two passages from Genesis in order to make his argument that what Moses permitted in Deuteronomy 24 does not reflect God's ideal. His design for marriage is that it be permanent and not split apart by men making clever arguments in order to satisfy their lusts and selfishness. Interestingly, the DSS not only take the same view; they make the same argument. Here is what we find in two scrolls:

God's design for marriage is that it be permanent and not split apart by men making clever arguments in order to satisfy their lusts and selfishness.

> The Shoddy-Wall-Builders who went after "Precept"—Precept is a raver of whom it says, "they shall surely rave" (Mic 2:6)—they are caught in two (traps): fornication, by taking two wives in their lifetimes though the principle of creation is "male and female He created them" (Gen 1:27) and those who went into the ark "went into the ark two by two" (Gen 7:9). Concerning the Leader it is written, "he shall not multiply wives to himself" (Deut 17:17). (CD 4:19–5:2a)

> If you would marry a wife in your poverty, take her from the children of . . . from the secret of the way things are. When you are united, live together with your fleshly helper. . . . For as the verse says, "A man should leave his father and his mother and adhere to his wife and they will become one flesh" (Gen 2:24). He has made you ruler over her, so . . . God did not give her father authority over her, He has separated her from her mother, and unto you He has given authority. . . . He has made your wife and you into one flesh. (4Q416 frag. 2, column iii, line 20–column iv, line 5).

John the Baptist, Jesus of Nazareth, and at least some of the men of Qumran took the marriage union very seriously and were highly critical of those who did not. Jesus and two Essene scrolls appeal to the same passages from Genesis in order to provide scriptural authority for their views.

Temple Tribute by Titan. Jesus said, "Give back to Caesar the things that are Caesar's, and to God the things that are God's."

Jesus and the Temple Tax

Jesus is well remembered for his clever answer to the question about paying taxes to the Roman Empire: "Give back to Caesar the things that are Caesar's, and to God the things that are God's" (Mark 12:17). Jesus was also once asked about the temple tax. This episode is recounted only in Matthew:

> When they came to Capernaum, those who collected the double-drachma tax approached Peter and said, "Doesn't your Teacher pay the double-drachma tax?"
>
> "Yes," he said. When he went into the house, Jesus spoke to him first, "What do you think, Simon? Who do earthly kings collect tariffs or taxes from? From their sons or from strangers?"
>
> "From strangers," he said.
>
> "Then the sons are free," Jesus told him. "But, so

we won't offend them, go to the sea, cast in a fishhook, and catch the first fish that comes up. When you open its mouth you'll find a coin. Take it and give it to them for Me and you." (Matt 17:24–27)

The temple tax (or ransom) is commanded in the book of Exodus, but how often it was to be paid was controversial in the time of Jesus. The passage reads as follows:

> The Lord spoke to Moses: "When you take a census of the Israelites to register them, each of the men must pay a ransom for himself to the Lord as they are registered. Then no plague will come on them as they are registered. Everyone who is registered must pay half a shekel according to the sanctuary shekel (20 gerahs to the shekel). This half shekel is a contribution to the Lord. Each man who is registered, 20 years old or more, must give this contribution to the Lord. The wealthy may not give more, and the poor may not give less, than half a shekel when giving the contribution to the Lord to atone for your lives." (Exod 30:11–15)

Peter told the temple tax collectors that Jesus paid the tax, but Jesus clearly had misgivings, as we see demonstrated in his provocative remark, "The sons are free." In context the "sons" are to be understood as the sons of God the king. Nevertheless, "so we won't offend them," Jesus instructed Peter to pay the tax.

The men of Qumran had an opinion about the matter also. They disagreed with those who argued that the temple tax was to be paid every year and not just once in a lifetime. Here is what one scroll says:

> Concerning the Ransom: the money of the valuation which a man gives as ransom for his life shall be half a shekel in accordance with the shekel of the sanctuary. He shall give it only once in his life. A shekel is twenty gerahs in accordance with [the shekel of the sanctu-

ary.] For the six hundred thousand, one hundred talents; for the third (that is, 3000), half a talent, [which is thirty minas; for the five hundred, five minas;] and for the fifty, one half a mina, [which is twenty-]five shekels. The total [is six thousand thirty five and one half of a] mina. . . . men for ten minas; . . . five shekels of silver are a tenth of a mina . . . the shekel is equivalent to twenty gerahs in accordance with the shekel of the sanctuary. A half of a shekel is twelve meahs and two zuzim. (4Q159 frag. 1, column ii, lines 6–12, with restorations; cf. 4Q513 frags. 1–2, column i, lines 2–4)

Line 7 makes clear Qumran's view on the matter: "He shall give (the temple tax) only once in his life." This could well have been Jesus' view—pay once and then as a son of the king (God) one remains forever free.

By the way, the hoard of Tyrian shekels and half-shekels found in the ruins of Qumran may have been set aside for payment of the temple tax. In light of what 4Q159 says in the quote above, I suspect the men of Qumran paid the tax one-half shekel per member of the community one time only and not annually as the temple establishment preferred. This would have been yet another source of tension between the Jerusalem priests and the Essene membership.

At many points the DSS shed light on Jesus' teaching. In the chapters that follow we shall see how the scrolls shed light on several NT writers.

A shekel from the second year after the Jewish revolt.

NEW TESTAMENT

The Scrolls and the New Testament

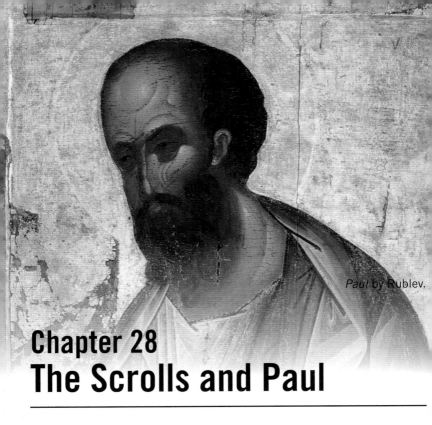

Paul by Rublev.

Chapter 28
The Scrolls and Paul

The Dead Sea Scrolls (DSS) help interpreters of Paul at many points, including understanding his stance on "works of the law" and justification by faith. Also, Paul and the DSS share much ecclesiastical and theological terminology in common. This does not mean that Paul had been a member of the Essene sect or that he borrowed doctrines and themes from them, but it does show that much of his language was not distinctive to the Christian Church. The commonalities and shared language between Paul and the Essenes were the joint property of all pious Jews who took their faith and their sacred Scriptures seriously.

Ecclesiastical Terminology and Order in Paul and the Scrolls

In a difficult part of his second letter to the Corinthian Church, Paul speaks about punishment and restoration in the community of believers. The HCSB rightly captures the sense of the Greek in 2 Corinthians 2:6 as "punishment by the majority," that is, the majority of the congregation in the church at Corinth. We find the same language in the DSS (though written in Hebrew, of course). For example, the Rule of the Community Scroll requires that "during the session of the general membership [lit. the many] no man should say anything except by the permission of the general membership [lit. the many]." (1QS 6:12b)

A few NT writers, including Paul, used the word "bishop" (Greek: *episcopos*). Its basic meaning is "overseer," which is the way it is translated in Acts 20:28. In Paul's letters the word occurs three times (Phil 1:1; 1 Tim 3:2; Titus 1:7). The Hebrew equivalent of the word (*mebaqqer*) occurs more than 40 times in the DSS and is used in essentially the same way that Paul used it. In fact, the word occurs in the same part of the Rule of the Community Scroll cited above: "No man should say anything except by the permission of the many, or more particularly, of the man who is the Overseer of the general membership" (1QS 6:11b–12a).
Thus two of the terms Paul used in an ecclesiastical sense are found together in a single sentence in a Qumran document that spells out the structure and organization of the Essene community. This commonality can be an aid to discovering the fullness of Paul's usage of these terms.

In both Paul and the DSS, we find teaching and regulations concerning order and decorum when the church is assembled. Photo: HolyLandPhotos.org.

In both Paul and the DSS, we find teaching and regulations concerning order and decorum when the church is assembled. Here is what Paul tells the Christians of Corinth:

How is it then, brothers? Whenever you come together, each one has a psalm, a teaching, a revelation, another language, or an interpretation. All things must be done for edification. If any person speaks in another language, there should be only two, or at the most three, each in turn, and someone must interpret. But if there is no interpreter, that person should keep silent

in the church and speak to himself and to God. . . .
But everything must be done decently and in order.
(1 Cor 14:26–28,40)

Paul's recommendations are similar to those found in the
Rule of the Community:

This is the rule for the session of the general membership, each man being in his proper place . . . each man
may state his opinion to the Council of the Community. None should interrupt the words of his comrade,
speaking before his brother finishes what he has to say.
Neither should anyone speak before another of higher
rank. Only the man being questioned shall speak in his
turn. During the session of the general membership no
man should say anything except by the permission of
the general membership, or more particularly, of the
man who is the Overseer of the general membership.
If any man has something to say to the general membership, yet is of a lower rank than whoever is guiding
the deliberations of the Council of the Community, let
him stand up. He should then say, "I have something
to say to the general membership." If they permit, he
may speak. (1QS 6:8–13)

Theological Terminology in Paul and Qumran

Certain words and phrases repeatedly crop up in Paul's writings. These are key expressions of his theology, and as it turns
out, many of the same theological phrases were important to
the men of Qumran also. Here are six examples:

- The "righteousness of God" in Paul (Rom 1:17; 3:21) and
  the DSS (1QS 1:21; 10:23,25; 11:12)
- The "grace of God" in Paul (Rom 5:15; 1 Cor 1:4; 3:10;
  15:10; Gal 2:21; Col 1:6) and the DSS (1QS 11:12)
- The "works of the law" in Paul (Rom 3:20,28; Gal 2:16;
  3:2,5,10) and the DSS (1QS 6:18; 4Q261 frag. 1, line 3;
  4Q265 frag. 4, column ii, line 6; 4Q398 frags. 14–17,

column ii, line 3 = 4Q399 frag. 1, column i, lines 11)

- The "church of God" in Paul (1 Cor 1:2; 10:32; 11:16; 15:9; 2 Cor 1:1; Gal 1:13; 1 Thess 2:14; 2 Thess 1:4) and the DSS (1QM 4:10; 4Q249g frags. 3–7, line 1)

- The "new covenant" in Paul (1 Cor 11:25; 2 Cor 3:6) and the DSS (CD 6:19; 8:21; 20:12; 1QSb 5:5, 21; 1QpHab 2:3; 1Q34bis frag. 3, column ii, line 6; 4Q509 frags. 97–98, column i, line 8)

- The "sons of light" in Paul (Eph 5:8 ; 1 Thess 5:5) and the DSS (1QS 1:9; 2:16; 3:13, 24–25; 1QM 1:1, 3 etc.)

Readers of Paul's letters often encounter the dichotomy between "flesh" and "spirit."

Readers of Paul's letters often encounter the dichotomy between "flesh" and "spirit." Whereas the flesh is weak and prone to sin and failure, the spirit is potentially strong, especially if empowered by God's Spirit. Paul discusses this topic at length in Romans 7–8. Here is one important verse in his discussion: "For those whose lives are according to the flesh think about the things of the flesh, but those whose lives are according to the Spirit, about the things of the Spirit" (Rom 8:5). We find similar ideas in Qumran's Rule of the Community plus another DSS:

> By His truth God shall then purify all human deeds, and refine some of humanity so as to extinguish every perverse spirit from the inward parts of his flesh, cleansing from every wicked deed by a holy spirit. Like purifying waters, He shall sprinkle each with a spirit of truth, effectual against all the abominations of lying. (1QS 4:20–21)

> And I am among those who fear God, who opens his mouth aided by His veritable knowledge, and . . . empowered by His holy spirit . . . truth for all these, and they became contentious spirits. Through the structures of statute and . . . of flesh. God has placed a spirit of knowledge and understanding, truth and

righteousness in the heart of . . . Be strong in the statutes of God so as to battle evil spirits. . . . (4Q444 frags. 1–5, column i, lines 1–4)

Paul, the Scrolls, and Veiling Women

The DSS may help us understand Paul's controversial and much-debated teaching about decorum in the assembled church. In 1 Corinthians 11:10 he says, "This is why a woman should have a symbol of authority on her head: because of the angels." What can this mean? Two Qumran scrolls may provide the answer. According to 1QM 7:6 and 1QSa 2:8–9, angels are present during holy war and during the assembly of the community. The implication seems to be that every aspect of human appearance and conduct must be holy during worship or service of God, for the angels are present to watch all that transpires.

Since in the Near Eastern culture at large the uncovered female head was viewed as inappropriate decorum, Paul meant for women to adorn themselves with modesty due to the sanctity of worship.[1] This conclusion makes sense of Paul's words and fits nicely with the known values of the age. Thus we should reject the popular interpretation of this verse which says that Paul wanted women to veil themselves so as to prevent the angels from lusting after them. This interpretative tradition grew out of speculations about the fallen ones mentioned in Genesis 6, but the DSS have helped us reach a more fitting conclusion.

Paul, the Scrolls, and "Works of the Law"

In his letters, especially Romans and Galatians, Paul argues passionately for salvation through faith, not through "works of the Law." In one place he says, "We know that no one is justified by the works of the law but by faith in Jesus Christ. And we have believed in Christ Jesus, so that we might be justified by faith in Christ and not by the works of the law, because by the works of the law no human being will be justified" (Gal 2:16).

Paul bases his argument on the precedent-setting faith of Abraham, the founding patriarch of the Jewish people who was counted righteous because he believed God (Gal 3:6; cf. Rom 4). In fact Paul quotes the all important passage, "Abram believed the Lord, and He credited it to him as righteousness" (Gen 15:6). But this is just one of two passages in the OT where "reckoned" and "righteousness" occur together. The other is found in Psalm 106, a psalm that recounts Israel's checkered history of sin and rebellion and God's grace in restoring his people. Along the way the psalm mentions the sin the Israelites committed in the wilderness at a place called Baal-peor, a sin that resulted in a plague (Num 25:1–13). We are told that an Israelite man and a Midianite woman brought pagan worship and practice (complete with some sexual activity on the side) right into the midst of the Israelite camp. A priest named Phinehas saved the day by killing the offenders. Psalm 106 refers to his zealous action: "But Phinehas stood up and intervened, and the plague was stopped. It was credited to him as righteousness throughout all generations to come" (Ps 106:30–31; cf. Num 25:6–15).

The men of Qumran and the apostle Paul held conflicting ideas on how a person could be declared righteous before God.

Of the two passages that Paul could have chosen to make his point about God's grace and the need to respond to this grace in faith, I can see why he chose the story of Abraham rather than that of the spear-wielding Phinehas!

The men of Qumran also were interested in how someone could be reckoned as righteous, but their thinking was very different from Paul's and so was their favored OT proof text.

Here is what one of their leaders said in a letter to some Jerusalem priests whom he hoped to persuade to his point of view:

> Now, we have written to you some of the works of the Law, those which we determined would be beneficial for you and your people, because we have seen that you possess insight and knowledge of the Law. Understand all these things and beseech Him to set your counsel straight and so keep you away from evil thoughts and the counsel of Belial. Then you shall rejoice at the end time when you find the essence of our words to be true. And it will be "reckoned to" you "as righteousness," in that you have done what is right and good before Him, to your own benefit and to that of Israel. (4QMMT C26–32 [4Q398 frags. 14–17])[2]

In our English translations it appears that the words rendered "reckoned to" and "as righteousness" could equally come from Genesis 15:6 or Psalm 106:31. In other words, they could be taken to allude to the faith of Abraham, which God reckoned as righteousness, or to the violent action of Phinehas, which God also reckoned as righteousness. However, the form of the Hebrew suggests that the author of 4QMMT had in mind the action of Phinehas rather than Abraham. You see, the Hebrew verb "reckon" in Genesis 15:6 is in the qal form; but in Psalm 106:31 *and* 4QMMT it is in the niphal form. (Forgive me for mentioning Hebrew grammar, but it actually is important!) The match in grammar between Psalm 106:31 and 4QMMT suggests that the Essene author was alluding to Psalm 106, not Genesis 15. Of course, as a religious group founded by ultra-conservative priests, the men of Qumran took the zeal of Phinehas as an excellent example of devotion and true priesthood.

What this implies is that the men of Qumran were committed to performing "certain works of the Law," which if performed would result in rejoicing "at the end time." They "reckoned" their works of the law would be counted as "righteousness." This works-based righteousness is the very thing Paul opposes so sharply in his letters to the Romans and Galatians. In the words of one DSS scholar, Qumran's 4QMMT provides interpreters of Paul with the "smoking gun" that proves the existence of a works-righteousness theology among the Jews of that era.[3]

The men of Qumran were committed to performing "certain works of the Law," which would be counted as "righteousness."

Paul, the Scrolls, and Human Beings as Molded Clay

In Romans 9 Paul likens a human being to a lump of clay that God has molded for his own purposes:

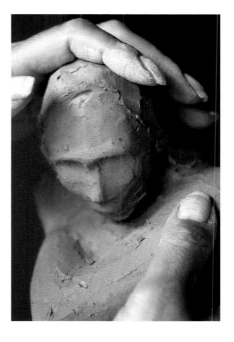

You will say to me, therefore, "Why then does He still find fault? For who can resist His will?" But who are you—anyone who talks back to God? Will what is formed say to the one who formed it, "Why did you make me like this?" Or has the potter no right over His clay, to make from the same lump one piece of pottery for honor and another for dishonor? (Rom 9:19–21)

We find similar imagery in the DSS, as we see here in the Rule of the Community:

You created from the dust for the eternal council. The perverse spirit You have cleansed from great transgression, that he might take his stand with the host of the holy ones, and enter into community with the congregation of the sons of heaven. And for man, You have allotted an eternal destiny with the spirits of knowledge, to praise Your name together with shouts of joy, and to recount Your wonders before all Your creatures. But I, a creature of clay, what am I? Kneaded with water, for whom am I to be reckoned, and what is my strength? (1QS 11:21–24a)

Stumbling Stone or Cornerstone?

In Romans 9:33 Paul quotes Isaiah 28:16, which says, "Therefore the Lord GOD said: 'Look, I have laid a stone in Zion, a tested stone, a precious cornerstone, a sure foundation; the one who believes will be unshakable.'" In Romans 12:1–2 he urges Christians to present themselves as a "living sacrifice, holy and pleasing to God," which is our "spiritual worship" (cf. Phil 2:17; 4:18). We find both of these elements (the stone of Isa 28:16 and humans figuratively offering themselves as living sacrifices) in another passage from Qumran's Rule of the Community:

When such men as these come to be in Israel, then shall the Council of the Yahad truly be established, an eternal planting, a temple for Israel, and—mystery!— a Holy of Holies for Aaron; true witnesses to justice, chosen by God's will to atone for the land and to recompense the wicked their due. They will be "the tested wall, the precious cornerstone" [Isa 28:16] whose foundations shall neither be shaken nor swayed, a fortress, a Holy of Holies for Aaron, all of them knowing the Covenant of Justice and thereby offering a sweet savor. They shall be a blameless and true house in Israel, upholding the covenant of eternal statutes. They shall be an acceptable sacrifice, atoning for the land and ringing in the verdict against evil, so that perversity ceases to exist. (1QS 8:4–10)

Paul's use of Isaiah 28:16 is influenced by Isaiah 8:14, which speaks of a stumbling-stone. Thus for Paul one's response to Christ (the stone) determines the function of the stone. If one responds in faith to Christ, he is indeed a solid cornerstone on which a secure spiritual house can be built. If one rejects Christ, on the other hand, he becomes a stone of stumbling. For the men of Qumran, the stone is interpreted as wholly positive. They identified their own community as the precious stone that God has laid in Zion, and their members were seen as a  "blameless and true house in Israel . . . an acceptable sacrifice, atoning for the land."

Summary

The findings from the DSS do not show that Paul depended on Essene thought or simply grafted it into Christian theology. After all, significant differences exist on fundamental issues such as the question of how one becomes righteous. However, the similarities that do exist between Paul's teachings and those of the Qumran community show us that Paul's

Christianity grew up from distinctly Jewish roots and not from pagan Greek beliefs.

creative use of OT Scripture resonated with the Jewish people of his time. This means Christianity grew up from distinctly Jewish roots and not from pagan Greek beliefs, as some critics have maintained.

Notes

1. For more on this interesting topic, see J. A. Fitzmyer, "A Feature of Qumran Angelology and the Angels of 1 Cor. 11.10," *New Testament Studies* 4 (1957), 48–58.

2. The document is called MMT because of the phrase *miqsat maʿasey ha-torah*, or "some of the works of the Law." Because there are fragments of six copies of the letter, scholars were able to compose a composite, which is what the letter C stands for in the citation.

3. For more on this important topic, see M. G. Abegg, "Paul, 'Works of the Law,' and MMT," *Biblical Archaeology Review* 20/6 (1994), 52–55, 82; J. D. G. Dunn, "4QMMT and Galatians," *New Testament Studies* 43 (1997), 147–53.

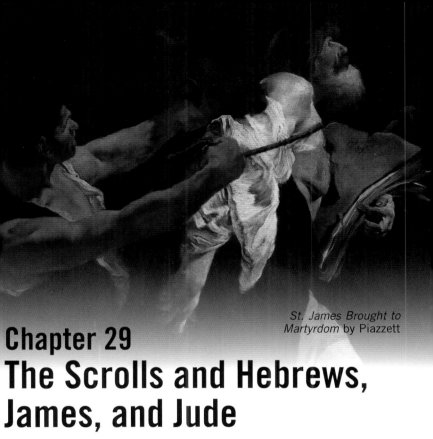

St. James Brought to Martyrdom by Piazzett

Chapter 29
The Scrolls and Hebrews, James, and Jude

The Dead Sea Scrolls (DSS) make important contributions to the study of NT letters that are very Jewish in their orientation. Lumped together, they are often called the General Letters. In this chapter we consider three of them: Hebrews, James, and Jude.

Hebrews

The book of Hebrews is in some ways the most difficult writing in the NT. We do not know who wrote it. It was not written by Paul, despite what some versions of the King James Bible say. One thing we do know is that it is Jewish to the very core. The letter was written to Jewish Christians (hence the name "Hebrews"). It makes many references to the prophets, angels, priests, sacrifices, and Israel's history. Many of its warning passages are framed in the light of this history, admonishing readers not to lapse into unbelief and apostasy as their forefathers had done. Below we examine two commonalities between the book of Hebrews and the DSS.

Melchizedek: Melchizedek makes an abrupt appearance in Genesis 14, shortly after Abraham's defeat of the tribal chieftains who had taken his nephew Lot and others hostage. We are told:

> After Abram returned from defeating Chedorlaomer and the kings who were with him, the king of Sodom went out to meet him in the Valley of Shaveh (that is, the King's Valley). Then Melchizedek, king of Salem, brought out bread and wine; he was a priest to God Most High. He blessed him and said: "Abram is blessed by God Most High, Creator of heaven and earth, and give praise to God Most High who has handed over your enemies to you." (Gen 14:17–20)

Meeting of Melchizedek and Abraham by Bouts the Older.

Melchizedek appears one other time in the OT:

> The LORD declared to my Lord: "Sit at My right hand until I make Your enemies Your footstool." The LORD will extend Your mighty scepter from Zion. Rule over Your surrounding enemies. Your people will volunteer on Your day of battle. In holy splendor, from the womb of the dawn, the dew of Your youth belongs to You. The LORD has sworn an oath and will not take it back: "Forever, You are a priest like Melchizedek." (Ps 110:1–4)

The author of Hebrews makes important references to Genesis 14 when discussing Melchizedek, but Psalm 110 captures his greatest interest. He argues that Jesus is the Davidic Messiah who sits at God's right hand (Ps 110:1) and also that he is a priest "in the order of Melchizedek" (Ps 110:4; Heb 5:6, 10; 6:20; 7:11,17) rather than the order of Levi, as was standard for priests. The author must argue this way since Jesus is of the tribe of Judah and of the family of David and not a descendant of Levi. If he is a priest, he can only be a priest after the special order of Melchizedek, who in Genesis 14:18 is identified as "priest to God Most High" and the "king of Salem," which is to say ancient Jerusalem. The author of Hebrews shows that Melchizedek is superior to Abraham and to the Levitical priesthood that would eventually spring from his line. After all, Abraham bowed before Melchizedek and paid him tithes (Heb 7:1–10). Therefore, since the priesthood of Jesus is "after the order of Melchizedek," who was superior to Abraham and the Levitical priesthood that issued from his descendants, Jesus' priesthood is likewise superior to that of the Levites.

The author of Hebrews shows that Melchizedek is superior to Abraham and to the Levitical priesthood that would eventually spring from his line.

The DSS may show that there is more to this argument than we previously realized. The author of Hebrews has taken pains to underscore Jesus' superiority to Moses, the angels, the prophets, and even the Levitical priesthood. To achieve the latter he links Jesus closely to the mysterious figure of Melchizedek. He says Melchizedek is "without father, mother, or genealogy, having neither beginning of days nor end of life, but resembling the Son of God" (Heb 7:3). This last part was poorly understood until scholars discovered the DSS. In what sense did Melchizedek resemble the Son of God? The Melchizdedek Scroll from Cave 11 helps us understand the larger context.

For this is the time decreed for "the year of Melchizedek's favor" (Isa 61:2), and by his might he will judge God's holy ones and so establish a righteous kingdom, as it is written about him in the Songs of David, "God has taken his place in the assembly of God; in the midst of the gods he holds judgment" (Ps 82:1). Scripture also says about him, "Over it take your seat in the highest heaven; God will judge the peoples" (Ps 7:7–8). (11Q13 2:9–11a, with restorations)

The author of the Melchizedek Scroll has modified the quotation of Isaiah 61:2 in an astounding way. Whereas Isaiah actually said, "The year of the Lord's favor," our author has changed it to read, "The year of Melchizedek's favor." The name "Lord" is the sacred name of God, Yahweh. By inserting Melchizedek's name here, the author implies that Melchizedek is in some way God himself.

The Melchizedek Scroll goes on to say that Melchizedek "will judge God's holy ones" and "establish a righteous kingdom." Furthermore, the author says that Melchizedek is the subject of some of the "Songs of David," meaning the Psalms. In one case (Ps 82:1) Melchizedek is identified as "God," who "has taken His place in the divine assembly; He judges among the gods." In another case Melchizedek is invited to take his "seat in the highest heaven" and as "God" he "will judge the peoples" (Ps 7:7–8). The author slightly modified this quotation of Psalm 7. In its original form it reads "the Lord judges the peoples." Here again, the "Lord" translates the divine name Yahweh. What the Melchizedek Scroll claims is simply astounding: Melchizedek is God himself!

These magnified presentations of Melchizedek in Jewish traditions antedate Christianity and probably help explain why the author of Hebrews finds it important to present Jesus as a heavenly high priest like Melchizedek.

In some of the fragments of the Songs of the Sabbath Sacrifice, Melchizedek appears in the role of a heavenly high priest (see 4Q401 frag 11, line 3: "Melchizedek, priest in the assembly of God"). These magnified presentations of Melchizedek in Jewish traditions antedate Christianity and probably help explain why the author of Hebrews finds it important to present Jesus as a heavenly high priest like Melchizedek.

Spiritual Sacrifice in Hebrews and the Scrolls: It is said of Jesus in Hebrews 13:15: "Therefore, through Him let us continually offer up to God a sacrifice of praise, that is, the fruit of our lips that confess His name." This is similar to ideas found in the Rule of the Community. Consider the following passages:

> Then indeed will he be accepted by God, offering the sweet savor of atoning sacrifice. (1QS 3:11)

> They shall be an acceptable sacrifice, atoning for the land and ringing in the verdict against evil, so that perversity ceases to exist. (1QS 8:10)

> They shall atone for the guilt of transgression and the rebellion of sin, becoming an acceptable sacrifice for the land through the flesh of burnt offerings, the fat of sacrificial portions and prayer, becoming—as it were—justice itself, a sweet savor of righteousness and blameless behavior, a pleasing free-will offering. (1QS 9:4–5)

James

The DSS shed light on the letter of James also. In the commentary on Habakkuk, we read of "those who do the Law" (1QpHab 7:10–11; 8:1). We also read about the "poor ones" and "the simple of Judah, doer(s) of the Torah" (1QpHab 12:4). In another scroll we have a fragment with a reference to "doing the words of the covenant" (4Q185 frag. 3, column i, line 3).

James, brother of Jesus, places similar emphasis on doing the Law. He admonishes his readers to "be doers of the word and not hearers only, deceiving yourselves" (Jas 1:22). Interestingly, the Greek word James uses for "doers" may reflect the Hebrew word meaning "those who do," which when spoken aloud in Greek or Latin could sound like "Essenes." This would fit well with the Essene emphasis on "doing the words of the covenant," and it may explain how the Esssenes got their name, a name which is otherwise meaningless in Latin and Greek.

Jude

Jude, another of Jesus' brothers, authored one of the smallest writings in the NT. He warns readers to avoid the moral and doctrinal errors of "ungodly" people who pervert the gospel (Jude 4). To make his case he appeals to many OT traditions, including some of those found in apocryphal and

Jude warns readers to avoid the moral and doctrinal errors of "ungodly" people who pervert the gospel.

pseudepigrapha works like the book of Enoch and the Testament of Moses. These works are quoted and alluded to in the following passages:

> Yet Michael the archangel, when he was disputing with the Devil in a debate about Moses' body, did not dare bring an abusive condemnation against him, but said, "The Lord rebuke you!" (Jude 9)

> And Enoch, in the seventh generation from Adam, prophesied about them: "Look! The Lord comes with thousands of His holy ones to execute judgment on all, and to convict them of all their ungodly deeds that they have done in an ungodly way, and of all the harsh things ungodly sinners have said against Him." (Jude 14–15)

Verse 9 paraphrases and quotes an incident described in a non-biblical work, only part of which has survived. Some call the work the Testament of Moses; others call it the Ascension of Moses. In any case, the part Jude quotes relates to Moses' death (Deut 34:5–8). In the century or so before the time of Jesus, speculation arose concerning the death and burial of Moses. A tradition arose that he ascended to heaven. Some even specu-

lated that the devil tried to prevent Moses from entering Paradise, accusing him of murder in the death of the Egyptians caused by plague and drowning in the Red Sea. The Bible of course says nothing about Moses ascending to heaven or being confronted by the devil.

In Jude 14–15 we have allusion to an incident related in the book of Enoch and a near verbatim quotation of Enoch 1:9. The passage that is quoted attributes to Enoch a prophecy of coming judgment on the wicked.

Brazen Serpent Sculpture at Moses' memorial atop Mt. Nebo, where Moses died. Photo: David Bjorgen.

Interpreters of the NT long wondered why Jude would make use of writings that did not gain entry into the canon of Scripture. Strictly speaking this question is anachronistic since the OT canon was not universally settled until after Jude was written, but in any event the DSS have shown us that apocryphal and pseudepigraphal writings were widely circulated and read in the NT era. Recall that 20 Enoch scrolls were found at Qumran as well as a host of Testaments and Apocalypses similar to the Ascension of Moses. Indeed, some scholars have wondered if the Ascension of Moses had originally been a part of the Qumran library but was somehow lost. Certainly the work would have fit nicely with known DSS documents.

Summary

One of the things the DSS have taught us is that religious writings were very common in the time of Jesus and the early Church.

One of the things the DSS have taught us is that religious writings were very common in the time of Jesus and the early Church.

Many of them were treasured, studied, and quoted even if they did not enjoy the same status as the books that came to be included in the canon of Scripture. For our purposes these books supply important contextual information, helping us understand the books that *are* a part of our canon.

St. James on Patmos by Bosch.

Chapter 30
The Scrolls and Revelation

One of the most interesting features of the book of Revelation is its description of new Jerusalem. John the seer writes: "Then I saw a new heaven and a new earth. . . . I also saw the Holy City, new Jerusalem, coming down out of heaven from God" (Rev 21:1–2). This vision is similar to Ezekiel's vision in which he saw the establishment of a new city and a new temple (Ezek 40–48).

John also says of new Jerusalem: "Her radiance was like a very precious stone, like a jasper stone, bright as crystal. The city had a massive high wall, with 12 gates. Twelve angels were at the gates; on the gates, names were inscribed, the names of the 12 tribes of the sons of Israel. There were three gates on the east, three gates on the north, three gates on the south, and three gates on the west" (Rev 21:11–13).

Sounds like a fantastically beautiful city, and this impression is only increased when we realize her dimensions: "The city is laid out in a square; its length and width are the same. He measured the city with the rod at 12,000 stadia. Its length, width, and height are equal" (Rev 21:16). How big are 12,000 stadia? It is estimated to equal 1,500 miles. The new Jerusalem is vast!

The New Jerusalem by Doré.

With the discovery of the scrolls, we have learned that the men of Qumran were also keenly interested in the appearance and dimensions of the new Jerusalem. At least six scrolls have been identified from five of the Qumran caves. (See the list in the text box.) All of these are in Aramaic (abbreviation: ar) and three of them (2Q24; 4Q554; 5Q15) preserve substantial chunks of text.

With the discovery of the scrolls we have learned that the men of Qumran were also keenly interested in the appearance and dimensions of the new Jerusalem.

New Jerusalem Scrolls
1QJN ar = 1Q32
2QJN ar = 2Q24
4QNJa ar = 4Q554
4QNJb ar = 4Q555
5QNJ ar = 5Q15
11QJN ar = 11Q18

Modeled after Ezekiel 40–47 and Isaiah 54:11–12, the scrolls present us with a vision that includes precise measurements and a look at the liturgical practices of the temple in new Jerusalem. Also, the new Jerusalem is said to be 100 stadia north to south and 140 stadia east to west (or 13.3 x 18.6 miles). That's pretty big, though much smaller than the vision related by John in the book of Revelation. Gates are also named in these scrolls, just as in Revelation:

He measured from the northeastern corner to the north gate, thirty-five stadia, and the name of this gate is called the gate of Simeon. From this gate to the middle gate he measured thirty-five stadia and the name of this gate is called the gate of Levi. From this gate he measured to the south gate, thirty-five stadia, and the name of this gate is called the gate of Judah. And from this gate he measured to the south eastern corner, thirty-five stadia, and from this corner westwards he measured to the east gate twenty-five stadia and the name of this gate is called the gate of Joseph. He measured from this gate to the middle gate, twenty-five stadia and the name of this gate is called the gate of Benjamin. (4Q554 frag. 2, column i, lines 11–20a, with restorations)

Whereas Revelation 21:12 simply tells us that the 12 gates bore the names of the 12 tribes of Israel, Qumran's New Jerusalem Scroll actually states the names, one by one. Some of the descriptions of the new city are very precise, down to information about the size of city blocks and streets. Here is another excerpt:

> Each block had a sidewalk around it, bordering the street, three staffs, that is, twenty cubits and one. And so he showed me the measurement of all the blocks: between each block was a street six staffs in width, that is, forty-two cubits. And the main streets that passed from east to west were ten staffs. The width of the street was seventy cubits, for two of them. A third street, which was on the north of the temple he measured at eighteen staffs in width, that is, one hundred twenty-six cubits. And the width of the streets that go from south to north, for two of them, nine staffs, with four cubits to each street, making sixty-seven cubits. And the middle street in the middle of the city he measured. Its width was thirteen staffs and one cubit, that is, ninety-two cubits. And all the streets and the city itself were paved with white stone. (5Q15 frag. 1, column i, lines 1b–6, with restorations)

The New Jerusalem scrolls and the vision of the new Jerusalem in Revelation 21 share many common features.

Although by no means identical in all that they say, the New Jerusalem scrolls and the vision of the new Jerusalem in Revelation 21 share many common features. The interest in the new and restored Jerusalem was keenly felt by the men of Qumran and by John the Seer, a man exiled on the island of Patmos because of his faith in Jesus as Messiah.

Cave 7. Photo: Albeiro Rodas.

Chapter 31
Are Some of the Scrolls from the New Testament?

Not long after the publication of the Cave 7 Greek fragments, of which only a few had been identified with any confidence, Spanish scholar José O'Callaghan claimed that he recognized several as belonging to the NT. In all, he identified six NT writings among nine Cave 7 fragments.[1]

Fragment 7Q5.

If O'Callaghan's identifications were correct, it would mean we now possess fragments of Greek NT manuscripts mostly dating to a time before AD 70, which would make them the oldest known NT manuscripts. O'Callaghan's identifications and suggested dates are presented in the following table.

José O'Callaghan's Identifications and Dates of Cave 7 Manuscripts

Manuscript	Identification	O'Callaghan's Degree of Certainty	Suggested Date AD
7Q4	1 Tim 3:16; 4:1,3	Certain	c. 100
7Q5	Mark 6:52–53	Certain	c. 50
7Q6, frag. 1	Mark 4:28	Certain	c. 50
7Q6, frag. 2	Acts 27:38	Probable	c. 60
7Q7	Mark 12:17	Probable	c. 50
7Q8	Jas 1:23–24	Certain	c. 50–70
7Q9	Rom 5:11–12	Probable	c. 50–60
7Q10	2 Pet 1:15	Possible	c. 60
7Q15	Mark 6:48	Possible	c. 50

Very few scholars have agreed with O'Callaghan's identifications.[2] Part of the problem is that these fragments are tiny. The most talked about fragment is 7Q5, which O'Callaghan thinks contains the last part of Mark 6:52 and the first part of 6:53. To make this identification he has to make two very doubtful letter identifications, assume that even when in pristine condition part of the passage was missing, and that one of the words is spelled in an odd way. All of this from a fragment that contains only one complete word: the Greek word for "and" (*kai*)!

In 1988 Wilhelm Nebe made a plausible case that 7Q4, which O'Callaghan took to be from 1 Timothy, was actually a fragment from the book of Enoch. A few years later Emile Puech and Ernest Muro published studies identifying other Cave 7 fragments with Enoch. These new identifications are as follows:

7Q11	1 Enoch 100:12
7Q4 frag. 1; 7Q12; 7Q14	1 Enoch 103:3–4
7Q8	1 Enoch 103:7–8
7Q13	1 Enoch 103:15
7Q4 frag. 2	1 Enoch 105:1 (or 98:11)[3]

These new identifications are probably correct. We know that the book of Enoch was in circulation prior to AD 70, and we know that it was appreciated by the men of Qumran (remember, 20 Aramaic Enoch scrolls were found in the Qumran caves). We also know that Enoch was translated and circulated in Greek, of which a few large fragments survive. Therefore, it is not at all surprising to find fragments of Enoch in one of the caves in which the men of Qumran deposited their scrolls. Moreover, other fragments in Cave 7 have been identified as belonging to the OT and OT Apocrypha. These are 7Q1 (=Exod 28:4–7) and 7Q2 (=Epistle of Jeremiah 43–44).

Finally, it is interesting that the men of Qumran placed all of their Greek scrolls in one particular cave. Not one scroll fragment in Cave 7 is in Hebrew or Aramaic. Some scholars wonder if what we have here is an instance of linguistic segregation, in which the non-Semitic language scrolls were viewed as less important or as in some sense unclean and therefore in need of segregation.

> *The men of Qumran placed all of their Greek scrolls in one particular cave. Not one scroll fragment in Cave 7 is in Hebrew or Aramaic.*

Summary

Since these fragments are from OT books and related writings rather than NT writings, we are not faced with the difficulty in trying to explain the presence of Christian writings in one of the Qumran caves.

Notes

1. J. O'Callaghan, "¿Papiros neo-testamentarios en la cueva 7 de Qumran?" *Biblica* 53 (1972), 91–100; English Translation: "New Testament Papyri in Qumran Cave 7," Supplement to the *Journal of Biblical Literature* 91 (1972), 1–14 (translated by W. L. Holladay).

2. See R. H. Gundry, "No *Nu* in Line 2 of 7Q5: A Final Disidentification of 7Q5 with Mark 6:52–53," *Journal of Biblical Literature* 118 (1999), 698–707.

3. For a study in English, see E. A. Muro, "The Greek Fragments of Enoch from Qumran Cave 7 (*7Q4, 7Q8, & 7Q12 = 7QEn gr = Enoch 103:3–4, 7–8*)," *Revue de Qumran* 18 (1997), 307–312.

Part X

Conclusion

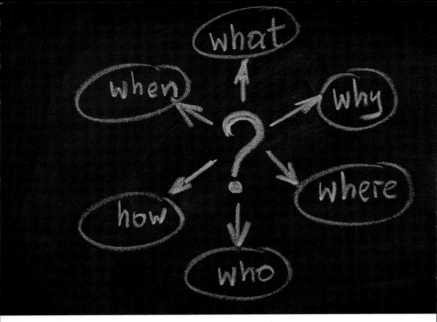

Chapter 32
Summary Q&A on the Dead Sea Scrolls

We have covered a lot of interesting ground. I suspect most readers had no idea how complicated the Dead Sea Scrolls (DSS) could be. We have run the gamut from dusty ancient scrolls to modern, high-tech science. On one hand we have reviewed learned, serious scholarship, while on the other hand we've surveyed and dismissed some silly theories as well. As the book draws to a close, let me recap some of the most important points that have been covered. I will do this by using a Q&A format.

Who wrote and collected the DSS?

When the first cave was discovered in 1947–1948, scholars believed the scrolls were written and collected by Essenes. Although some scholars have since disputed this conclusion, suggesting instead that the DSS were written by Christians or various Jews in and around Jerusalem possibly as late as the Middle Ages, most today believe that the scrolls are indeed the lost library of the Jewish sect called Essenes, written 2,000 years ago.

Did Essenes live at Qumran, where most of the DSS were found?

Ongoing archaeological work has tended to confirm the link between the ruins at Qumran and the scrolls found in the nearby caves. Suggestions that the ruins are those of a fortress, farm, or villa have not persuaded many. Most scholars and archaeologists still think that the inhabitants of the compound were indeed Essenes, who collected, wrote, and studied the DSS.

How old are the DSS?

Study of the handwriting, comparison with historical events, and carbon-14 testing have all confirmed that the scrolls range from as early as third century BC to the middle of the first century AD. Most of the scrolls date to the first century BC.

Do the DSS mention Jesus or early Christians?

Neither the name of Jesus nor any other Christian appears in the scrolls. The scrolls tell us nothing directly about Jesus or his early followers. Nor is Jesus referred to indirectly, by means of some sobriquet, such as "Teacher of Righteousness" or "Wicked Priest." These suggested identifications have been rejected by all qualified scholars.

Have New Testament books been found among the DSS?

Although a few scholars have tried to match a dozen or so of the Greek fragments from Cave 7 with New Testament writings, the majority of scholars find the proposals completely unconvincing. Recently some of these Greek fragments have been plausibly identified as from the book of Enoch, a book we know was prized at Qumran.

Was there a conspiracy to hold back from the public some of the DSS?

In short, no. Because of long delays in publishing a number of fragmentary texts from Cave 4, rumors began to circulate suggesting that there was a conspiracy (perhaps centered in the Vatican) to prevent some of the DSS from seeing the light of day. It was suggested that, among other things, the scrolls tell Jesus' life story in a way that conflicts with the New Testament, for instance that he was married to Mary Magdalene and had children (e.g., Dan Brown's novel). In reality, there was no conspiracy to suppress the publication of the DSS. The problem was one of practicality: there were just too many fragments for too few scholars working on them. When the Scrolls team was expanded in the early 1990s, the pace of publication quickened; and when all of the DSS and fragments were finally published, it became clear that there were no embarrassing secrets that needed to be kept from the public.

Do the DSS confirm the reliability of the Old Testament?

Yes. The DSS show that the standard Hebrew text (called the Masoretic Text) that underlies today's Old Testament has in fact been well preserved. However, the scrolls also demonstrate that there were other versions, slightly different from the standard version. One of these versions agrees with the Greek translation of the Old Testament, which New Testament authors frequently cited.

What role has science played in work on the DSS?

As already mentioned, science has helped date the scrolls. DNA testing has also identified the types of animal skins used in making the scrolls and has helped scholars know which fragments belong together. Various types of imaging technology have aided scholars in reconstructing the fragments and recovering words and letters no longer visible to the naked eye.

How is Scripture interpreted in the DSS?

Scripture is often interpreted in a futuristic and allegorical way. In their commentaries (called *pesharim*) the men of Qumran believed that the prophets spoke of their (the Essenes') time, a time on the very brink of coming judgment.

What are the key beliefs of the authors and collectors of the DSS?

The men of Qumran were very critical of the aristocratic priest-hood in Jerusalem. They refused to worship at the temple and anticipated a coming judgment and destruction of this priest-hood. They anticipated the coming of the Messiah, who will support the true high priest, a priest likely hailing from the ranks of the Essenes. At this time there would be a great battle in which the Romans would be defeated. Indeed, the Messiah will kill the Roman emperor. The Essenes also interpreted Scripture in a very strict manner. They evidently regarded the Pharisees as liberal and "wishy-washy" in their understanding of the Law.

Was John the Baptist an Essene?

Although at points John's preaching and lifestyle cohere with Essene values, most scholars doubt John was an Essene. Even if he had once been an Essene, the New Testament makes clear that he had departed from them.

Was Jesus an Essene?

Very unlikely. Jesus' remarkably open teaching and surprisingly inclusive lifestyle, especially with regard to tax collectors and people called "sinners," were completely at variance with the teaching and sequestered lifestyle of the men of Qumran. Essenes are not mentioned in the Gospels in all probability because they had no interest in Jesus and his ministry.

Did Jesus borrow ideas from the Essenes?

There is no evidence that Jesus borrowed any ideas or teachings from the Essenes. Overlap between Jesus' teaching and the teaching of the Essenes was likely due to the common pool of Jewish beliefs. After all, both Jesus and the Essenes took Scripture seriously and believed that all that the prophets foretold would be fulfilled. In the interpretation of the Law, however, Jesus differed sharply with the Essenes.

Did Jesus read any of the DSS?

There is no evidence that Jesus ever read or even saw a DSS. The 900 or so scrolls found in the region of the Dead Sea represent only a tiny fraction of the number of scrolls that circulated in Israel in the time of Jesus. There is no reason at all to think that the scroll of Isaiah from which Jesus read (Luke 4) was one of the scrolls of Isaiah from Qumran. There is no evidence that Jesus ever even had a conversation with an Essene.

Do the DSS shed light on the ministry and teaching of Jesus?

Indeed they do. The scrolls attest the existence of long strings of beatitudes, just as we find in Jesus' famous Sermon on the Mount (Matt 5; Luke 6). The scrolls attest the expectation of healing, raising the dead, and proclaiming good news in the messianic age, which we see in the teaching and ministry of Jesus. The scrolls argue for the sanctity of marriage by appeal to passages from Genesis, just as Jesus argued.

Do the DSS shed light on the letters of the apostle Paul?

Indeed they do. In his letters (esp. Galatians and Romans) Paul asserts that no can be made righteous by works of the Law. Some critics in the past accused Paul of creating a straw man. In other words, they say that no Jews believed they could be made righteous by obeying the Law. However, scrolls from the Dead Sea have proven that some Jews did believe that certain works of the Law had to be performed in order to be declared righteous in the sight of God.

Do the DSS shed light on other New Testament writings?

Indeed they do. The scrolls anticipate the coming of Melchizedek, a figure who evidently represents God himself and whose work will cleanse Israel of sin. This expectation sheds light on the role of Melchizedek in the book of Hebrews. The scrolls also speak of those who do the Law, which sheds light on the admonition in James that believers be "doers" of the word and not hearers only. The DSS also help us understand why Jude quotes from the book of Enoch. The presence of so many copies of the book of Enoch among the DSS shows us how important this book was in the time of Jesus and the early Church.

Thus Jude quoted a book that was popular in the Jewish consciousness.

What work still needs to be done?

Scholars are still sifting and sorting out the many fragments. The hope is to piece together small fragments and create larger fragments, so that enough text is recovered that they can be read and interpreted. Of course, interpretation and reinterpretation are also ongoing tasks. Much has been learned in recent years, with the result that some older conclusions need to be revised or abandoned altogether. There is still hope to recover fragments of scrolls still in the possession of Bedouin and private individuals. And, of course, there remains the possibility of the discovery of yet more caves containing DSS.

How important are the DSS for Christian faith?

The scrolls neither make nor break Christian faith. What they do is clarify important aspects of Christian origins and theology. The scrolls clarify prophetic and messianic expectations. They help us understand more clearly issues surrounding the interpretation of the Law of Moses and why the men of Qumran broke with the Jerusalem temple establishment. Also, the DSS have disproved a few skeptical theories, such as the idea that Jesus' reply to the imprisoned John the Baptist (Matt 11:2–6; Luke 7:18–23) was not messianic or the idea that calling Jesus the Son of God did not reflect genuine Jewish hopes but a Greco-Roman idea based on worshipping the emperor. Scroll 4Q521 refutes the first skeptical theory, while 4Q246 refutes the second. In the end the scrolls show how well Jesus, his movement, and the writings we call the New Testament authentically fit into the world of first-century Israel. To read and understand the DSS is to understand Jesus and the New Testament much better.

Appendix 1
Major Scrolls Publications

The number of publications related to the Dead Sea Scrolls is enormous and continues to grow larger every month. Below I provide a select list of recent English works that will help the beginner. I also cite some useful computer software. I annotate select entries.

For Basic Introduction to the Scrolls
E. M. Cook, *Solving the Mysteries of the Dead Sea Scrolls: New Light on the Bible* (Grand Rapids: Zondervan, 1994).

J. A. Fitzmyer, *Responses to 101 Questions on the Dead Sea Scrolls* (New York: Paulist, 1992).

F. García Martínez and J. Trebolle Barrera, *The People of the Dead Sea Scrolls: Their Writings, Beliefs and Practices* (Leiden: Brill, 1995).

C. M. Pate, *Communities of the Last Days: The Dead Sea Scrolls, the New Testament, and the Story of Israel* (Downers Grove: InterVarsity, 2000).

E. M. Schuller, *The Dead Sea Scrolls: What Have We Learned?* (Louisville: Westminster John Knox, 2006).

H. Shanks (ed.), *Understanding the Dead Sea Scrolls: A Reader from the Biblical Archaeological Review* (New York: Random House, 1992).

J. C. VanderKam, *The Dead Sea Scrolls Today* (London: SPCK; Grand Rapids: Eerdmans, 1994; revised 2009).

J. C. VanderKam and P. W. Flint, *The Meaning of the Dead Sea Scrolls: Their Significance for Understanding the Bible, Judaism, Jesus, and Christianity* (San Francisco: HarperCollins, 2002). The best book of its kind, highly recommended.

For Accounts of the Discovery of the Scrolls

H. Shanks, *The Mystery and Meaning of the Dead Sea Scrolls* (New York: Random House, 1998).

J. C. Trever, *The Dead Sea Scrolls: A Personal Account* (Westwood, NJ: Fleming H. Revell, 1965; repr. Piscataway, NJ: Gorgias Press, 2003).

Hebrew and Aramaic Texts of the Scrolls

Discoveries in the Judaean Desert (36 vols., Oxford: Clarendon Press, 1955–). The official, international publication series of the Scrolls, highly technical.

F. García Martínez and E. J. C. Tigchelaar, *The Dead Sea Scrolls Study Edition* (2 vols., Leiden: Brill, 1997–1998). Provides Hebrew/Aramaic and English facing pages.

D. W. Parry and E. Tov (eds.), *The Dead Sea Scrolls Reader* (6 vols., Leiden: Brill, 2004–2005). Provides Hebrew/Aramaic and English facing pages.

English Translations of the Scrolls

M. G. Abegg, P. W. Flint, and E. Ulrich, *The Dead Sea Scrolls Bible: The Oldest Known Bible Translated for the First Time into English* (San Francisco: HarperCollins, 1999). A collocation of the Bible scrolls from Qumran; convenient way to look up what parts of Scripture survived and how they read.

F. García Martínez, *The Dead Sea Scrolls Translated: The Qumran Texts in English* (Leiden: Brill, 1994).

G. Vermes, *The Complete Dead Sea Scrolls in English* (rev. ed., London and New York: Penguin Books, 2004).

M. O. Wise, M. G. Abegg Jr., and E. M. Cook, *The Dead Sea Scrolls: A New Translation* (San Francisco: HarperCollins, 1996).

Research Tools Related to the Scrolls

M. G. Abegg Jr., *The Dead Sea Scrolls Concordance* (with J. E. Bowley, E. M. Cook, and E. Tov; Leiden: Brill, 2003).

J. A. Fitzmyer, *A Guide to the Dead Sea Scrolls and Related Literature* (Grand Rapids: Eerdmans, 2008). Very useful, reliable tool produced by a member of the original team of scholars who worked with the Scrolls.

C. Martone, "Research Tools," in L. H. Schiffman and J. C. VanderKam (eds.), *Encyclopedia of the Dead Sea Scrolls* (2 vols., Oxford: Oxford University Press, 2000), 2:760–64.

F. García Martínez and D. W. Parry, *A Bibliography of the Finds in the Desert of Juda 1970–95: Arranged by Author with Citation and Subject Indexes* (Leiden: Brill, 1996).

S. A. Reed, *The Dead Sea Scrolls Catalogue: Documents, Photographs and Museum Inventory Numbers* (ed. M. J. Lundberg, with M. B. Phelps; Atlanta: Scholars Press, 1994). Very useful reference work.

L. H. Schiffman and J. C. VanderKam (eds.), *Encyclopedia of the Dead Sea Scrolls* (2 vols., Oxford: Oxford University Press, 2000). Only work in its class; immensely helpful.

CDs and Software

Accordance (Oaktree Software). Hebrew/Aramaic modules for all biblical and nonbiblical Scrolls, lexically and grammatically tagged; English translations included; primarily designed for Macintosh platform, it can also function on the PC platform.

T. H. Lim (ed.), *The Dead Sea Scrolls Electronic Reference Library* (with P. S. Alexander; Oxford: Oxford University Press; Leiden: Brill, 1997).

Logos Bible Software. Hebrew/Aramaic modules, lexically and grammatically tagged; English translations included; designed for the PC platform.

E. Tov (ed.), *The Dead Sea Scrolls on Microfiche: A Comprehensive Facsimile Edition of the Texts from the Judean Desert* (Leiden: Brill and IDC Microform Publishers, 1992).

Major Conference Volumes

J. H. Charlesworth (ed.), *The Bible and the Dead Sea Scrolls: The Princeton Symposium on the Dead Sea Scrolls* (3 vols., Waco, TX: Baylor University Press, 2006).

J. J. Collins and R. A. Kugler (eds.), *Religion in the Dead Sea Scrolls* (Grand Rapids: Eerdmans, 2000).

F. H. Cryer and T. L. Thompson (eds.), *Qumran Between the Old and New Testament* (Sheffield: Sheffield Academic Press, 1998).

P. W. Flint and J. C. VanderKam (eds.), *The Dead Sea Scrolls after Fifty Years: A Comprehensive Assessment* (2 vols., Leiden: Brill, 1998–1999). Probably the most important collection of studies on the Scrolls.

R. A. Kugler and E. M. Schuller (eds.), *The Dead Sea Scrolls at Fifty: Proceedings of the 1997 Society of Biblical Literature Qumran Section Meetings* (Atlanta: Scholars Press, 1999).

T. H. Lim, with L. W. Hurtado, A. G. Auld, and A. Jack (eds.), *The Dead Sea Scrolls in Their Historical Context* (Edinburgh: T & T Clark, 2000).

D. W. Parry and E. Ulrich (eds.), *The Provo International Conference on the Dead Sea Scrolls: Technological Innovations, New Texts, and Reformulated Issues* (Leiden: Brill, 1998).

S. E. Porter and C. A. Evans (eds.), *The Scrolls and the Scriptures: Qumran Fifty Years After* (Sheffield: Sheffield Academic Press, 1997).

L. H. Schiffman, E. Tov, and J. C. VanderKam (eds.), *The Dead Sea Scrolls: Fifty Years After Their Discovery. Proceedings of the Jerusalem Congress, July 20–25, 1997* (Jerusalem: Israel Exploration Society and the Israel Antiquities Authority, 2000). Another very important collection of studies.

E. Ulrich and J. C. VanderKam (eds.), *The Community of the Renewed Covenant: The Notre Dame Symposium on the Dead Sea Scrolls* (Notre Dame: University of Notre Dame Press, 1994).

M. O. Wise, N. Golb, J. J. Collins, and D. G. Pardee (eds.), *Methods of Investigation of the Dead Sea Scrolls and the Khirbet Qumran Site: Present Realities and Future Prospects* (New York: The New York Academy of Sciences, 1994). No conventional collection of studies; includes panel discussion of ethics relating to copyright and publication of the Scrolls.

Scholarly Journals Devoted to the Scrolls

Dead Sea Discoveries (Leiden: Brill, 1994–)

Qumran Chronicle (Krakow: Enigma Press, 1990–)

Revue de Qumran (Paris: Gabalda, 1958–)

Appendix 2
Major Scrolls Players

This appendix introduces major players in the discovery, publication, and analysis of the Dead Sea Scrolls. Many of these names have been mentioned in this book. The list below is not a long one. I could easily add another two or three dozen names. My apologies to those who think I omitted someone who should have been included!

Abegg, Martin G.

Martin G. Abegg Jr. (1950–) made headlines around the world in 1991, when he reconstructed unpublished texts of the DSS by inputting words and phrases from a set of index cards that Raymond Brown, Joseph Fitzmyer, and others had prepared in the 1950s and 1960s. Abegg was dubbed the "Scrolls buster." He and his doctoral advisor Ben Zion Wacholder published three facsimile volumes of previously unpublished texts, thus ending what many regarded as the scrolls monopoly. Abegg is on the faculty of Trinity Western University in British Columbia, Canada, where with his colleague Peter Flint he heads up the Dead Sea Scrolls Institute and teaches the Scrolls and Hebrew Bible. He eventually joined the International Committee for Editing the Dead Sea Scrolls, which is entrusted with the publication of the scrolls in the Discoveries in the Judaean Desert (DJD) series. Recently Abegg was appointed Ben Zion Wacholder Professor of Biblical Studies.

Albright, William F.

William Foxwell Albright (1891–1971) was long recognized as the North American dean of Old Testament archaeology and Semitic linguistics. He taught at Johns Hopkins University, where he served as the W. W. Spence Professor of Semitic Languages from 1930 until his retirement in 1958. When the first scrolls discovery came to light in 1948, he wrote to John Trever: "My heartiest congratulations on the greatest MS discovery of modern times! There is no doubt whatever in my mind that the script is more archaic than that of the Nash Papyrus. . . . I repeat that in my opinion you have made the greatest MS discovery of modern times—certainly the greatest biblical MS find."

Allegro, John M.

John Marco Allegro (1923–1988) acquired degrees in Oriental studies from the University of Manchester (England). He was appointed to the International Committee for Editing the Dead Sea Scrolls in 1953. He was successful in having the Copper Plaque (or Copper Scroll) opened in 1956. In 1968 he published the fifth volume in the DJD series, which turned out to be badly flawed. After making strange and sensational claims to the press, he fell out with other scrolls scholars and was dropped from the team. He gained notoriety when he published his book *The Sacred Mushroom and the Cross* in 1970, the year he resigned from the faculty of Manchester. He went on to publish *The Dead Sea Scrolls and the Christian Myth* (1981). In these books the disgraced former professor claimed a hallucinogenic drug lay behind Christian and Gnostic mysticism. Regrettably these strange ideas are exploited by various irresponsible sensationalists in today's popular media.

Baillet, Maurice

Maurice Baillet (1923–1998) studied Semitic languages in Paris, Rome, and Tübingen (Germany) and joined the International Committee for Editing the Dead Sea Scrolls in 1958. He served on the staff of the Centre National de la Recherche Scientifique from 1959 to 1993. He published most of the scroll fragments from Caves 2, 3, 6, 7, 8, 9, and 10 (the so-called "minor caves") in the third volume of the DJD series. He went on to publish several Cave 4 documents (i.e., 4Q482–4Q520) in the seventh volume of the series. Baillet gained the distinction of publishing the texts entrusted to him in a timely and careful manner.

Barthélemy, Dominique

Dominique Barthélemy (1921–2002) entered the Dominican order in 1939 and went to graduate studies in Paris and Jerusalem at the École Biblique Biblique et Archéologique Fançaise in Jerusalem. From 1957 to 1991 he was professor of Old Testament at the University of Fribourg in Switzerland. He was widely recognized as an authority in textual criticism of the OT, including the various Greek translations. With J. T. Milik he holds the distinction of publishing the first volume in the Discoveries in the Judaean Desert series.

Brooke, George J.

George J. Brooke (1952–) studied under William Brownlee at Claremont Graduate School, where he received his doctorate in 1978. Brooke's dissertation, published in 1985, investigated 4QFlorilegium (4Q174) and biblical interpretation in the scrolls. Brooke acquired and conserved the library and papers of Brownlee and some years later published John Allegro's extensive set of scrolls photographs. Brooke, who serves as the Rylands Professor of Biblical Criticism and Exegesis at the University of Manchester, has been commissioned to replace Allegro's flawed edition of the pesharim (Qumran's commentaries on Scripture).

Brownlee, William H.

William H. Brownlee (1917–1983) received his doctorate from Duke University in 1947, under the direction of William F. Stinespring. Upon completion of his doctoral studies, he traveled to Israel (or Palestine) to pursue further study in the Ugaritic language, as part of his preparation for major work in the prophet Ezekiel. He and John Trever had the good fortune of being shown some of the scrolls found in 1947. Brownlee holds the distinction of publishing one of the first studies on the scrolls: "The Jerusalem Habakkuk Scroll," *Bulletin of the American Schools of Oriental Research* 112 (1948),

8–18. Brownlee went on to publish seminal studies of the Rule of Community Scroll (1QS) and commentary on Habakkuk (1QpHab). Brownlee spent most of his scholarly career on the faculty of Claremont Graduate School, where he served from 1959 until his retirement in 1982.

Carmignac, Jean

Abbé Jean Carmignac (1914–1986) founded *Revue de Qumran* in 1958, the first scholarly journal devoted to the study of the Dead Sea Scrolls. Carmignac achieved distinction also by publishing early on, with colleagues P. Guilbert, É Cothennet, and H. Lignée, two volumes of translation and commentary on the major scrolls. After his death a special edition of *Revue de Qumran* (vol. 13, 1988) was prepared in his honor.

Collins, John J.

John J. Collins (1946–) earned his doctorate from Harvard in 1972. Collins has served on the faculties of the University of Notre Dame and the University of Chicago and since 2000 serves as the Holmes Professor of Old Testament Criticism and Interpretation at Yale University and Divinity School. Collins has served as editor in chief of *Dead Sea Discoveries* and the *Journal of Biblical Literature*. He is a member of the International Committee for Editing the Dead Sea Scrolls. Collins gained early distinction for his work in Jewish apocalyptic and messianism. His book, *The Scepter and the Star: The Messiahs of Apocalypticism in the Dead Sea Scrolls* (1995), is an outstanding example.

Cross, Frank Moore

Frank Moore Cross Jr. (1921–) earned his doctorate at Johns Hopkins University in 1950, under the direction of William F. Albright. After serving on the faculty of McCormick Theological Seminary, Cross was appointed to the faculty of Harvard University in 1957, where from 1958 to 1992 he has served as the Hancock Professor of Hebrew and Oriental Languages in the Department of Near East Languages and Civilizations. He also served as the curator of the Harvard Semitic Museum from 1958 to 1961 and then as director of the museum from 1974 to 1987. Cross has served on the International Committee for Editing the Dead Sea Scrolls since 1953. Cross gained distinction for his work in paleography (study of ancient writing), by which the scrolls could be dated. Scientific methods of dating, such as Carbon-14 and its newer form AMS (Accelerator Mass Spectrometry), have confirmed the accuracy of Cross's work. Cross also has the distinction of directing several Ph.D. students who have gone on to do important work in scrolls research.

de Vaux, Roland

Father Roland G. de Vaux (1903–1970) was a French Dominican priest and director of the École Biblique et Archéologique Fançaise in Jerusalem. He and colleagues excavated the ruins at Qumran from 1951 to 1956. In 1953 he was appointed to the International Committee for Editing the Dead Sea Scrolls and served as editor in chief of the Discoveries in the Judaean Desert series (1954–1970), seeing the first five volumes through the press. For a number of years, he was editor in chief of *Revue de Qumran*. Regrettably de Vaux failed to publish the greater part of his field notes and findings relating to his excavations.

Dupont-Sommer, André

André Dupont-Sommer (1900–1983) studied epigraphy and history at the Sorbonne in Paris. He spent time at the École Biblique et Archéologique Fançaise in Jerusalem and took part in archaeological excavations. He published early introductions to the scrolls, which were well done and well received. But Dupont-Sommer's theory of the Essene origin of the Christian movement, complete with suggestions that aspects of the life and death of Jesus are somehow adumbrated in the scrolls, is eccentric and has not persuaded other scrolls scholars.

Fitzmyer, Joseph A.

Father Joseph A. Fitzmyer, S.J., (1920–) received his doctorate at Johns Hopkins University in 1956, under the direction of William F. Albright. In the early 1950s Fitzmyer was added to the International Committee for Editing the Dead Sea Scrolls. His principal assignment was the preparation of an index of all nonbiblical scrolls, a task he undertook in 1957 in the room dubbed the "scrollery" in the Palestine Archaeological Museum in east Jerusalem (now the Rockefeller Museum). Father Fitzmyer is an Aramaic specialist and is well known for his excellent Anchor Bible commentaries on Luke, Acts, and Romans. He gained notoriety when he published the Aramaic text of the so-called "Son of God" text (4Q246). He acquired the text when J. T. Milik put it on a screen while giving a public lecture. The publication of this remarkable text in the early 1970s fueled hopes for the publication of the remainder of the many fragments from Cave 4. Fitzmyer is now professor emeritus at Catholic University of America in Washington, DC.

Flint, Peter W.

Peter W. Flint (1951–) received his Ph.D. from the University of Notre Dame, under the direction of Eugene Ulrich. His dissertation on the Psalms at Qumran, published in 1997, is highly regarded. Since 1995 Flint has been on the faculty of Trinity Western University, where with Martin Abegg he directs the Dead Sea Scrolls Institute and edits the Studies in the Dead Sea Scrolls and Related Literature series. Recently Flint has been installed in the Canada Research Chair of the Dead Sea Scrolls.

García Martínez, Florentino

Florentino García Martínez (1942–) is on the faculty of Katholieke Universiteit Leuven (Belgium), is one of the contributors to the Discoveries in the Judaean Desert series, and serves on the editorial boards of *Dead Sea Discoveries* and, with Martin Abegg and Peter Flint, Studies in the Dead Sea Scrolls and Related Literature. He is also the director of the Qumran Institute at the University of Groningen in the Netherlands. García Martínez has published extensively on the scrolls in English, Dutch, and Spanish. He has also translated most of the scrolls into Spanish.

Harding, G. Lankester

Gerald Lankester Harding (1901–1979) held the post of chief inspector of antiquities in Amman, Jordan, and director of antiquities of the Jordanian Department of Antiquities of the Amman Museum from 1936 to 1956. Early on he confirmed the antiquity of the newly discovered scrolls and promoted and participated in excavations of the ruins, the search for more caves, and in the piecing together of the fragmentary scrolls. He was the leading figure in assembling in 1953 the International Committee for Editing the Dead Sea Scrolls.

Milik, J. T.

Józef Tadeusz Milik (1922–2006) began studying and translating scrolls while he was a student at the Pontifical Biblical Institute in Rome. Roland de Vaux invited Milik to join the International Committee for Editing the Dead Sea Scrolls. Milik transcribed, translated, and published a great number of fragmentary scrolls, but because he was unable to publish many others entrusted to him (nor would he let others see them), he was criticized by scholars and in the popular press. In time his unpublished texts were taken from him and were given to others.

Puech, Émile

Father Émile Puech (1941–) began working with Jean Starcky in the archaeology of Qumran. Puech is the director of research at the Centre National de la Recherche Scientifique and is on the faculty at the École Biblique et Archéologique Française in Jerusalem. Puech has published several scroll fragments in the Discoveries in the Judaean Desert series and a learned book on the theme of resurrection in the DSS. He has also assumed Jean Starcky's archaeological work.

Sanders, James A.

James A. Sanders (1927–) studied in Paris, earned degrees at Vanderbilt University and Divinity School, and the Ph.D. at Hebrew Union College in 1955. He served as professor of biblical studies at Colgate Rochester Divinity School (1954–1965), as Auburn Professor of Biblical Studies at Union Theological Seminary in New York (1965–1977), and as professor of intertestamental and biblical studies at the Claremont School of Theology and the Claremont Graduate School (1977–1997). In 1965 Sanders published the Cave 11 Psalms Scroll as the fourth volume in the Discoveries in the Judaean Desert series. At Claremont, Sanders founded the Ancient Biblical Manuscript Center (ABMC) and served as its president. The ABMC houses photographs, negatives, transparencies, and even a few original manuscripts of ancient biblical texts, DSS, and related writings.

Schiffman, Lawrence

Lawrence Schiffman (1948–) received his Ph.D. from Brandeis University and is the Ethel and Irvin A. Edelman Professor of Hebrew and Judaic Studies at New York University. Schiffman has organized conferences on the scrolls, edited the journal *Dead Sea Discoveries*, coedited with James VanderKam the *Encyclopedia of the Dead Sea Scrolls*, and is a member of the International Committee for Editing the Dead Sea Scrolls. He has specialized in how the Law of Moses was understood at Qumran and has pointed to links between the scrolls and the Sadducees.

Skehan, Patrick W.

Father Patrick William Skehan (1909–1980) was one of the original members of the International Committee for Editing the Dead Sea Scrolls. In 1954 he was appointed to the team responsible for the publication of scrolls from Qumran's Cave 4. He taught Semitic and Egyptian Languages and Literature at Catholic University of America from 1938 until his retirement in 1980. Some of the work that he left behind was published by Eugene Ulrich and Peter Flint.

Starcky, Jean

Father Jean Starcky (1909–1988) studied Semitics and Oriental Languages at several institutions, including the Pontifical Biblical Institute in Rome and the École Biblique et Archéologique Française in Jerusalem. He taught New Testament at the Institut Catholique in Paris. In 1953 he joined the International Committee for Editing the Dead Sea Scrolls in Jerusalem and began examination of the many scroll fragments from Cave 4. Starcky was later appointed to the Centre National de la Recherche Scientifique and recruited Maurice Baillet to assist his work with Cave 4 materials. One of his most interesting studies in the scrolls was a work that attempted to trace the development of messianism at Qumran.

Strugnell, John

John Strugnell (1930–2007) graduated from Oxford University in 1952 and, at the recommendation of Godfrey Driver in 1954, was appointed to the International Committee for Editing the Dead Sea Scrolls. Strugnell proved to be a gifted transcriber and translator of the scrolls but published little of his work. He was on the staff at the Oriental Institute in Chicago (1957–1960), at Duke University (1960–1967), and then at Harvard University (1967) until his retirement. In 1984 he was appointed head of the International Committee for Editing the Dead Sea Scrolls. In 1990, after making anti-Semitic remarks during an interview that was published in *Ha'aretz*, he resigned.

Sukenik, Eleazar

Eleazar Lipa Sukenik (1889–1953) received his Ph.D. from Dropsie College in 1926 and then was appointed as an archaeologist at Hebrew University in Jerusalem. He published important works on synagogues and Jewish tombs and ossuaries. In the fall of 1947, he was shown scrolls from the first cave, which he rightly recognized as ancient. He was able to purchase the War Scroll (1QM), the Hymn Scroll (1QHa), and two tall jars believed to have contained scrolls. He later acquired the second Isaiah Scroll (1QIsaiah^b).

Tov, Emanuel

Emanuel Tov (1941–) received his Ph.D. from Hebrew University in Jerusalem in 1973. His field of specialty concerns Jeremiah and Baruch, in both the Hebrew and Greek traditions. In 1980 he became the first Israeli to be appointed to the International Committee for Editing the Dead Sea Scrolls. In 1990 he was appointed to head the committee. Under Tov's direction the publication of volumes in the Discoveries in the Judaean Desert dramatically accelerated. There is now almost nothing left to publish. Tov is the J. L. Magnes Professor of Bible at Hebrew University.

Trever, John

John C. Trever (1915–2006) received his Ph.D. from Yale University in 1943. An excellent photographer, he traveled to Palestine in 1947 in order to photograph some mosaics that had been recently excavated. Trever was housed at the old American School on Saladin Road in Jerusalem. On Sunday, February 15, 1948, Millar Burrows, director of the school, left Jerusalem for a two-week trip to Baghdad. He appointed Trever as acting director. The following week Acting Director Trever met with agents who had in their possession some of the major scrolls from Cave 1. Trever recognized their antiquity and importance and made arrangements to photograph them. The rest, as they say, is history.

Ulrich, Eugene

Eugene Ulrich (1938–) received his Ph.D. from Harvard University in 1975. He has been on the faculty of the University of Notre Dame since 1973, where he is now the John A. O'Brien Professor of Hebrew Scripture and Theology. Since 1985 Ulrich has served as the associate editor of the Discoveries in the Judaean Desert series. A specialist in the text and canon of Scripture, including the Greek translation (the Septuagint), Ulrich has published or contributed to several volumes in the DJD series. With Martin Abegg and Peter Flint, he is also editor of *The Dead Sea Scrolls Bible*.

VanderKam, James

James C. VanderKam (1946–) received his Ph.D. from Harvard University in 1976. In 1991 he joined the faculty at the University of Notre Dame, where he is now the John A. O'Brien Professor of Theology. VanderKam has published important studies in Enoch and Jubilees, works that apparently were treasured by the men of Qumran. Coeditor of the *Encyclopedia of the Dead Sea Scrolls*, a contributor to several volumes in the Discoveries in the Judaean Desert series, and coauthor, with Peter Flint, of *The Meaning of the Dead Sea Scrolls*, VanderKam is respected for his careful work.

Vermes, Geza

Geza Vermes (1924–) received his doctorate from Louvain in 1953 and from 1965 to 1991 was professor of Jewish studies at Oxford University. A prolific author, since 1962 Vermes has produced ever expanding English translations of the DSS, the most recent in 2004. He is also well known for books on the historical Jesus, beginning with *Jesus the Jew*, which was published in 1973.

Yadin, Yigael

Yigael Yadin (1917–1984), son of Eleazar Sukenik, served in the Israeli army, excavated Masada, Nahal Hever, and other sites, and published a number of works on the DSS (in Hebrew and in English), notably impressive critical editions of the War Scroll (1QM) and the Temple Scroll (11Q19). Yadin is famous for his acquisition of the scrolls Mar Samuel put on the market in the United States in an ad that appeared in *The Wall Street Journal*. He is also famous for the way in which he acquired the Temple Scroll in October 1967, some months following the Six Day War. Bethlehem and other parts of Palestine fell into Israeli hands following the war. Yadin dispatched agents to the home of a Bethlehem antiquities dealer named Kando, who was rumored to be in possession of the Temple Scroll. Kando was forced (at gunpoint?) to relinquish the scroll. G. Ernest Wright, president of the American Schools of Oriental Research (ASOR), wrote Yadin in November 1967, gently rebuking him in the matter of the "confiscation of the Scroll."

NCHORING CHRISTIANS
all ages in the truths of Scripture.

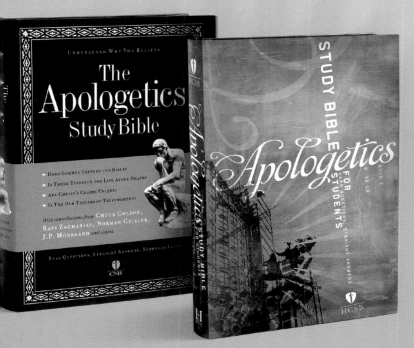

Apologetics Study Bible line features unique articles and contributions from modern ogists, along with book introductions, study notes on "problem" passages, sidebars, comparisons. The Apologetics Study Bible for Students includes dozens of articles cted from today's most popular youth leaders, along with 25 tactics against com- anti-Christian arguments, 20 top five lists to help younger Christians remember key ogetics topics, notable quotes, and more.

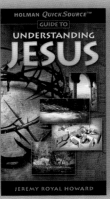
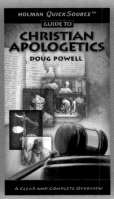

Learn more at ApologeticsBible.com.
Available at bookstores nationwide.

The ECPA Award Winning
HCSB STUDY BIBLE

A visual Bible that is comprehensive, easy to read, and easy to use, with features and formats specifically designed to enhance your Bible study experience. A vast collection of notes provide insight into the meaning of every page of the *HCSB Study Bible*.

HCSB   HOLMAN
BIBLE PUBLISHERS

Every *Word* Matters
BHPublishingGroup.com